ACKNOWLEDGEMENTS

This book has grown from my personal belief in the need for more sustainable practices in fashion and textile design which was further developed through activities and workshops convened during my 2004–2005 project Interrogating Fashion. This research project was part of the Designing for the Twenty-First Century Initiative funded by two UK research councils: Arts and Humanities, and Engineering and Physical Sciences. I am grateful to all who took part in the Fashion Paradox workshops for their stimulating contributions, including Susannah Dowse (TRAID Remade), Rebecca Earley, Claudia Eckert, Kate Fletcher, Kate Goldsworthy, Katharine Hamnett, Derek McKelvey (previously of M&S), Phil McKeown (Unilever), Lucy Orta, Phil Patterson (M&S), Kay Politowitcz, Sarah Ratty (Ciel), Phil Sams (Unilever), Helen Storey and Mathilde Tham. I also acknowledge the many other colleagues who joined the debate, and the encouragement from the research department of London College of Fashion.

I am indebted to all the designers, photographers and companies featured for generous cooperation in providing images, interviews and information, too many to include here individually. Thanks are due to Fatemeh Eskandarypur for her assistance with research and the resources section, and to Raven Smith for his commitment to the project. Thanks also to Fatemeh and to Frances Geesin for comments on the text, and support and encouragement when needed. I would like to extend my gratitude to the editorial team at Black Dog, past and present: Ziggy Hanaor for initiating the project, and Blanche Craig, Nadine Monem and Safiya Waley for their editorial advice and support. Finally, much appreciation goes to my friends and family, especially to Morris, for unfailing support and encouragement.

PROFESSOR SANDY BLACK

Professor of Fashion and Textile Design and Technology
London College of Fashion
University of the Arts London

Massive thanks to everybody whose momentous support and continuous patience made this book possible—there are too many of you to name. A huge thank you goes especially to my friend and colleague Nadine Monem for her encouragement and also to the ever supportive and insightful Aaron.

RAVEN SMITH

Editor
Black Dog Publishing

ECO-CHIC
THE
FASHION
PARADOX

Sandy Black

black dog
publishing

Gary's Harveys newspaper
dress is part of his collection
of recycled couture gowns.
Photograph by Robert Decelis.

CONTENTS

CHAPTER ONE

THE GREENING OF THE FASHION INDUSTRY

THE GREENING OF THE FASHION INDUSTRY

The fashion industry is many things to many people. Fashion's multiple facets mean that we engage with fashion in different ways at different times, for example, casual street styles, major high street offerings or luxury international designer brands. Unlike previous eras, fashion is now pluralistic—any number of looks may be simultaneously in vogue, and rapid turnaround is the norm.

The key used to be status and wealth—fashion was only for the elite and 'trickled down' to the masses as described by Georg Simmel at the start of the twentieth century in classic fashion theory.[1]

Mens' and womens' casual fashions, Spring/Summer 2007, from socially responsible clothing label Edun, who work with African businesses to encourage sustainable production and trade. Image courtesy Edun

Fashion is perplexing, intriguing, irritating and above all, compulsive. Like it or not, fashion exerts a powerful hold over people— even those who eschew it. While reactions to fashion are ambivalent, there is no doubt that clothes matter.[2]

Like today, fashion was aspirational and based in the fundamental process of change. For consumers, being seen to be 'up to date' and not 'out of fashion' was key. Parisian couturiers held sway as leaders of fashion from the mid-nineteenth century to the mid-twentieth century, allowed the diffusion of their fashions by selling calico *toiles* and patterns of their 'models' to be copied for the newly emergent department stores. These stores catered to private clients and to manufacturers. Patterns were also reproduced for personal tailoring and home dressmaking, and published in the growing number of women's magazines meeting demand for fashionability on a budget. Then, at the start of the twentieth century (stimulated by the need for military uniforms), came mass-production and the first signs of democratisation in fashion.

More practical but stylish clothes became available, led this time by the rise of the US ready-to-wear industry. In the 1940s and 50s, influential US designer Clare McCardell established a casual look that became known as 'sportswear'. Factory made clothes became highly desirable and within the reach of more and more working people. Home dressmaking steadily declined from the 1950s when the teenage 'youthquake' began to turn the established order upside down and young talented designers like Pierre Cardin, Courreges and Mary Quant looked to a new future. Elite, designer-led fashion was still the domain of the privileged, but couture became far less influential than in its heyday and the French houses launched their own *prêt-a-porter* lines. The consumer society began to emerge. In the 1970s and 80s fashion started travelling in the opposite direction, as fashion rebellion made an appearance in youth style tribes such as punk and goth.[3] These styles in turn inspired high level designers such as Versace, Jean Paul Gaultier and Zandra Rhodes. Since the 1960s, mass-produced casual sportswear (jeans, t-shirts and baseball caps) based on the US casual style has gradually developed as a global uniform of the young. The dictates of rigid seasonal styles promoted by magazines such as *Vogue* and *Tatler* had to relinquish their hold as new style-driven publications emerged. Fashion was fragmenting—the rules were to be broken and barriers between high fashion elites and ordinary folk, designer and everyday wear began to disappear.

1   Simmel, G, "Fashion", *On Individuality and Social Forms*, 1971, University of Chicago Press. (Simmel's article was first published in 1904.)

2   Jennifer Craik, *The Face of Fashion*, 1993

3   Polhemus, Ted, *Streetstyle*, Thames & Hudson, 1994. Also documented in the accompanying exhibition at the Victoria and Albert Museum co-curated by Amy de la Haye and Ted Polhemus.

LEFT:
Mary Quant designed the
bold check fabric and the
clothes for this 1964 outfit.

RIGHT:
The rigid seasonal styles
promoted by magazines
can be seen here with
these Dior Winter coats.

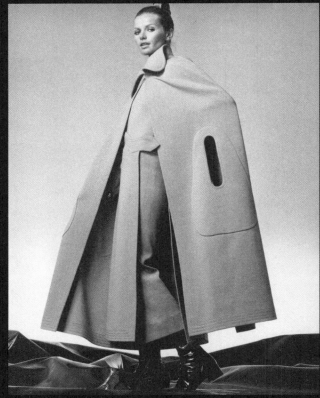

LEFT:
Hardy Amies Spring/Summer
1970. Dinner dress in purple,
black and beige printed silk,
with matching fringed turban
for a bohemian look. Image
courtesy of London College of
Fashion/Woolmark archive.

RIGHT:
Sharp geometric lines in a
glamorous cape and apronned
jumpsuit from Pierre Cardin,
1970. Image courtesy of
London College of Fashion/
The Woolmark Company.

Futuristic design from 1965 by Andre Courreges, which stopped "well above the kneecaps". Image courtesy of London College of Fashion/ The Woolmark Company.

During the 1980s, when conspicuous consumption was at its height, designer labels became the symbols of aspirational status. However, this cachet was diffused in a second wave of democratisation of luxury fashion in the 1990s, when aggressive marketing and expansion made designer brands available to a much wider audience. The brands were purchased by less affluent consumers and worn alongside basic clothing, creating the inevitable dilution of the luxury brand image, epitomised by the changing position of Burberry fashion. The eclecticism within contemporary fashion has, however, continued and personalisation of fashion is an expression of the new individuality. Sometimes it is appropriate to differentiate between 'fashion' and 'clothing'—fashion being based on desire rather than need, clothing being more of a commodity—however this ceases to be relevant in a consumer society where most people have far more clothes than meet their needs, and shop to refresh their wardrobes. This book therefore encompasses clothing within the term fashion, and fashion within the term clothing.

Fast Fashion

In the last 15 years, fashion has become faster and cheaper. Global communications and marketing, together with increased competition and the growth of offshore manufacturing, have fuelled demand and higher consumer expectations. This has resulted in faster and faster fashion cycles. This is an unsustainable position for fashion in both the medium and long term. The production and consumption of fashion represent the two extremes of a very long, fragmented and complex supply chain that transforms fibre into yarn and fabrics, which is mediated by designers, manufacturers and buyers into the clothing on offer at retail. There are issues to be dealt with at each stage of the process, well before the customer finally makes their own selection, wears, washes and finally throws away the items. As Katharine Hamnett reiterates: "How we consume shapes the future of the planet."

The current focus on fashion and sustainability is due to the convergence of many environmental and commercial factors, together with changing cultural and social norms. Fashion has always been a global affair; seeking out the unusual or the exotic for its rarity and prestige. It is worth remembering that international trading in luxury goods is an ancient practice; textiles and other goods were brought to the EU from China from as early as the first century BC. By Medieval times precious commodities such as spices, coffee and silk were traded to the West by a complex sequence of international transactions with merchants of the Byzantine Empire at its centre. In the late nineteenth century, Arthur Lazenby Liberty set up his emporium in London to provide luxurious and exotic items from the mysterious Orient for a bohemian and fashionable clientele.

The recent sharp increase in overseas manufacturing, particularly in China and India, is a direct result of the change in international trade agreements which came into play in January 2005 (when the Multi-fibre Arrangement (MFA) and General Agreement on Trade and Tarrifs (GATT) which had previously been in force, regulating import and export quotas between countries, came to an end). Individual markets (including the UK) were protected from competing cheap imports (from China for example) but now cheaper goods can flood the market, disrupting the previous status quo.

Sharp styling, intricate details and strong colours for John Smedley's fine merino wool knitwear, Autumn/Winter 2007.

As a consequence, many developing countries such as Bangladesh and Cambodia entered the garment manufacturing trade. Although some interim quotas were still in place, the new trading relationships could still be fraught with difficulty—in 2005 the so-called 'bra wars' dispute broke out over millions of Chinese-made clothes which were blocked at EU ports until China agreed it would not export any more pullovers, trousers and bras that year and count half the blocked items against its 2006 quota.[4]

One of Ciel's classic designs from Unsung Heroes. Photograph by Ben Gold. Image courtesy of Cari-Johan Paulin.

The Fashion Paradox

The clothing and textile sector is a significant economic player, employing over a billion people worldwide (2.7 million employed in the EU alone) and selling to millions more. Relative to income, clothes are now far cheaper than they were a few decades ago. Clothing sales have increased by 60 per cent in the last ten years.[5] We now consume one third more clothing than even four years ago, according to a Cambridge University report, and discard it after wearing just a few times or indeed, even once.[6] There has been a shift in the way clothing and fashions are sold in the UK, with the rise of 'value fashion' available in supermarkets with the weekly groceries, and high street stores such as Primark and Matelan who sell specifically on low prices, rather than longevity. The stampede at the opening of Primark's flagship Oxford Street London store in Spring 2007 showed just how popular this cheap fashion is. Cheap fashion means disposable fashion, and encourages more consumption, creating a vicious circle. More importantly, fast fashion also puts pressure on the clothing manufacturers and their suppliers to squeeze more output in less time, impacting those at the bottom end of the production chain who actually make the clothes. How can we change this to a more virtuous cycle? This book outlines some of the major issues involved and examines the complex sequences of events inherent in producing our clothes and the textiles that make them.

SOME OF THE KEY QUESTIONS:
How can fashion become more environmentally and ethically sound?
How can we slow down fashion?
How can consumers make a difference?
How can designers make a difference?
Can conflicting interests be reconciled in a fast moving industry like fashion?
What ecologically sound choices are available in fabrics?
What would be the impact on the fashion industry if everyone kept their clothes or longer?
Can we resolve the fashion paradox of transience and sustainability?

This is a difficult agenda. Until very recently sustainability issues have largely been sidestepped by the fashion and textile industries. However, the groundswell of consumer awareness and media coverage of global environmental issues and concerns about ethical practices in the supply chain has created pressure, which has now precipitated action by the large clothing companies such as M&S, Gap and H&M. There has been a fundamental paradigm shift as we enter a new era of ethical

4   "EU and China in bra wars deal", *The Guardian*, 6 September 2005, p. 7. 48 million pullovers, more than 11 million bras and 18 million pairs of trousers, along with eight million t-shirts and other items, were held in warehouses at EU ports.

5   *Recycling of Low Grade Waste*, 2006, Oakdene Hollins and Salvation Army Trading Company Ltd, p. 10.

6   *Well Dressed?*, University of Cambridge Institute for Manufacturing, 2006, p. 10.

From the Sans Autumn/
Winter 2007 Collection.

consumption. Consumers are demanding to know more about how and where and in what conditions their clothes are made. In a dramatic turnaround in corporate social responsibility in textile, dyeing and manufacturing businesses, companies that were previously seen as a major part of the environmental problem are now becoming part of the solution. With similarities to the organic food movement, lobbying over a period of time by small eco-fashion companies and campaigning organisations has now taken hold and new thinking is beginning to emerge on a much more comprehensive scale, impacting all levels of the supply chain. The UK fashion industry is going green, especially on the high street. TopShop, doyen of fast fashion, has adopted corporate social responsibility in a recent mission statement, and Primark have joined the Ethical Trading Initiative, a consortium of major retailers and campaign organisations, stating they are "committed to monitoring and progressively improving the conditions of the people who make products for Primark" on signs displaying their one pound t-shirts. Media interest and campaigning on working conditions in garment factories has risen to the top of the news agenda. Several reports have recently been published on the fashion industry, and newspaper coverage of labour issues has reached the front pages. Almost every magazine and trade journal from *Vanity Fair* to *Business Week* and *Time* has published a 'Green Issue' since 2005.

Do we know what drives fashion? Fashion is full of contradictions—it is ephemeral and cyclic, referencing the past but constantly embracing the new; it represents an expression of personal identity and difference, while also demonstrating belonging to a group; it can be both an individual act of 'performing' ourselves, and a collective experience; fashion exists for the few as one-off couture pieces or tailor-made bespoke clothing, and for the many as mass-produced volume clothing. Alternatively, make-it-yourself and customised individual pieces have recently captured the imagination of a younger generation and grown in popularity—directly mimicking the hippie revolution of the 1970s and its hand-crafted clothing. The desire to be fashionable, for constant change and renewal, expresses itself in all areas of contemporary lifestyles, have created over-consumption and obsolescence. This is paradoxically what fuels the industry on which many millions depend for their livelihoods in both the developing and developed world, from cotton farmers to garment workers and shop staff. For those living below the poverty line in countries such as China and Bangladesh, jobs in clothing factories often offer a better alternative to subsistence farming, although wages may be no more than the bare local minimum. Western consumers have come to realise that complex ethical issues are hidden behind all our fashion purchasing decisions. Some of these fashion stories are told in the following chapter and further reading can be found in the resources section.

Given this background and the myriad of meanings and interpretations attached to fashion as a cultural, economic or social phenomenon, the concept of 'eco-fashion' may seem a contradiction—an oxymoron in itself. The pioneering but short-lived eco-fashion wave of the early 1990s associated the archetypal natural and 'wholesome' image with environmentally sound fashion. Today's eco-fashions are based on combining ecological and ethical principles with concept innovation and a high level of design aesthetic. Whether made from totally organic cotton, recycled vintage fabrics or designed for less waste and longer life, a new wave of stylish designs is changing the way sustainable and ethically sourced clothing is perceived—eco-fashion is becoming chic! The groundwork of previously initiatives has paved the way for more development of textile materials and greater infrastructure is in place, including certification and legislation on chemicals for example. Demand has risen and both designers and consumers now have more choices for sourcing ecologically-produced goods.

In today's context of increased concerns about global climate and environmental issues, scarcity of energy resources and ethical production, there is a new sensibility that conspicuous consumption of faster and faster fashion must slow down. However, the fashion and textiles industries are hugely important economically; accounting for one person in six in employment worldwide, from fields to factories. The desire for novelty and credible fashion status is deeply rooted in our psyche and the constant turn of fashion cycles, which drives demand and fuels the industry, will never disappear; nor should it. However, alternatives have to be developed. Buying things that have been made more considerately is a choice we are prepared to embrace, but different issues arise when businesses have to contemplate the impact of a decline in their sales. This then is the fashion paradox—how to reconcile the transience and inherent obsolescence of fashion's constant change with the imperatives of sustainability and social justice, and fashion's economic importance with diminishing resources? How can we consume clothing with a clear conscience?

This book presents some different possible solutions to these dilemmas. A number of pioneering clothing companies such as Katharine Hamnett, People Tree, Gossypium and Ciel and have been creating and developing eco-philosophy fashions since the 1990s, particularly focused on organic cotton production or recycled materials. Now several smaller design-led companies have sprung up, creating alternative approaches to eco-clothing, with an increasing focus on style and fashion, rather than an overtly campaigning message. These companies appeal to the highly design conscious and fickle Western consumer, who now has endless choice in shopping. While only a few of these small designers will sustain a larger or more long term business, they can all influence the agenda enormously; just compare the similar phenomenal growth in organic food sales. We now have a marketplace that is reminiscent of the tale of David and Goliath—the small companies raising consciousness, stimulating demand and gathering a growing consumer public following, to such an extent that the large companies have had to act. Larger high street chains and global companies such as Nike, Gap and M&S were previously accused of unethical practices in clothing and footwear production but are now embracing the imperatives for traceability to find ethical and environmental solutions to the paradox. The buying and production power of these large companies means that even a small percentage shift towards ethical and ecological sourcing, such as including a proportion of organic cotton in their fabric, can make a massive difference. This is where fundamental and lasting change in the fashion industry must come from. Eco-fashion must aspire to being the norm—not the exception—and requires a re-examination of all the principles and processes of producing, designing and marketing clothes. Consumers can be a great influence for positive change, once they are made aware of the issues, and are offered alternatives which meet acceptable ethical and fashion standards.

We are witnessing the convergence of a number of wider political and Non Governmental Organisation (NGO) initiatives such as Make Poverty History, Forum for the Future, Pesticide Action Network, Clean Clothes Campaign and Labour behind the Label and the Fair Trade Movement, together with the key impact of the Stern Report in the UK and Al Gore's *An Inconvenient Truth* in the US, assessing the potentially disastrous economic, environmental and social effects of climate change. In the textiles sector, there has been a proliferation in eco-labelling certification across different countries and fibres such as the Oeko-Tex 100 fabric label system, SKAL, GOTS, Fairtrade and the Soil Association organic cotton certification. The recent establishment of UK campaigning organisations the Ethical Fashion Forum and the project Fashioning an Ethical Industry have begun to make an impact in the UK's higher education sector—raising awareness among tutors and the next generation of fashion and textile designers. The London College of Fashion has now instigated a Centre for Sustainable Fashion to provide a focus and resource for further educational and industry activities.

Within the fashion business there have been new initiatives. The last-minute establishment of an eco-fashion designer grouping Estethica at London Fashion Week in September 2006 (now established as a regular feature), So Ethic in the Pret-a-Porter Paris trade exhibition, and Slowhite in Milan, show how 'fashionable' ethical and eco-fashion has become. Ethical Fashion shows have taken place in recent years in Paris, London and New York as the trend for ethical and environmentally-aware fashion spreads. Surely the long term aim must be for ethical fashion not to be singled out, to get to the point where it no longer needs its own separate event to raise awareness. However, in order that green is not just the new black, information is required to assist and inspire the next generation of fashion designers and students. We are in a transitional period, one in which there is real opportunity for lasting change, with more transparency essential in the way clothing is produced and reaches the shops at the price it does. The ethics of clothing production have come more and more to the foreground of media debate, featuring prominently in the press and broadcast media. BBC Radio 4 featured an edition of *The Moral Maze* in July 2007 which asked: "What, if any, is our moral responsibility to those who make the clothes we buy?" The programme concluded that there was often over simplification of the issues by external commentators and the local context such as levels of poverty had to be recognised, commenting that actions such as boycotts could damage livelihoods in the longer term.

For its third showing September 2007, London Fashion Week's Estethica ethical fashion show-within-show was sponsored by Monsoon.

The Evolution of Eco-Fashion

The eco-fashion movement has had previous incarnations: first as part of the hippie revolution in the mid-1970s, when it might be considered more as an anti-fashion stance. The movement was characterised by opting out of mainstream commercial activities and setting up 'alternative' lifestyles, with homemade, ethnic and hand-crafted fabrics and clothes the norm. This type of eco-fashion, embracing fabrics such as hemp and natural dyeing, can still be see in the modern incarnation of 'new-age traveller' communities and other alternative lifestyles. The second wave of eco-fashion appeared in a more commercial manner in the 1990s, one of whose

Green dress by Debbie Little, made from a parachute, and brown dress by Juste, made from fair trade silk which is naturally dyed in Bangladesh. Photograph by Yuri Anderegg.

Poster for 2007 Ethical Fashion Show, which is now held annually in Paris.

champions was the US fashion company Esprit, an eco-aware company based in San Francisco since the 1960s (the cradle of the hippie culture). Designed by Lynda Grose (who still is an active campaigner today), Esprit launched their Ecollection in 1994. At this time, there was a substantial amount of eco-activism in California and outdoor clothing companies such as Patagonia and J Crew had already started to develop environmentally-sensitive ranges. In the UK, the fashion trade magazine *Drapers Record* included a special report "Going Green" in June 1994, highlighting eco-lines (mainly t-shirts) available in the high street from Next, H&M and others. At this time legislation was just being put in place in the EU to regulate the effluent standards from dye houses and was a matter of concern to the industry, due to increased costs. But the concept of eco-fashion was still an oxymoron five years later. *The Independent* newspaper ran an article on fashionable young eco-clothing designers, featuring designs by Conscious Earthwear (now Ciel), Jessica Ogden, Komodo and Patagonia and knitwear from Amano made by women's groups in Bolivia in January 1999. The article asked:

Is it possible to be both fashionable and environmentally friendly? Environmentalism is still associated with the 'new age' look of the early 1990s, with natural hemp and wooden love beads, or with the traveller trends of dreadlocks, combat gear and Peruvian sweaters.

In the last few years, more small, ethical and ecologically-motivated fashion companies have sprung up and the momentum and debate has grown exponentially. In 2006, the Craft Council's Well Fashioned exhibition, curated by Rebecca Earley of Chelsea College of Art & Design, assembled some of the smaller designer fashion companies working in the UK and especially in London's fashionable East End. This did a great deal to raise consciousness particularly among younger people, simultaneously creating a massive amount of press and publicity for the cause. However, in the long term, the major commercial impact will be from the difference that the large high street and designer brand companies can make throughout their decision-making and value chains, due to their purchasing power and economic significance. After much preparatory work, M&S announced in January 2007 a bold environmental strategy for the entire company, that has helped set the agenda for others to follow.

PASSIONATE ECO-CAMPAIGNER

LYNDA GROSE

LYNDA GROSE *worked as a knitwear designer for Esprit in 1990. The womenswear company, based in California—the hotbed for environmentalism—made the enlightened management decision to investigate the issues and develop an ecologically sound collection of women's clothing. This was to be known as the Ecollection and the main drive came from Esprit CEO, Peter Buckley, who set up an 'eco-desk' to carry out a company-wide audit of activities and materials, involving all the staff.*

GROSE BEGAN to research and create the designs together with 'thinker' Dan Imhoff (now author of many environmental farming publications) who developed the eco-criteria by which the collection would operate. By 1992, the first clothes were in the shops, and unusually for a fashion company, the collection was not expected to make any initial profit. However, the Ecollection generated six million dollars worth of sales, and broke even by 1994. Their environmental charter was ambitious and wide-reaching, including plans to:

Maximise product life through classic design and durable construction; Eliminate or minimise the use of manmade fibres;

Portrait of Lynda Grose.

OPPOSITE TOP:
Autumn 1992 brochure page detailing the Esprit Ecollection philosophy and showing natural coloured undyed clothing and post-consumer Donegal tweed jacket. Image courtesy Lynda Grose.

OPPOSITE BOTTOM:
Outfit made of post industrial recycled wool. Image courtesy Lynda Grose.

Minimise load on landfills—use recycled and biodegradable materials; Encourage sustainable agriculture and farming; Work with businesses that share our ethical and environmental goals; Influence the fashion industry.

THE COLLECTION was considered, using US naturally coloured organic cotton. organic and recycled wool, linen, Tencel and also sourced handmade items such as buttons and jewellery made from natural and recycled materials, by artisan groups in Ghana and Ecuador to support their livelihoods. The collection was immediately successful but, in retrospect, Grose now feels there was a compromise on the issue of colour. Although low impact dyes were favoured to minimise the impact of the dyeing process, predominantly un-dyed and unbleached fabrics were used in the collection, contributing to one of the lasting stereotypes of eco-fashion. Despite the initial success, this groundbreaking initiative became vulnerable. The Ecollection was planned to be absorbed into the main collection, but—subject to not just the changing moods of fashion but also to the inevitable changes in senior management it closed in Autumn 1995 when Peter Buckley left the company (as Grose says "fashion cannot survive on beige alone").

 GROSE WAS spurred on by the issues that she uncovered during her time at Esprit which were reiterated in her subsequent role at Patagonia. Grose now designs, teaches and activates both in California and overseas. She also consults for Aid for Artisans in Armenia, Peru and Kyrgestan, where she works with local producer groups.

THE FAIR TRADE FASHION PIONEER

PEOPLE TREE

WELL KNOWN *as one of the original ethical trading companies, the strap line on the People Tree catalogue reads "the Fair Trade fashion pioneer". People Tree was founded in 1997 by Safia Minney while she was living in Japan She built on her previous work by establishing the catalogue,* Global Village. *By the mid-1990s,* Global Village *had grown into a company trading green products to 500 outlets. The trading arm of* Global Village *evolved into the Fair Trade Company which later became a member of the International Fair Trade Association (IFAT).*

AFTER SEVERAL years trading eco-products, fashion was added to the Fair Trade Company's range (based on ecological and organic textiles) and the People Tree collection was born. The People Tree ethos therefore began with the premise of sustainable development for excluded and disadvantaged people in developing countries, and not from the idea of starting a fashion company. In 2001, the company set up operations in the UK and is the first clothing company in the UK to have both Fairtrade and Soil Association accreditation on their designs.

    PEOPLE TREE creates close and sustainable partnerships with organic farmers and artisans working in small-scale village units in many countries including India, Bangladesh, Chile and Kenya. Producing handmade textiles, clothing and jewellery. An entire village may have 150 to 600 people engaged in embroidery or hand-weaving

A stylish and attractive, checkered monochrome People Tree top.

OPPOSITE TOP:
A Richard Nicoll design for People Tree in collaboration with Vogue Japan.

OPPOSITE BOTTOM:
People Tree Cable Waistcoat

and the company gives technical assistance and also supports local social projects. Through the catalogue, the company has helped to find new western markets for these products and kept traditional local skills alive. However, in those pioneering days, when the market was more conservative, People Tree sold t-shirts and casual wear to 'handicrafts types' who were predominantly in their 40s. Now the market for ethical and ecologically-produced goods has become more competitive and fashion aware across all age groups.

SAFIA MINNEY says: "Fashion is political, that's got to be part of the reason why people buy the clothes. If you buy a dress from People Tree, you do so in the knowledge that you are helping to distribute wealth more widely around the world." Each catalogue tells a story of one aspect of production—perhaps organic cotton growing in Bangladesh or natural dyeing in southern India. However, this is not enough for today's fashion consumer faced with numerous choices, not all of them ethical. Buying decisions are often based on price as much as design. A shift has recently taken place in which ethical production has begun to unite with mainstream fashion.

WHEN TOPSHOP decided to embrace ethical fashion and join the 'green bandwagon', People Tree was one of three ethical fashion companies given floor space for Fairtrade Fortnight in March 2006. The success of this is evident, as the flagship store in central London maintained its People Tree concession. Jane Shepherdson, former buying director of TopShop is quoted saying: "The clothes need to be more exciting, more directional, so they stand for something [other than saving the planet]." Shephersdon left TopShop and joined the advisory board of People Tree in 2007. A greater fashion influence in now evident in the catalogue pages and one project saw the collaboration of People Tree, Vogue Japan and directional designer Richard Nicoll and others designing an exclusive collection. From now on it is clear that fair trade and fashion need not be mutually exclusive.

THE ICONIC UK RETAILER

MARKS & SPENCER

MARKS & SPENCER *(M&S) developed into a national institution from its beginnings in the late nineteenth century as a 'Penny Bazaar' market stall in Leeds, Yorkshire. M&S is known equally well for its clothing and food lines, particularly for keeping the nation fully supplied in underwear and gourmet sandwiches. M&S also built a reputation for quality and value in basic clothing and in its materials and manufacturing, imposing stringent standards on all its suppliers via its team of 150 clothing technologists.*

ORIGINALLY, THE company prided itself on manufacturing (through its suppliers) the majority of its clothing in the UK, with a small proportion made in Israel (a country with which the company has always had close links). However, this changed in the 1990s due to shifts in global economics which, although M&S resisted much longer than its competitors, inevitably led to overseas sourcing.

As the biggest clothing retailer in the UK, with 520 stores, due to its buying power, many supplier companies had become over-dependent on M&S business, and the M&S withdrawal was a significant contributing factor to the decline of much of the UK garment manufacturing sector. Well known for its mainstream clothing for the middle market, M&S was initially slow to create lines to attract younger and more fashion-conscious older consumers, and underwent a period of declining sales at the turn of the century.

This was redressed with the development of new lines such as Per Una, 2001, designed by Next founder George Davis, and the Autograph series designed by guest designers such as Betty Jackson, Julien MacDonald and Timothy Everest. Per Una's profile has also been raised through advertising campaigns using a selection of fashion icons such as 1960s model Twiggy and modern *model-du-jour* Lily Cole. Other marketing initiatives included the abandoning of the famous St Michael brand and the recent creation of a more personalised concept and logo: Your M&S.

UNDER THE leadership of chief executive Stuart Rose, the company has developed a public reputation as a progressive actor on environmental and ethical issues throughout its operations. However behind the scenes, and for many years, M&S has developed policies on safety and environmental aspects of clothing such as the elimination of harmful chemicals and dyes from the textiles it sources.[6] It has developed its own environmental, chemical and factory minimum standards and codes of practice, which have become something of a benchmark within the fashion industry for other brands and manufacturers to follow. M&S joined the Ethical Trading Initiative in 1999, and company activities in these key ethical and environmental areas recently reached a stage where they were confident to 'go public' and speak openly about them. In 2006, the issues of sustainable garment production rose to the top of the media, public and business agendas. The marketing concept Look Behind the Label sought to address the increasing demand from M&S consumers for information about its products, via adverts and a dedicated website. In January 2007 Stuart Rose announced the groundbreaking Plan A, a bold statement on the company's intentions on five key areas of environmental and ethical policy over a five year period. This was a major step for a high street retailer which others have followed, and has gained the company a number of business awards. In the

M&S supply a vast range of men's fashion alongside their predominant womenswear. Shown here is a cashmere jumper, cossack hat and red scarf accessories Autumn, 2007.

OPPOSITE:
A model shows off a metalic-effect bikini from the M&S Spring/Summer 2008 range.

6   Derek McKelvey, Interrogating Fashion seminar presentation at the LCF, July 2000.

**7   For further details
refer to the M&S website:
www.marksandspencer.com**

LEFT:
Fair trade Cotton boxer
shorts for men.

RIGHT:
Laura Bailey models the
M&S five pound fair trade
t-shirt.

OPPOSITE TOP:
Iconic model Twiggy shows off
the M&S sustainable, fair trade
cotton collection with Laura
Bailey and Erin O'Connor.

OPPOSITE BOTTOM:
M&S washcare label
promoting lower temperature
of 30° as part of Plan A.

contemporary climate it is no longer sufficient for a retailer to sell goods—they also have to take responsibility for the stages involved in their manufacturing process. *The Guardian* recently produced their Green List of FTSE 100 companies. Only two high street clothing brands revealed their carbon emissions, one of which being the retail giant M&S.

PLAN A comprises a hundred commitments on five areas: climate change, waste, sustainable raw materials, fair partnerships and health.[7] One of its main commitments is to become carbon neutral, and to be sending nothing to landfill sites by 2012. With regard to clothing, Plan A has committed to launching organic cotton, linen and wool lines and is trialling recycled polyester fleece for 2008. The aim is that, by 2012, all its polyester products, from clothing to homeware, will be made from recycled plastic bottles.

HAVING PROMOTED a Fairtrade Fortnight in 2007, including clothing lines, commitment number 81 of the hundred listed, states they will convert 20 million garments to fair trade cotton. When factoring in the popularity of their five pound cotton t-shirts, this

shift is equivalent to ten per cent of all the cotton used by M&S. Furthermore, Mike Barry, head of Corporate Social Responsibility, announced that M&S had purchased a third of all the fair trade cotton production for 2008. In 2008 the company will also start to benchmark its suppliers as gold, silver and bronze depending on their ethical trading status and adoption of the new M&S Supplier Exchange Initiative for best practice.

WITH THE opening of a series of restructured 'green' stores —the first in Bournemouth—M&S has made public pledges on environmental and ethical trading practices, and the day-to-day operation of its business. It is campaigning on many fronts, including the reduction in recommended washing temperatures from 40C (degrees Celsius) to 30C on its garment labelling. This can reduce energy consumption significantly. So far the initiative has had positive response in the industry and it remains to be seen how Plan A succeeds with consumers, and how they will buy into the new ethics of the M&S brand, which, ultimately, must translate into sales.

Katharine Hamnett, UK Fashion Designer of the Year 1984, meets Prime Minister Margaret Thatcher.

OPPOSITE:
Katharine Hamnett show Spring/Summer1985. Oversized T-shirts featured slogans 'EDUCATION NOT MISSILES', and 'STAY ALIVE IN '85'. Image courtesy of Katharine Hamnett.

THE UNCROWNED QUEEN OF ETHICAL FASHION

KATHARINE HAMNETT

KATHARINE HAMNETT, *since her early days in fashion in the 1980s, has always been an independent voice. Hamnett has become well known as a campaigner for human rights and a political activist, using fashion as her medium. It was she who became famous for wearing a t-shirt declaring '58% DON'T WANT PERSHING' to meet prime minister Margaret Thatcher at a Downing Street fashion reception and, in so doing, launched the slogan t-shirt, which is now ubiquitous. In keeping with many fashion trends which have re-emerged from the 1980s, Hamnett recently re-issued her vintage t-shirts such as 'CHOOSE LIFE' and 'BRING BACK GOD', the style of which have been copied in high street stores and market stalls everywhere.*

THERE IS of course much to campaign about in the traditional fashion manufacturing and supply chain. In 1989 Hamnett commissioned some research on the environmental impact of the textile and clothing industry she was involved in, and found appalling facts about deaths from pesticides and contaminated water supplies, and dreadful working conditions in garment factories. This deeply affected the course of Hamnett's business, in an industry that was at that time reluctant to take any of these issues on board. After 'wrestling' with her manufacturers for many years (to try to get them to comply with ethical and environmental standards), she pulled out of the fashion

system altogether: "I decided I didn't want to make a living from the people suffering at the bottom of the supply chain. So I cancelled my licences and decided I would go back into manufacturing, which I hate, in order to source and produce an ethical collection and make it as environmental as I can possibly get it."[8]

SINCE HER epiphany at the end of the 1980s, Hamnett has collaborated with Pesticide Action Network in their campaign films which she is proud to say were featured on CNN across the US. Unusually for a fashion designer, she worked directly with cotton producers, fabric weavers and garment manufacturers around the world, sourcing organically grown cotton, trimmings and threads to deal with every aspect of her clothing manufacture. The global nature of the textile and fashion supply chain is highlighted throughout the production cycle: Hamnett's cotton may be grown in Africa, spun in Germany, woven in India or the UK, and garments manufactured in India, Portugal or Italy. She categorically states, however, that she will not use China to outsource either fabrics or manufacturing because of its poor ethical and human rights record.

NEARLY GIVING up from exhaustion and frustration, Hamnett persevered, and in September 2006, launched her new, online only, menswear and womenswear ranges. She did this under the Katharine E Hamnett label and showed the collection at the first ever Estethica show at London Fashion Week. Her approach is to create a desirable, wearable and durable evolving fashion collection—not one that changes every season—which is as ethically and environmentally sound as possible in its production, hence the 'E' in the new brand. On a spectrum of 'shades of green' the Katharine E Hamnett collection is extremely dark green and aiming for perfection. Having been somewhat marginalised in recent years by the fashion industry, which she criticises in many respects, Hamnett has remained steadfastly independent, enabling her to fight for her causes in the way she wants,

8 Katharine Hamnett, speaking at the Interrogating Fashion Symposium, London College of Fashion, 29 November 2005.

9 Authour Interview, 27 July 2007.

— 34 —

and she now finds that her time has come again. This time round though, there has been a "sea change, a paradigm shift in consumer attitudes which is irreversible—this is not a trend".[9]

HAMNETT IS passionate about organic cotton, which comprises the majority of her collection, including the new range of canvas sneakers she is developing. She is critical of the Fairtrade mark, finding it "superficial" and not reaching far enough to benefit farmers directly in the same manner that the health benefits and premium price for organic cotton can achieve. However, she does recognise that bad practice can occur in all areas of production, including organic cotton.

ONE OF Hamnett's most recent projects, and arguably her most significant in terms of potential impact, was with the Tesco supermarket giant. Once again there has been controversy. During her third season designing an organic cotton range of clothing—shirts, dresses, t-shirts, shorts and so on for men and women—she decided not to renew her contract. By "wringing out the supply chain" (dealing directly with the cotton growers and factories in India and Sri Lanka) she persuaded Tesco to commit to buying the cotton six months ahead of season. Tesco cut out the wholesalers and agents (and their profits) to enable a higher quality product to be sold at a reasonable price level compared with their normal products. This organic cotton collection was to be sold at a lower profit margin in order to gain market share. This type of collaboration contributes to Hamnett's aim: to achieve fashion for the widest group of consumers—both in sizing and ages. Hamnett enjoys the challenge this kind of designing brings, designing clothes which will be long lasting (perhaps 40 years) that are well made using high quality materials; utilising both her skill and restraint to create fashion that will become classic. Of course the publicity value for both parties is potentially great if the products are successful in the marketplace, although she emphasises there was no budget allocated to publicity for the Tesco collection. Lack of marketing was one of the

Part of the advertising campaign for the Katharine Hamnett Denim Collection.

OPPOSITE:
Model wears iconic 'CHOOSE LIFE' slogan t-shirt. Image courtesy of Katharine Hamnett.

8   **For further details refer to the M&S website:** www.marksandspencer.com

reasons for the terminating of the Tesco agreement. The recent pairing of TopShop with model Kate Moss—not a designer—is a very different case but a telling comparison in the publicity stakes. Attention to detail is key in her new product development. During the Tesco collaboration, working directly with fabric suppliers and the buying-power of a major supermarket enabled Hamnett to produce particular fabrics including a blend of organic cotton with four per cent recycled polyester. The polyester allows the fabric to be permanently pleated, extending the longevity of the fashion garment.

CREATING HER ethical and environmentally sound collections has been—and still is—a lifetime's work for Katharine Hamnett. From the time she struggled to obtain threads and zip tape for the manufacturing of her collections which reached the same high standards as the organic cotton cloth, she has now experienced working with the force of a major brand with the ability to place significant volumes of orders for fibre and cloth. Hamnett believes fashion is a fundamental function to societies and humanity—people adorn themselves as part of the mating ritual—and fashion will never go away.

WITH HER Katharine E Hamnett line, she has reached the point where she is once again looking to license manufacturing but this time in a very different commercial climate. The difference in consumer attitudes, their demand for more information and higher expectations is now driving forward into the mainstream an agenda which has been at the heart of Hamnett's work for nearly two decades. Retailers are highly sensitive to consumer influence and the importance of ethical issues to purchasing decisions are now being recorded in numerous surveys. Hamnett believes we are moving from, "a moral imperative to an economic imperative"—which has finally galvanised the larger corporations into action.[10] She is very fond of statistics and cites them with ease to justify her stance on ethical and environmental

10 Authour Interview, 27 July 2007.

issues within textiles and clothing production: the World Health Organisation and Pesticide Action Network figures for deaths caused by pesticide use in Africa are compelling in their horror. Hamnett is currently working with the United Nations' Better Cotton Initiative on developing a new certification for ethically and environmentally sound clothing to supersede the proliferation of other individual standards. The new mark, free to farmers, suppliers and manufacturers, will include standards for both materials, production and labour processes. This will be the first certification of its kind in the clothing arena.

THE KATHARINE Hamnett company has become a campaigning organisation and Hamnett speaks excitedly about the new t-shirt campaign aimed at encouraging young people to vote and become engaged in politics once more—"SAVE THE WORLD—VOTE". Long may she reign.

CONTINUING TO RAISE THE BAR FOR ETHICAL FASHION

SARAH RATTY

SARAH RATTY *is the designer behind the eco-philosophy fashion label Ciel whose fans include celebrities such as Cate Blanchett and Sienna Miller. Ratty has championed ecologically sensitive fashions since her debut collection Touch the Earth, 1992, which featured unbleached organic cheesecloth and mud hand-prints. Ratty continues to create clothes which combine funky style with sustainable fabrics and azo free dyes. In her words the brand is:*

A hip, luxurious and special womenswear label that unites intelligent eco-design with socially conscious production methods for the thoughtfully style led.

BORN AND raised in Brighton, Ratty grew up surrounded by fashion. Her mother taught fashion at the local college—one of her students being Barbara Hulanicki, founder of seminal label Biba, in the 1960s. Ratty went on to study fashion in Bristol but, always one for asking too many questions, she was soon ploughing her own furrow and making her own way as a largely self-taught designer of eco-philosophy fashion. Working from a friends' studio, she started her own fashion line in 1990, and became one of a pioneering band of designers

Vintage Ciel coat. Image courtesy of Sarah Ratty.

OPPOSITE:
From the Spring/
Summer Collection.

who staged their own 'alternative' fashion shows in a warehouse in London's Camden Town. Compatriot, Maggie Pinhorn, negotiated the use of derelict spaces in London and still runs the now established Alternative Fashion Show in London's ultra-fashionable East End. Ratty's breakthrough came when she was offered the use of a shop space in the centre of London near the famous Liberty store. For a month she staged a fashion installation designed by an architect friend, which caught the eye of many fashion stylists—a case of being in the right place at the right time. Early projects included working with Oxfam to design their No Logo clothing range, at which point Ratty started working with waste knits such as Aran sweaters (creating new patchworks of old materials salvaged by Oxfam's Wastesavers operation). She continued to create recycled fashion, under her Conscious Earthwear label, by working with old sleeping bags and denim which went on to feature in the fashion press such as *i-D* and *The Face* and sell in prestigious fashion boutiques Browns and Whistles. A complete outfit (including one of a patchworked coat, skirt and top from the White Goddess collection made of old Aran sweaters) was featured in the key 1994 V&A exhibition Street Style, representing the new raw energy in street fashion. She says:

This style of remaking and remodelling from old clothes was really exciting as there was no precedent and there were no limits to innovation and creative freedom—if I wanted a particular pocket I simply cut one off something and incorporated it into the design. It was very organic and intuitive.[11]

OPPOSITE:
Ciel smock dress in fine organic cotton mousseline, Spring/Summer 2007 Collection. Photograph by Ben Gold.

11 Authour Interview, 27 July 2007.

One of Ciel's classic designs: 'Hollywood' biker jacket in Oeko-tex certified fake leather and faux fur fabrics, with alpaca sweater and satin culottes. Photograph by Ben Gold.

OPPOSITE:
From one of Ciel's earliest collections. Image courtesy of Carl-Johan Paulin.

UNUSUALLY FOR many pioneering eco-designers, Ratty's designs crossed the invisible line into fashion and she showed her first label of ecologically inspired clothes—Conscious Earthwear—at London Fashion Week in 1996 (gaining prestigious stockists in both the UK —Harrods, Harvey Nichols—and Japan). Although aiming for ethically and environmentally sound production, Ratty was partly driven to using recycled materials because of the difficulty of sourcing ecological fabrics such as organic cotton. At that time, the minimums were too high for a small designer-led company, a situation which has now begun to improve considerably. One of the most popular designs was her 'boarding parka' padded coat, inspired by old sleeping bags. Ratty's current collection, under the label Ciel, have a more feminine mood, and include hemp/silk blend fabric, cotton and linen fabrics, bamboo lingerie and alpaca knitwear. Alpaca and cotton are sourced from Peru where traditional production methods can be said to be naturally 'organic'. In 2006 Ratty visited southern India to work with Lambani embroiderers for a range of accessories and tops, for Ciel Spring/ Summer 2007. The Spring/Summer 2008 Collection included silks, block printed by hand, personally sourced in Karnataka India, helping to keep artisan skills alive.

THE CURRENT climate for fashion designers is far better than it was in the early 1990s when there were no azo free dyes, and organic cotton was only available in white or undyed. However, the new wave of eco-designers have often been grouped together in eco-shops (such as Equa or online outlets such as adili.com or mywardrobe.com) whereas Ratty prefers Ciel to also be seen within the general fashion marketplace. This success is evident by regular press coverage in the fashion pages.

SPEAKING ABOUT fabric sourcing, Ratty is of the opinion that organic cotton should not necessarily be grown in Africa where water is such a problem. She also believes it is also not necessary to demonise China as there are good and bad factories everywhere. Ratty's approach is a stark contrast to that of Katharine Hamnett who refuses to work with China due to its poor human rights record. Ratty's views are sought by several organisations whose committees she advises on, such as the Soil Association organic textile certification programme. She believes we need to make compromises in order to achieve the eco-philosophy agenda, and that the constant quest for perfection (as sought by some campaigners and designers) negates the progress that has been made over the last decade. She says:

The best thing fashion designers can do at present is to offer a better choice to consumers—we must accept that a dark side exists and 'there is no shape without shadow'—but demonisation is not the way forward.

SARAH RATTY has at last received recognition for her pioneering stance on eco-fashion: Ciel was presented with the first UK Exports Ethical Fashion Award and was shortlisted for the *Observer's* 2007 Ethical Awards in the ethical fashion category. The philosophy that "Ciel designs from the inside out" has paid off and as the *Evening Standard* wrote in November 2006: "Ciel is a fashion label that continues to raise the bar for ethical fashion". A year later the *Observer* cited Ciel as an "ethical label we really love and aren't just buying because we feel obliged to".[12]

12 Ciel was listed no 24 in the *Observer* Womens' Alternative Style awards, November 2007.

Today, consumers and designers are faced with a bewildering array of labelling and terminology. Terms such as 'sustainable', 'organic', 'green', 'fair trade', 'ethical', 'eco', 'bio' and 'environmental' need to be understood so consumers can make comparisons and informed choices. Fashion purchasing decisions are based on desire more than need—in the West we have more than enough clothes for our basic needs. If sustainable principles are inbuilt, clothes will be less environmentally harmful and still appeal to the consumer. We need to achieve some balance between the many factors in operation in the market, so clothes regain some of their long term value to last longer (some to become heirlooms of the future) and therefore be less disposable. The role that design and aesthetics play in this transformation is crucial—purchasing decisions are generally made on visual and fashion appeal, not on their do-good credentials. Therefore new design thinking is increasingly important throughout the fashion and clothing industry. Consumers need to be offered great fashion that has, almost incidentally, been ethically made on environmentally sound principles as a new standard of added value. Although there are many good examples, we are still a long way from this position, especially at the middle market and designer levels.

Eco-chic presents designs covering an international selection of fashion and clothing companies including jewellery, footwear and accessory makers. From small to large, this book features designer and company profiles to illustrate some of the ways in which 'eco-chic' can be achieved. The chapters illustrate the many links in the textile and fashion supply chain from fibre production to garment manufacturing and retail, highlighting the important role of design choices and the power of the fashion buyer. We discuss the concept of 'shades of green' and raise questions of a 'trade-off' between various problems such as travel miles and organic production, fair trade and higher cost materials, low cost or luxury goods.

If a company introduces eco-fashion lines, what impact does this have on their non-eco goods? Many axes of decision-making are involved in the design process involving material choices, performance and longevity, aesthetics, manufacturing process and aftercare, all within a given cost constraint, whether bespoke, handmade or small batch production, designer level or for mass-production and the high street consumer. This book will help to inform and inspire people to understand the complexities and how everyone can make their contribution.

Issues in the Fashion Industry

The fashion business is often completely unpredictable: months ahead of release dates, trends have to be anticipated and interpreted for the retail customer by designers and buyers. The traditional textile and fashion supply chain comprises many levels: fibre to yarn to fabric (including dyeing and finishing processes), design, sourcing fabric and garment manufacturing, through to the range planning, buying, production, wholesaling, marketing and retail consumption stages.

Fashion buyers perform a hidden but pivotal role in selecting and ordering the styles and ranges which actually appear in the shops. Ordering from manufacturers must of course be done in advance and is, by the nature of fashion, speculative. Actual sales are uncertain, fluctuating massively; due to the operation of fashion cycles, the influence of trends and also the volatile factor of the weather. Therefore, buyers are under business pressures, and try to finalise their orders as close to their seasonal needs as possible, responding to emerging trends up to the last minute, making changes in colours or specifications, sometimes cancelling orders or re-ordering at short notice. Factories are given seasonal work, which may not be repeated, as sourcing typically moves around to find the best prices and schedules. Therefore season-to-season continuity for workers is not guaranteed. Decisions made remotely at head office can therefore have a major impact on what happens at factory level, an issue now recognised by global companies such as Gap. In addition to this volatility, fashion cycles are inherently wasteful—much stock is unsold even after being put 'on sale'. Waste comes from both pre-consumption and post-consumption phases and surplus stock is sold on to discounters, burnt, dumped or traded to the developing world through the charity shops networks. Over a million tonnes of textiles and clothing (including household textiles) are discarded annually in the UK, 70 per cent of which is dumped into landfill, although up to half of this is still reusable.[13]

More sustainable approaches to fashion design need to consider the whole life cycle—that is, all stages from production to consumption and disposal. Issues which have to be addressed, either in small or large increments, or sometimes by radical change, include:

PRODUCT DESIGN AND DEVELOPMENT
fibre and materials selection and combination
reduction in wastage including materials and energy
environmental impact of dye pollution, water and energy usage
re-usability or recycle ability
design for entire life cycle
good design solutions and aesthetics
new technologies and processes.

PRODUCTION AND MANUFACTURE
global sourcing locations and international trade agreement
increasing competition and fast fashion
ethical sourcing of production, audits and compliance
codes of conduct and supply chain management
value for money and efficiency.

PROFITABILITY AND INVESTMENT IN RESEARCH
retail and consumer facing
education on environmental and ethical issues
communication and transparency
traceability of production chain
social responsibility and justice
end of product life—new responsibility and take-back.

Each of these areas is in itself highly complex, needing to be broken down into components and matched with possible solutions and new approaches in the

13 Recycling of Low Grade Waste, 2006, Oakdene Hollins and Salvation Army Trading and Nonwovens Innovation and Research Institute, 2006

context of sustainability. In the last two decades, much has been debated and written about green design, design for sustainability, design for the environment and eco-design (see booklist in resources section) but this literature has focused on product design and rarely touched substantially on fashion.

This book attempts to throw light on the way the fashion system works, especially in relation to the UK, with analysis of some of the fundamental items of clothing in our wardrobes, and how they arrive in the shops. The aim is to give more insight into the complex circumstances and the inter-dependence of the different aspects of the textiles and fashion industry. In this book, fashion is an inclusive word that covers clothing, footwear, and accessories but also incorporates aesthetics, attitudes to lifestyle and the designed environment. Fashion is a powerful communicator with which we exhibit status, sexuality, and signal specific messages. We use it to enhance our self-esteem and express identity, through belonging to a group or being different. We can use it to blend in or stand out, make radical statements or hope to be cool. Fashion functions as social catalyst in many situations, and everyone has an intimate relationship with their clothes, whether subconsciously or more overtly.

Approaches to the Fashion Paradox

Many strategies can be adopted to minimise environmental impact within the design and production of fashion. At all stages of design and production decision-making there are trade-offs to be made, reconciling fashion and style with available materials, costs and time constraints. Throughout the examples shown, many different approaches are evident, often several are enlisted at the same time, greatly enhancing the reduction of environmental impact. Some examples of these are:

RE-THINKING DESIGN FOR THE ENTIRE FASHION LIFE CYCLE
design concern for use and end-of-life and possible re-use or disassembly

RECLAIM AND RE-USE WASTE MATERIALS
design with materials that would otherwise be discarded

RECYCLE
design using already reprocessed waste materials

UPCYCLE
design using reprocessed or waste materials to make a product of equal or higher, not lower, quality

REPAIR AND REMODEL
make good an existing item fit for new purpose

RECREATE
creatively re-think, customise or re-design an existing design concept

REDUCE
design for minimal use of energy, minimise or eliminate waste materials

USE ECOLOGICAL MATERIALS
design choices for environmentally benign fibres, fabrics and other materials, seeking to minimise impact

USE MONO MATERIALS
use of only one material to facilitate recyclability

HARNESS NEW TECHNOLOGY
apply technology to achieve reductions in energy, materials or develop more efficient new process

LONGER LASTING FASHION
design with high quality materials and making, with aesthetic durability creating emotional bonds in addition to function

MULTIFUNCTIONAL CLOTHES
designs with more than one use or configuration

DESIGN FOR DELIGHT
creating new and sustained feel-good relationships with clothes to be valued

Above all, design for delight and wellbeing are essential if eco-fashion is to be successful, incorporating as many principles of eco-design as possible. This list could never be exhaustive, but indicates some of the thinking which can be applied at the design stage of the fashion cycle. Other initiatives, such as take back of clothes by shops, have begun to emerge as new strategies for the end of the fashion life cycle (which is of course much shorter than the end of the garment's life), and which has now become part of the overall responsibility of the entire fashion industry. Many of the large companies have now introduced eco-lines, using organic cotton for example, but these can reflect negatively on the rest of their fashion offering, a difficult problem creating a major barrier to eco-fashion, but one which is being tackled by several retailers and manufacturers. There can now be some optimism that the greening of the fashion industry is at last underway in earnest.

RE-DESIGNING FASHION

This chapter looks at some of the wider issues and design context in which fashion and clothing are situated how we relate to things in our world, and how innovations in design and production can help turn the tide of severe over-consumption and environmental disharmony.

Product design determines the way everything we use around us works, looks and feels, from humble objects such as clothes pegs to highly engineered devices like vacuum cleaners, and the more obviously 'designed' kitchen appliances of Alessi or Philippe Starck. Innovations like the Dyson vacuum cleaner propel functional objects onto a new plane. James Dyson fundamentally redesigned

Designs from Noir Spring/ Summer 2007 collection, Cotton Couture, created to make cotton luxurious and sexy, using certified African cotton. Image courtesy of Noir.

the vacuum cleaner, which operates differently and looks completely unlike its predecessors—a radical paradigm shift. Dyson's re-thinking of design changed the relationship of person to appliance and has permanently influenced other areas of domestic design. In fashion, the revolutionary concept of A Piece of Cloth (APOC) clothing first launched by Issey Miyake and Dai Fujiwara in 1999, creates clothing which is almost complete as it rolls off the knitting or weaving machinery. Designed to reduce waste fabric, the garments then need minimal sewing and finishing. The APOC process eliminates the need to use sample fabrics and garments can be made on demand; reducing the need for stockholding. This collection concept is unique in the fashion industry and represents a re-thinking of fashion through creative development of manufacturing technology. These examples illustrate the way new paradigms emerge through innovative design thinking.

Gradually, over the last few decades, concepts within a sustainability agenda (longer lasting goods, low energy and environmental footprint, reduced wastage, or recyclable materials) are now routinely considered as part of contemporary architecture and product design. However, the same approach has not yet been automatically and comprehensively applied to fashion design, which is also a form of product development but one which operates within its constantly changing remit. Clothing must be functional, suited to its market and purpose, it has to fit the body in a wide range of sizes, it has to be laundered or cleaned and it has to fit within a pricing bracket determined by the market. At the same time, fashion must inspire delight and desire through novelty and originality. However, design choices in style, cut, fit, and fabric are infinite, and there are no absolutes, only timeless 'classics' which remain benchmarks for the periodic shifts which move fashion forward.

There is a polarisation evident in the fashion market between the highly influential and radical fashion designers and the eco-pioneer companies. The forward thinking designers such as Issey Miyake, Comme des Garcons, Yohji Yamamoto, Martin Margiela and Hussein Chalayan create major shifts in thinking about fashion, inventing new body proportions, often using innovative materials, technologies and processes. At the other end of the scale the smaller eco-pioneer companies are generally less interested in changing fashion *per se*, but rather passionate about ecology and the ethics of clothing production and particular fibres such as hemp or organic cotton, for example. The global brands like Nike, Gap and Timberland and large multiple stores like M&S are now beginning to act on ethical and sustainability issues for the mass-market. However, there is still a large proportion of companies for whom sustainability is not yet fully on the radar. Given the convergence of environmental and social justice issues, we can no longer ignore the imperatives for re-thinking our whole relationship with clothes and the way we design fashion. More clothing companies are beginning to ask what they should be doing. There are enormous barriers to be overcome, particularly the costs of setting up different systems, sourcing new materials, greater monitoring of suppliers, learning about and working more closely with people at the beginning of their supply chain and so on. This then poses new challenges for the design of fashion to help solve the paradox of consumption, business and sustainability.

APOC Issey Miyake Making
Things exhibition, Tokyo
2000, with roll of industrially
produced knit fabric for the
APOC collection. Image
courtesy of Issey Miyake Inc.

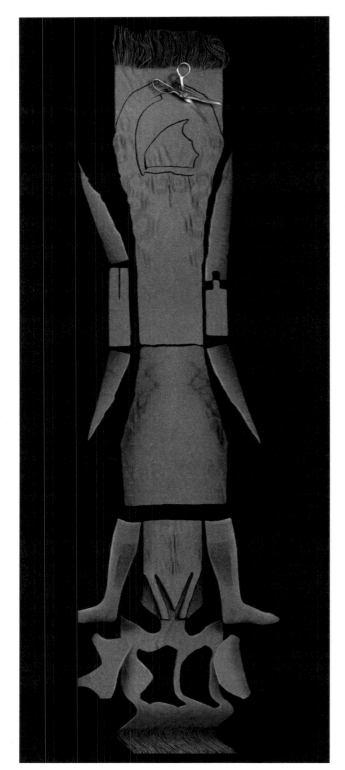

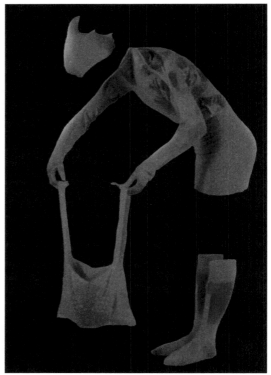

APOC Queen, Spring/
Summer 1999. An animated
sequence showing the
release of an entire wardrobe
embedded in the knitted
cloth. Photography by Pascal
Roulin. Images courtesy of
Issey Miyake Inc.

The Role of Design and Designers

The *Cox Review of Creativity in Business*, December 2005, pragmatically defines design as "...what links creativity and innovation. It shapes ideas to become practical and attractive propositions for users and customers. Design may be described as creativity deployed to a specific end." Whereas Richard Florida in *The Rise of the Creative Class* suggests an economic imperative:

Human creativity is the ultimate economic resource. The ability to come up with new ideas and better ways of doing things is ultimately what raises productivity and thus living standards.

Several design theorists such as Victor Papanek, Ezio Manzini, Michael Braungart and William McDonough, have proposed radical ideas about the way we must now re-think design more holistically, by being both innovative design collaborators, and responsible consumers. John Wood, Professor in Design at Goldsmiths College, London, suggests designers are "finally becoming recognised as important catalysts for economic growth" but not enough are able to "think deeply about ethics or know much about eco-design methods".[1] This realisation led him to develop his concept of "metadesign"—a holistic approach looking at the entire context in which the designer and the intended design operate. Sustainable design-theorist Ezio Manzini advocates the concept of emerging design networks in which "everybody designs", comprising individual people, enterprises, non-profit organisations, and local and global institutions. Braungart and McDonough—chemist and designer, respectively—developed the concept of "cradle-to-cradle" design which creates products that become ingredients for new products at the end of their useful life, an 'up-cycling' approach rather than 'recycling' or 'down-cycling'. They also radically re-thinking design solutions, creating new systems in order that allow them to produce good design rather that just 'less bad' design. Droog Design, a Dutch collective are known for radical designs which turn existing design conventions upside down, often with a great deal of humour. However, product designers are now moving closer to providing design services and designing systems rather than simply products—a washing machine which is hired for a certain number of washes and then recharged for example. New ways of living and consuming have to be proposed. The slow design movement, championed by Alistair Fuad-Luke, author of *The Eco-Design Handbook*, has gained in momentum, in tandem with the ideology of slow food, promoting experience over speed and engendering wellbeing.[2] However, little attention has been given to the specific eco-issues within fashion and textiles, although publications are beginning to appear, such as Kate Fletcher's *Sustainable Fashion and Textiles*.

1 *Agents of Change: A Decade of MA Design Futures*, Goldsmiths College, 2005, p. 11.

2 www.slowdesign.org

Part of the Droog Design
team's Fluid Functions series,
which explores the multi-
purposes of designed objects.

LEFT:
Clothes hanger lamp by Hector Serrano 2007. By hanging your own garment you create a personalised lamp. Image courtesy of Droog Design.

BOTTOM LEFT:
A selection of products from Droog Design design. Image courtesy of Droog Design.

BOTTOM RIGHT:
Droog design Dishmop by Gijs Bakker, which has a replaceable foam ball head.Image courtesy of Droog Design.

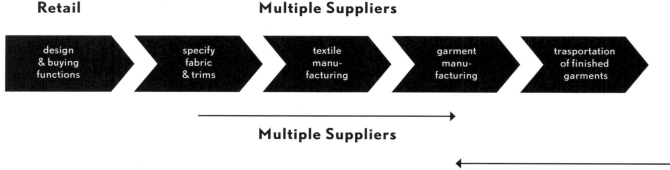

Retail　　　　　　　　**Multiple Suppliers**

| design & buying functions | specify fabric & trims | textile manu-facturing | garment manu-facturing | trasportation of finished garments |

Multiple Suppliers

Garment Suppliers

RETAIL SUPPLY CHAIN DIAGRAM

Could the paradox of 'slow fashion' become a new reality? It is up to both consumers and the emerging generation of new design thinkers to be the catalysts to energise and implement a range of new approaches. This 'eleventh hour' crisis we find ourselves in is not a set of problems with one right answer. The circumstances are hugely complex and many different strategies working simultaneously can contribute to lasting change. Some of the ways in which fashion might play its part are outlined in the following sections, with examples of different ideas and fashion products already being produced. This is just the beginning of what must become mainstream very quickly, and this time around, eco-fashion cannot afford to be a passing phase.

Fundamental shifts in behaviour by consumers and in design, manufacturing and economic processes have now become essential to survival, although this may be a difficult process. As there is so much to be done, incremental improvements can have some immediate value, even though these will be too slow on their own. A new paradigm means no turning back. Emotional engagement helps: there are many advocates now suggesting different measures of human progress, other than the Fordist/capitalistic economics of industrial growth, such as happiness, personal fulfilment and ecological sustainability as part of the bottom line of economic accounting. Jonathan Porritt—formerly of Friends of the Earth—now programme director of Forum for the Future, writes on restructuring global economics in his book *Capitalism as if the World Matters*. There is now a burgeoning number of books on the concept of happiness in terms of economics and sustainability.

The role of the designer inherently has ethical and ecological implications as it carries with it crucial responsibilities for choices in materials and processes, and is currently changing to embrace broader issues around sustainable technology and manufacturing. For designers it is hard to be categorical, and in many situations, choices have to be made between options, or the benefits of one strategy have to be offset by another. Compromises effecting sustainability have to be made in the fast

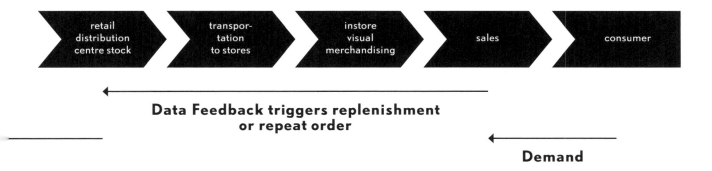

retail distribution centre stock → transportation to stores → instore visual merchandising → sales → consumer

Data Feedback triggers replenishment or repeat order

Demand

commercial world of fashion, bound by constraints of cost and timing in one of the most time-sensitive commercial industries. Even small changes towards more ecologically sound materials and processes within a large company can have a major impact, due to their scale of operations and buying power. Important choices made by fashion design and buying teams can therefore positively influence future manufacturing and business.

A new role for creative designers has also emerged in spotting new opportunities by looking at things in new ways. Design thinking is now becoming more important to the business agenda; with significant implications for repositioning of design centrally within company organisations. Designers are connecting new materials, technologies and processes together or collaborating to make new products by engaging different disciplines to work directly together. Can better design seduce more consumers into buying ethically and environmentally sound products? Can ethically and environmentally sound clothing and fashion be reconciled with the economic realities of the mainstream fashion business, or is it destined to be only a niche market, itself subject to the whims of fashion? Designers can enable positive change in the mindset that sees environmental issues as constraints, rather than as new opportunities. Smaller companies often feel they are too small to consider looking into more eco-friendly/environmental products and procedures as they do not have the budget and believe that their impact is minimal or insignificant and it is more of a concern for the larger companies.

There are new ways of thinking about clothes, with new technologies, materials and processes bought together by design, and there is huge potential for more sustainable products to be developed which will impact the fashion industry now and into the long term future.

The Life Cycle of Clothing

It is easy in our contemporary consumer society, with seemingly infinite choice, to know nothing of any garment's origin. We consider a piece of clothing as somehow 'born' in the shop, having its brief fashion moment and then it is thrown away. As Braungart and McDonough suggest, the flaw in this perception is that there is no 'away'. Our things do not dematerialise. Our dress, t-shirt or trainers are the product of a long chain of events—a 'cradle-to-grave' life cycle: from fibre to fabric production, design, manufacturing and distribution through the wholesale and retail channels, then, after purchase, laundering or dry cleaning, and a final 'end of life' choice: dustbin or charity shop. The final resting place for our garments may be in another person's wardrobe in the UK or anywhere across the globe; feeding markets in developing countries, a landfill site, or an incinerator, each of which has further environmental consequences. Although it is commonly accepted that the greatest environmental impact of a product is in its materials and production phase, recent research by Cambridge University, and by Kate Fletcher, has proved different in relation to clothing.[3] When taking into account carbon footprints and energy usage, it is suggested that the major environmental impact of a typical piece of everyday clothing, a t-shirt say, is in fact from the laundering and aftercare phase, rather than its materials, manufacturing and distribution. This is assuming the item is washed, tumble-dried and ironed. What actions can we take to reduce this impact?

The average piece of underwear or next to skin layer of clothing such as a t-shirt may be washed around 30 times (a figure used in testing fabrics) and the extent of energy used depends on the temperature of the wash and whether it is tumble dried. According to the Cambridge report, if the t-shirt is washed 25 times at 60C, tumble dried and ironed, the energy used in the laundering is 65 per cent of the total energy profile for the t-shirt, far outweighing the materials and transportation. Over recent decades, washing temperatures have come down with consumers using lower temperatures, especially with the increase in manmade fibre clothing, and there is a noted decline in the 'boil wash' used as standard in previous eras. However, the frequency of washes has increased as we wash clothes to refresh them, not to get them clean. As part of their new environmental plan M&S have started a campaign in stores and in garment labels for washing at 30C. Therefore a combination of washing less frequently at lower temperatures, and line drying, can significantly decrease the energy impact of our clothes. Of course fashion can sometimes help—the vogue for crumpled clothing which was prevalent in the early 1990s must have unwittingly diminished energy use!

Dry cleaning our clothes has a different type of impact, mainly derived from emissions and residues from the solvents and energy used in the process. The most usual solvent is polychloroethylene, which is a possible carcinogen if not handled in controlled and closed loop systems. 'Green' chemicals are currently in development for use by the dry cleaning industry, including a liquid carbon dioxide process, one based on liquid silicon and an ultrasonic cleaning system. Ironically, one of the ways being explored to reduce toxic emissions is a 'wet' dry cleaning process which uses water in a controlled manner.[4]

3   "Well Dressed", IFM Cambridge. See also: www.katefletcher.com and *How to do Eco Design: A Guide for Environmentally and Socially Sound Design*, German Federal Environmental Agency, 2000.

4   "Profile of the Dry Cleaning Industry", US Environmental Protection Agency, 1995.

Designers need to take into account the care of the fabrics used in their designs in terms of suitability for use and durability, particularly if there are special finishes or a number of different fabrics used together. However, this has traditionally been the extent of the design cycle, and the consumer then takes responsibility for the garment and its disposal. This is beginning to change as the impact of the 'end of life' phase becomes more apparent to all. Recent EU legislation on restricting the use of landfill sites has helped to raise awareness of the waste in discarded textiles and clothing.[6] New design thinking is emerging, some of which can be seen in this book, which considers end of life or further lives for the clothing, which, in combination with choices of fabrics, can help to alleviate problems of clothing waste.

The Fashion Supply Chain: Fashion Stories

In order to affect the environmental impact of buying fashion, it is helpful to understand the complex chain of activities (the 'supply chain') and stages through which clothing passes to reach the shops. Here are the stories of some basic regularly worn, everyday fashion items.

The T-Shirt

T-shirts became popular in the 1950s as clothing items in their own right, having transformed from the male undergarment worn as part of military uniform. Originally the t-shirt was designed to be unseen, but a comfortable basic layer worn next to the skin. This popularity coincided with the relaxation of formal dress codes and the rise of casual clothing that was to be the hallmark of a new code of dressing, especially in the US. Iconic film stars such as Marlon Brando and James Dean cemented the cool, stylish and sexualised image of the white t-shirt. The t-shirt it is now one of the most universal garments of both male and female, adult and children's wardrobes, worn everywhere around the world, penetrating even to the most remote tribes of the Amazon.

The plain white has given way to colours, printed logos and campaigning slogans, in fitted or loose styles, often made from a polyester/cotton mix, but the best quality, classic t-shirt is still made of a hundred per cent brushed cotton with sleeves above the elbow. We now ask how this wardrobe staple is manufactured. The t-shirt has become a commodity item, made and sold in very large quantities. The next chapter looks in detail at the issues of cotton growing, but let us assume the cotton has been conventionally cultivated, possibly from genetically modified seeds, and spun into yarn in the US. The yarn would have been knitted into fine cotton jersey fabric, previously in the US perhaps, until the 1990s, but now it is highly likely to be transported to a cheaper labour country such as China or Nicaragua for knitting, dyeing and cutting bulk fabric. It is then delivered to a garment factory where it is cut and sewn (using twin thread cover-stitch machines), by a series of individual workers on a production line. The t-shirt is then finished,

5   The Landfill Directive, 2004, sets demanding targets to reduce waste sent to landfill. For the UK's response see www.defra. gov.uk/environment/waste/ topics/landfill-dir.

pressed, labelled, packed and shipped in a bulk consignment, or possibly air freighted back to the US or the EU, to meet tight fashion season deadlines. Environmentally, much depends on the cotton production—conventional cotton cultivation relies on large amounts of agro-chemicals used in growing, whereas as an organic cotton t-shirt would eliminate that problem. However, as the weight of fibre in a t-shirt is only around 250 grams, there are other more important aspects of the t-shirt's life cycle, such as laundry. It is impossible at retail level to trace back the production source and travel miles associated with the t-shirt, and although clues might be given in the packaging, labelling and possibly point of sale information, these are not comprehensive. When it has been worn, the t-shirt will be washed, dried and ironed, up to perhaps 40 times before the colour and the print fades, the fabric looks limp and baggy and the t-shirt is discarded.

In October 2005 the London-based design consultancy Better Thinking began its own experiment. Without any previous knowledge in the fashion industry and in collaboration with consultant Dr Kate Fletcher, they decided to create their own fully sustainable coloured t-shirt. Their experience was telling and highly informative, exposing the complexity of the decision-making and trade-offs between the benefits and problems, which always have to be taken into account. The 'least worst' solution is sometimes all that can be achieved, but it was important to the company to strive for perfection, creating higher standards overall.

The project—intended to create 'the perfect t-shirt'—particularly investigated dyeing methods, including natural dyes as well as synthetics. However, due to the polluted-effluent problems with synthetic dyes and the heavy metal mordants of natural dyes, they finally found the most sustainable solution was to leave the t-shirt unbleached and undyed—a compromise on initial intentions. They also investigated a range of strategies for manufacturing, including local sourcing and manufacture, recycled materials, socially responsible sourcing, and a novel disposable t-shirt concept, asking the public to vote on their choice. Finally, two years on, Better Thinking joined forces with UK knitwear manufacturers John Smedley to produce their perfect shirt. Their final design, two and a half years after the idea's conception, employed undyed cotton grown and spun in Peru, using minimal water, and was available in a commercial context from Spring 2008.

AN ALTERNATIVE HEMP T-SHIRT

THTC: THE HEMP TRADING COMPANY

ALMOST BY *accident, London company The Hemp Trading Company (THTC) started producing t-shirts made from knitted, a hundred per cent hemp, fabric. Founder Dru Lawson had been looking for a way to combine his environmental and political interests and began to campaign for the legal cultivation of industrial hemp while studying environmental politics at university*

HAVING STARTED by promoting his t-shirts in the hip-hop music industry, the business now makes 50,000 hemp t-shirts per year. Lawson personally sources his hemp fibre and fabric directly from China, visiting the hemp growers and selecting and working with modern garment factories to ensure they meet the company's ethical standards. The t-shirts are then transported back to the UK where they are printed by a subcontracted company as needed for the range, in response to sales. As the hemp is grown without the massive chemical or water input of conventional cotton it is a more sustainable, and cost effective, fibre solution. The knitted fabric is similar to a hundred per cent cotton t-shirts, a little heavier but of better quality than most, and as hemp is also very hardwearing, the t-shirt will survive laundering better, perhaps reducing consumption overall, compared with standard cotton t-shirts. Until bans on cultivating hemp are lifted in the US and UK, hemp cannot be grown in these countries, and the Chinese hemp is cheaper overall.

DJs wearing THTC hemp/
cotton blend t-shirts. Image
courtesy of THTC.

ECO-CHIC: THE FASHION PARADOX

Sweaters produced by John Smedley established in 1784 in the Lea Valley, Derbyshire. Image courtesy John Smedley.

A Knitted Sweater

Created by Oliviero Toscani, Benetton's controversial advertising from the 1980s and 1990s featured provocative images on issues such as race and religion.

Take a merino wool sweater made by John Smedley, or a lambswool sweater by Benetton. What is the difference in their manufacturing processes? John Smedley is a vertically integrated knitwear company, which controls all its own processes from spinning yarn to knitting garments on one site in the UK. It has been operating in the same factory premises in Derbyshire since 1784, and is still family owned, with continuous production through eight generations since the beginning of the industrial revolution. It now produces around half a million items per year from its main Lea Mills site and two others locally.

The company started with spinning cotton then expanding to hosiery and knitwear in 1795. Smedley spins its own worsted wools for its sweaters using high quality merino fleece which, since 1995, it has imported from five dedicated sheep stations in New Zealand; a country which has a strong animal welfare record. The company now operates a completely traceable sourcing system, each garment being labelled with the name of one of the sheep farms. Before knitting, the yarns may be top-dyed in Germany or hand-dyed on site. Top-dyed yarn is dyed in the pre-spinning stage, with waste water treated and cleaned before being returned to the water course. However, for cotton knitwear, the garment pieces will be dyed after knitting and before making up. Meeting customer requirements for lasting quality, the yarn is treated for shrink proofing, then knitted into very fine gauge sweaters, using both old and new machinery. The separate pieces are precisely shaped or 'fully fashioned' as they are made, which reduces waste compared to cut and sew methods. Within the factory, the high value yarns are preserved as any waste knitting (for example with faults) is unwound and re-used. Highly skilled handworkers then assemble the knitted pieces through special 'linking' processes. The sweater is finished by washing in the spring water from the factory site (a contributor to the soft touch it is claimed), and after three stages of pressing and steaming the garments, is distributed to wholesale and retailers directly. Over 70 per cent of the firm's production is exported to 35 countries, the rest is sold in the UK. Aside from the importing of the wool fleece, the transportation costs in manufacturing are very low, as most operations are carried out on one site. The woollen yarn in the sweater is a biodegradable fibre and has been treated to be machine washable at 40C but tumble-drying is not recommended, keeping laundering energy down. Although wool is produced in the UK, its quality is inferior to the fine merino wool grown in Australia and New Zealand, and would not be high enough quality to be used in Smedley's premium ranges.

Benetton is a global clothing brand, founded in 1965 with headquarters and manufacturing mainly in Italy, but also Hungary, Croatia and Tunisia, and worldwide distribution. Originally manufacturing knitwear but now manufacturing fashion and leisure wear lines, Benetton is a publicly quoted company. In 2004 their annual turnover was 2.2 billion dollars on 108 million units of clothing.[7] Benetton has, until now, imported its wool from Australia, but as a major user of this wool, it has been targeted by the organisation PETA (People for the Ethical Treatment of Animals) who are campaigning for ethical wool through better treatment of Australian sheep. In June 2007, Benetton agreed to boycott Australian wool and seek other sources, until the controversial practice of mulesing is stopped.

6   Benneton annual report 2005–2006: http://sec.edgar-online.com/2005/06/29

Sharp styling, intricate details and strong colours for John Smedley's Autumn/Winter, 2007, fine merino wool knitwear. Images courtesy of John Smedley.

Benetton is well known for its use of colours in knitwear, which was a key signature of its brand; extended to celebrate different skin colours in its advertising and brand name United Colours of Benetton. In order to achieve rapid fashion changes in colours, Benetton knits its sweaters in undyed yarns, and then dyes the completed garments to particular shades as required in each of the markets it supplies (currently over 5,000 stores worldwide). This process eliminates overstocking of unwanted colours. The company has a quick response to changing fashions, enabling a total store restock in seven to 15 days. This is possible because Benetton uses its 15 Italian manufacturers representing a mix of subcontracted and directly controlled factories. In sustainability terms, the recent shift away from Australian wool is a very public commitment in the face of overwhelming evidence of animal welfare issues, indicating that companies now must be seen to be doing the right thing ethically and environmentally.

The Fleece

The 'fleece' is both a fabric and a garment. First developed in 1979 fleece has now usurped most of the functions previously fulfilled by thick woollen sweaters or jackets. Fleece creates outdoor garments, which are warm, light, comfortable and hardwearing. Malden Mills in the US was the original company to develop the fabric under the brand name Polarfleece. It was initially used in military clothing and outdoor sports such as skiing and mountain climbing, but has now become accepted generally as everyday outdoor casual wear, and as the company suggests, "forever changed the way the world dresses for cold weather". The fibre which makes up the fleece fabric is normally a hundred per cent polyester, which helps to account for the decline in wool and rise in polyester fibres in world production.

The original petrochemical-based polyester fibres may come from many parts of the world, such as Korea and Japan, and are spun into conventional yarns, which are then knitted in another factory to create a loop pile. This is shaved to give the velour surface, which traps a great deal of air for thermal insulation, and as the polyester fibre wicks away moisture, these properties make the fabric highly suitable for active sports use. This type of synthetic fibre fleece is now made by other companies and has almost generically become known as polar fleece. Previously, traditional fleece fabric was made from knitted cotton jersey with inlaid yarns, brushed to raise the surface (see the inside of standard cotton sweatshirts). The polyester fleece garment itself is very light weight for its bulk, but like wool and acrylic fibres, can be subject to pilling through abrasion in wearing, and static cling may be an issue. Several Polartec fabrics now claim 'anti-pilling' finishes and others such as water resistance or UV protection. In the laundry phase polyester fleece it is quick drying, without requiring tumble-drying, or ironing, as the polymer is hydrophobic. Polyester fleece does not absorb water into its structure, unlike wool, which is rather absorbent. This means that the energy used in cleaning polyester is much lower than that involved in conventional material. Dyeing of polyester and other synthetics does however require a high pressure process to achieve depth of colour desired for outerwear.

Practical fleece jacket and Organic cotton t-shirt from Patagonia, who converted all their cotton to organic from Spring 1996. Images courtesy of Patagonia.

Specialist outdoor sportswear company Patagonia, based in the US and founded by mountain climber Yvon Chouinard, was instrumental in the further refinement of early fleece fabrics. Working with Malden Mills, Patagonia developed an exclusive double-faced fabric, Synchilla, which became the second-generation fleece fabric, Polartec, in 1987. Malden Mills has recently adopted Polartec as the company name, manufacturing three hundred types of fabrics based on the original synthetic fleece.

It also comes as a surprise to some that fleece fabric can also be made from recycled polyester fibres, usually from recycled plastic water bottles, which consist of the polymer PET (polyethylene terephthalate). This was an early 1990s breakthrough for recycling when it was first introduced in the US by Wellman under the Ecospun brand. Recycling diverted considerable amounts of plastic waste from landfill—it takes five large bottles to make one fleece—and reduced petroleum use. Fleece had become significant in Patagonia's sales, and in collaboration with Wellman and Dyersburg fabric mill, they were once again pioneers, using recycled polyester fleeces in all their clothing ranges. In the EU, one of Italy's long established companies, Calamai, mainly known for recycled fibres, also started to make recycled fleece in 1986, claiming to be the first in the field.

In theory, the polymers derived from petrochemicals should be infinitely recyclable, as synthetic garments, especially polyester, can be reprocessed into chips to start the process again. In practice new material may also be required to boost quality. In 2005 Patagonia introduced a groundbreaking 'closed loop' returns facility under their Common Threads Recycling Programme in which they take back any unwanted Polartec branded fleece garments to be recycled in the unique Eco-Circle process developed by Teijin Fibres in Japan.

Therefore, despite originating from petrochemicals, the sustainability credentials for the fleece garment are much better than might be expected, but particularly when made from recycled fibre. According to Patagonia, recycling the polymer material takes around 75 per cent less energy than making it from scratch and it can be recycled to original quality, using the correct processes

Denim Jeans

The ubiquity of jeans is astonishing, making them one of the most significant items of clothing overall. Globally the denim business is huge and worth a staggering 60 billion dollars. The major US organisation for cotton growers are Cotton Inc who, in a survey of US women in 1996, showed that each woman owned an average of seven pairs of denim jeans plus another nine other denim garments, and wore denim on average four days of the week. In the UK in 2006, 81 million pairs of jeans were sold at a value of 1.5 million pounds and due to the volume produced at the lower end of the market, the average price of jeans has continued to drop.[7] The US denim market is polarised between premium designer brands, selling at around 150–200 US dollars, and the standard market, where the average price is 40 US dollars, with the majority spend being 21–30 US dollars.[8] In the UK, value retailers such as Tesco and Primark sell jeans for six to ten pounds, or less. How can they do this?

7 Figures from Mintel, 2006.

8 Denim for all Womankind, Cotton Inc., 2007.

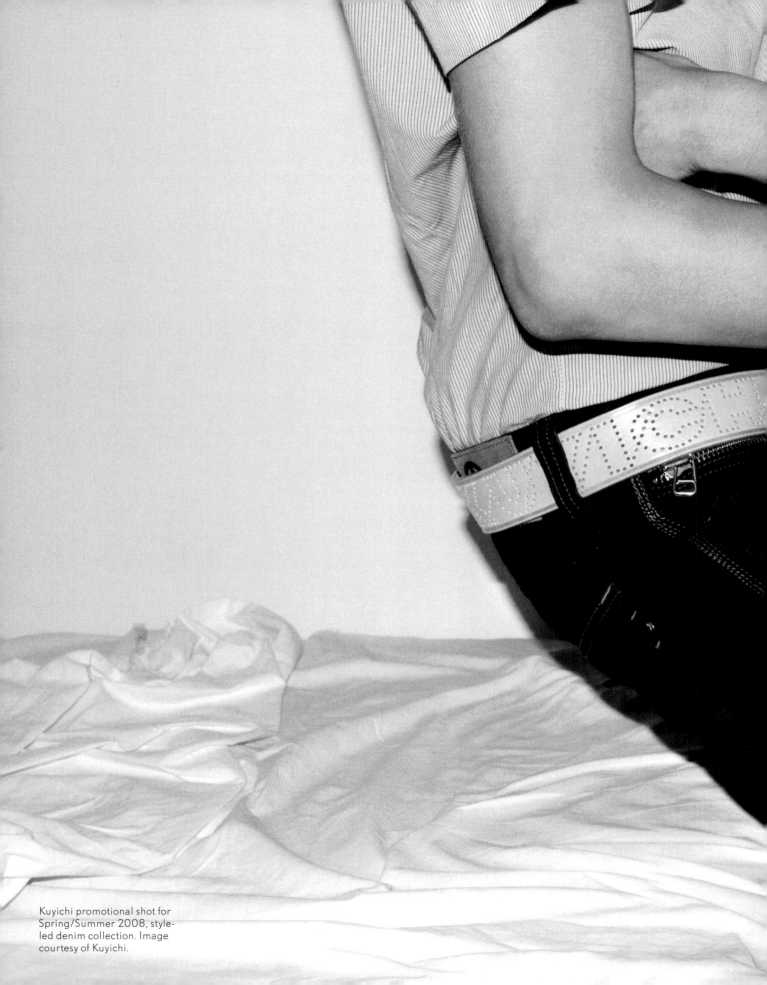

Kuyichi promotional shot for Spring/Summer 2008, styleled denim collection. Image courtesy of Kuyichi.

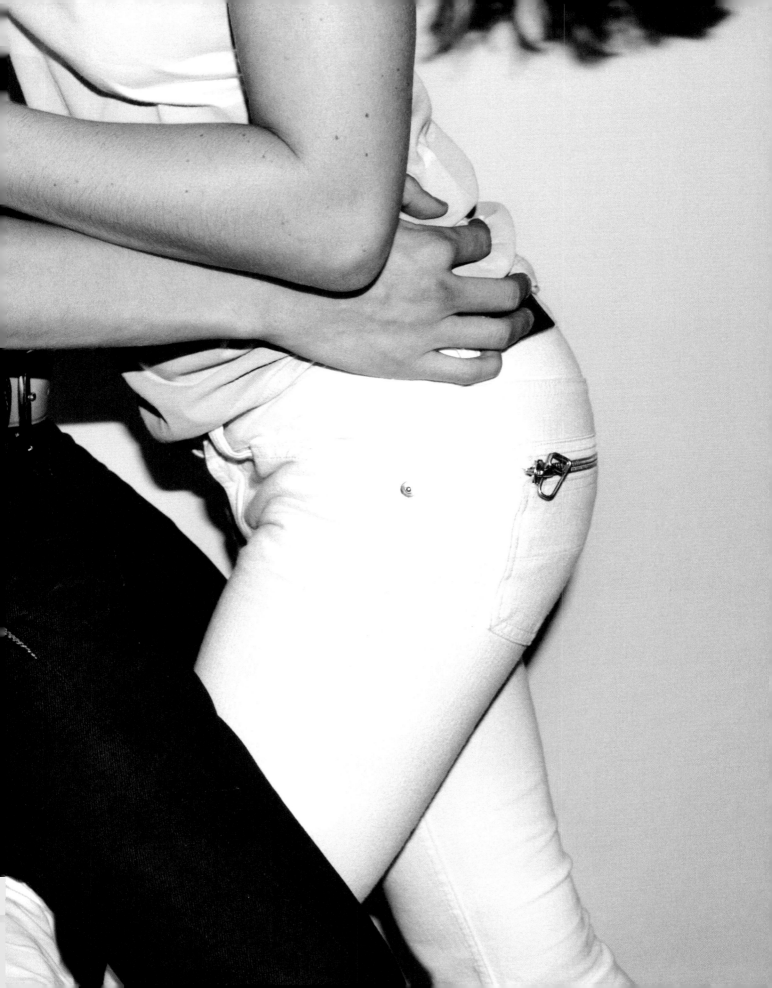

A classic pair of Levis denim jeans today might be made using conventionally cultivated US cotton, then shipped to China to be spun, dyed with synthetic indigo colour, woven, manufactured and finished. Denim fabric is made of a hundred per cent cotton, which creates huge demand for cotton fibre, and contributes to the phenomenal growth in cotton production in recent years. The uniform quality of denim fabric on such a vast scale is a testament to the successful methods of mass-manufacturing.

In 2001, Fran Abrams and James Athill (*The Guardian* journalists) tracked a pair of 20 pound Lee Cooper jeans sold in a high street store in the UK on its global journey of 40,000 miles by land and sea, starting from the fibre grown in Benin in West Africa to the manufacturing in Tunisia.[9] This is a summary of their findings. The jeans label could have said "Made in Tunisia, Italy, Germany, France, Northern Ireland, Pakistan, Turkey, Japan, Korea, Namibia, Benin, Australia and Hungary", as all these countries were involved in some way. Distributed to the UK from a centre in France, the jeans were made in a town called Ras Jebel, Tunisia, which had three factories owned by Lee Cooper. The oldest one had been making jeans for 25 years, and employed 500 women in its eight production lines. Despite most of the women belonging to the local trade, unions wages were said to be below the average for Tunisia. Abrams and Antill observed that "each (woman) functions like an automaton, pulling a garment from a trolley by her side, throwing it on to her sewing machine, roaring down the seam at full throttle, ripping it off, throwing it back. Over and over. Bonuses depend on it." The denim fabric came from Italy, dyed with synthetic indigo to a dark shade of blue which, by the end of the day, coloured the womens' hands. However, it was at the less well equipped Tunisian factory where the finishing took place. The workers there stone washed the colour from the jeans for the fashionable worn and faded look, using pumice stone from Turkey, which creates tonnes of waste sludge. Excess indigo dye (which itself is benign) can easily enter into water systems, affecting conditions for fish and plants. The cotton fibre for the denim fabric was grown in Benin, West Africa, by smallholder farmers and sent to Italy for weaving and dyeing, then back to Tunisia for cutting and sewing the fabric. The farmers found it hard to make a living, due in part to local corruption, and had to depend on free family labour and harmful pesticides to achieve the crop. Interestingly, cotton fabric for the jeans pockets came from a different source in Pakistan or Korea. The cotton-covered polyester sewing thread had also travelled a journey originally being "made in Lisnaskea, in Northern Ireland, as well as in Hungary and in Turkey... dyed in Spain and wound on to spools in Tunis before being delivered to Ras Jebel". Polyester for thread and for the zip tape came from Japan, but the tape was manufactured in France. The brass zip teeth were also made in Japan but the all-important signature metal rivets and buttons were made in Germany from raw materials (copper and zinc) supplied by mines in Namibia and Australia respectively.

This is a typically complex fashion supply chain story behind one seemingly innocuous pair of jeans in a UK high street. The jeans are representative of the global journeys and varied livelihoods touched upon in a remarkably diverse set of scenarios, with ethical, social and environmental issues appearing at every stage. The normal wholesale pricing structure comprises all materials, overheads and labour. Taking this into account, in 2001 the factory-gate price of the jeans was equivalent to five pound, whereas their full UK retail price was roughly 30 pounds

9   Arams, Fran, and James Astill, "The Story of the Blues", *The Guardian*, 29 May 2001.

before markdown, (apparently selling at up to 50 pounds in France), which takes into account the shipping, wholesale and retail overheads and profit margin. "You can't compare our salaries with the salaries in France and you can't compare the prices. It isn't the same", explained a factory worker to one of the journalists.

A number of newer, smaller companies such as Del Forte, Loomstate and Kuyichi have started to address some of the issues identified in the supply chain for denim jeans. They are creating transparency in their chains and alleviating some of the social and environmental problems by using organically grown cotton, and developing kinder finishes for the jeans to satisfy the desire for new trends. Relatively small players such as these companies can however have a big influence.

Even Levi's launched organic cotton denim jeans in Spring 2006 as part of their Engineered Jeans range. Levi's were responding to the new mood in consumer behaviour, their research showing that customers are willing to make a contribution to a better world when choosing a product. However, sometimes a bold move of this kind can reflect negatively on the rest of a company's ranges, exposing factors such as price difference and raising many questions. In order to do this with credibility an entire factory line has to be given over to organic production, otherwise the organic status of the product is compromised. Therefore in 2006, Levis product development and design teams in the EU collaborated to produce a better product sustainable throughout the entire supply chain. The new product eliminated metal rivets, opting for reinforced stitching instead. The jeans employed non-galvanised metal buttons and innovative non-chemical finishes using starch or Marseille soap, to comply with the Control Union EKO standard in EU production. Some are also made with a substantial amount of organic cotton and others are dyed with natural indigo. The Levis Eco-Jeans were rolled out in 20 of the EU and US stores in autumn 2006 at retail prices around 140 pounds or 250 US dollars. Only 30,000 pairs were produced, and this much higher price bracket is expected to reduce to forty to 60 pounds in future. Lines were also introduced which used just a proportion of organic cotton at a more standard price.

Since 2001, Dutch denim company Kuyichi has created a directional style-led denim collection made in a hundred per cent organic cotton. Kuyichi proudly promotes its social conscience and sustainability credentials, as the clothes are SKAL certified under the Sustainable Textile Production programme, which covers fibre to production. They collaborate with Dutch NGO Solidaridad to stimulate durable local economics in the countries producing their cotton—Peru, Turkey and India. Kuyichi respects both the communities and the land they work on, and have SA8000 accreditation for soil quality. They work to a fair social plan that affords clean air, clean soil, fair wages, safe and healthy working conditions and no child labour, exploitation or discrimination. In order to make their production process transparent, the company has now introduced an ambitious traceability programme for each garment, under the new umbrella organisation, Made-By, that supports a group of ethical fashion brands, including Edun, to develop socially responsible supply chains. After buying your jeans, you can visit the website www.made-by.org and input a code printed on the care label of your garment. Instantly you will be able to see which companies have been involved in creating the denim, including the cotton pickers. This type of initiative, similar to the John Smedley sweater, looks set to develop, but it remains to be seen how much it captures the public imagination.

Kuyichi promotional shot for
Spring/Summer, 2008.
Image courtesy of Kuyichi.

ORGANIC COTTON DENIM JEANS

DEL FORTE

AS A *designer for one of the top Californian denim companies Tierra del Forte began her line of organic cotton denim jeans after a substantial period working in the fashion industry. Having trained in design and merchandising at the San Francisco Fashion Institute, her role designing ranges for the mass-market had a six week turnaround on jeans.*

COMPANY PRODUCTION moved—from US cotton mills and manufacturing in Mexico to a hundred per cent production in China. Del Forte travelled to China to personally work with the fabric mills and factories. Her experience of the overwhelming noise levels there and the fact that the workers did not have ear protection were a huge influence on her work. Immediately she began to research the entire process of garment manufacture and intensive investigative approach.

THIS RESEARCH led to the decision to start her own company and create an environment within which she took control of every aspect of the manufacturing. Del Forte started with organic cotton, and took fabric production and manufacturing back to the US in order to minimise miles travelled. Independently supported by friends and family, Del Forte's first jeans were delivered in 2006. For her organic cotton fabrics, Del Forte works with one of the oldest denim manufacturers, Cone Mills, in North Carolina, and three other companies, sourced through the US-based Organic Cotton Exchange.

—76—

ABOVE AND OPPOSITE:
Organic cotton denim
collection by Delforte,
Spring/Summer 2008

DEL FORTE takes great care over the finishes which are applied to Del Forte garments after they are made. She eliminates the harsh chemicals normally employed by using a minimal hand-based 'rinse wash' with liquid soap and low impact softening agents, rather than detergents. The traditional process of stone washing uses pumice stones, usually sourced from Central and Southern America. These stone should ideally be left in their natural habitat to aerate the soil for crops and removal of them from their nataural habitat is therefore deemed 'unsustainable'. This method is bypassed by Del Forte who instead applies finishing by hand with sandpaper, and as an alternative to harsh chlorine bleaches she uses lower impact hydrogen peroxide to achieve the same effect. Compared to standard jeans, the labour component of the wholesale price is much higher (around 75 per cent) and based on ethical principles. With Del Forte acting as design director, the company now produces 20 new styles every season, selling in the premium denim market at around 200 US dollars (a market segment which accounts for two to three per cent of US denim sales). These sales are set to grow steadily over the coming years.

THE COMPANY had acquired 150 sales accounts by its third season, built up from an original six, and now shows at international ethical fairs such as Estethica in London. As jeans are one of the items that stay in the consumer's wardrobe longest, fit and style are the key—these jeans sell on their strong fashion design and quality, not primarily on their eco-credentials, which is an added value for the customer. Currently Del Forte is developing a 'reJeaneration' project in which the company will reclaim jeans after use and offer either a discount on a new purchase, or donate ten per cent to the Organic Cotton Exchange. Del Forte is a prime example of a new wave of small enterprise, built on responsibility and good design, which will continue to influence the wider market with its organic cotton luxury denim.

Slowing Down Fashion

This section looks at the opportunities for fashion which does not have a rapid turnaround. This 'slower' fashion is presented by bespoke and longer life products, and new definitions of luxury and appreciation of craftsmanship. The current 'fast fashion' ethos of cheaper and faster clothes is inherently unsustainable and cannot continue indefinitely—in fact signs show that this paradigm is reaching its limits. Garment factories have been pushed to their capacity in many places, and consumers have become more aware of the issues this brings. Front page exposés in the media are effective in raising this awareness and calling into question the industry and consumer practices that enable the situation to perpetuate. As a direct contrast to faster, cheaper, 'disposable' fashion, the concept of 'slow fashion' comprises less obsolescence in a number of ways. Slow fashion encompasses design for long term use and wear, intelligent and innovative choice of materials for minimal impact and waste, aesthetic, functional and emotional value, and concern for the entire life cycle of the product. 'Disposable' is a euphemism for 'use once and throw away' describing items that are made in bulk from cheap materials, but which have a lasting impact in landfill waste. Disposable has come to means 'no value' in contemporary society and now, thanks to fast fashion such as the one pound t-shirt, or six pound jeans, this applies to cheap clothes. Slow fashion could mean many things and chimes with a new 'slow' movement current in food and culture generally; an antidote to our consumer- and technologically-driven society. In order to achieve longer lasting and 'low maintenance' clothing, the fabrics could have technical coatings to keep them cleaner for longer and, as a consequence, would change change the relationship we have with our clothes. But how does keeping clothes for longer square with the 'must have' imperative for constantly changing fashions?

Fast and Slow Clothes

Mathilde Tham of Goldsmiths College London and sustainability consultant, Kate Fletcher, have studied women's behaviour in relation to particular items of their wardrobes.[10] Their findings propose that we have different attitudes and relationships with our clothes depending on the type of clothing and the way in which we use it. Some items of fashion can be considered fast, but others are slower as they progress through our wardrobes.

Tham and Fletcher studied the life cycles of a coat, a pair of jeans, a party top and underwear, and the relative environmental impact of each. For example, a coat is worn regularly for one or two seasons, is not cleaned too often, and could enter the secondhand market; therefore its main environmental impact may be in its production phase. Underwear is, of course, washed very often, so its impact comes from laundering. Jeans last a very long time in the wardrobe and become completely individualised. They are washed less often than underwear, improve with age and washing, and may even be customised by their owner with embellishments. On the other hand, party tops are worn only once or twice for their novelty and aesthetic impact, and therefore have a very short wardrobe life. These scenarios

10 **Workshop Presentation: Interrogating Fashion, London College of Fashion, July 2005. See also Fletcher, K, and M Tham, "Clothing Rhythms",** *Externally Yours: Time to Design,* **in E Van Hinte ed., 010 Publishers, 2004, pp. 254–274.**

illustrate that the way we bring individual meanings and personal feelings to dressing, sets it apart as a social and cultural activity, far removed from the original purpose of clothing for warmth and protection. This is why new behaviours are impossible to impose, and fashion consumers' needs must continue to be met at the same time as environmental and ethical issues are addressed. Delight and desire are the key motivations in the fashion mainstream market, rather than doing the right thing. However, there is evidence in the press of the beginnings of a backlash in attitudes to green issues, which can be criticised as niche, middle class and pretentious; the subject of superficial 'greenwashing'. Design will play an increasingly important role in reconciling these diverse agendas.

Luxury Goods

Luxury goods have a significant and interesting place in the spectrum of contemporary fashion and can be defined as items with high exclusivity and cost, high aesthetic values, craftsmanship and perceived heritage and status. Luxury brands such as Dior, Gucci and Louis Vuitton have a significant influence on the market through powerful advertising. Originally available only to the affluent, there has, in recent years, been a clear democratisation of luxury, as the major brands have sought wider markets through increased retail presence.

An example of the luxury brand: high-end chic and stylish accesories by Louis Vuitton.

The meaning of luxury is constantly evolving to match the changing socio-cultural norms and attitudes within a particular country or region. Luxury no longer needs to be ostentatious—it can be about superb quality and value, and it can also be experiential and sensory, foregrounding appreciation for intangible qualities. In a faster society, luxury can now be interpreted as time, or in the form of a unique experience—such as eco-tourism to remote areas to work on a project, leaving a minimal environmental footprint. Within the fashion arena, conscience consumption and responsible luxury are now buzz words as the luxury sector, in tandem with the mainstream fashion industry, wakes up to the need to adopt a more transparent and philanthropic attitude to its indulgent lifestyle. This sector has been slow to respond to the *zeitgeist* and to the potential influence of luxury brands in terms of responsibility, integrity, morality and ethics—truth, trust and transparency being the watchwords. At present, actions might take the form of consumption of ethically sourced, fairly traded goods made by indigenous people, using more sustainable materials, carbon offsetting, or contributions to local communities. As a report commissioned by American Express, *Twenty-first Century Living* cynically says, "a combination of wealth and eco-awareness is creating entirely new categories of conscience-driven luxury". Having previously been associated with excess rather than discreet consumption, the concept of responsible and conscientious luxury consumption is somewhat paradoxical in itself, and could be superficial conscience salving rather than a change in attitude from the super rich minority—a 'green is the new gold' attitude. There is, however, another perspective, in that buying long-lasting craftsmanship, highest quality and unique items means they will be treasured for a long time, becoming heirlooms of the future, and contributing to a lower rate of consumption.

TIMELESS MODERN CLASSICS

STEVEN HARKIN

STEVEN HARKIN *personally crafts high quality, distinctively designed bags of leather or more unusual materials like aluminium. The bags are hand-stitched and are aesthetic sculptural objects in themselves, which enables them to become a part of daily life, rather than a temporary fashion accessory. Their timeless designs, materials and functionality combine to become modern classics.*

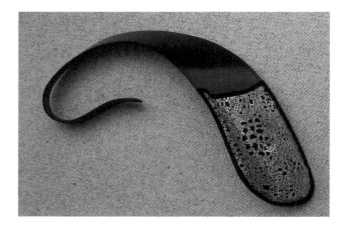

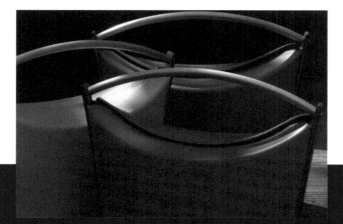

Experimental bag by Steven Harkin combining hand-crafted leather with silver fabric by Frances Geesin. Photograph by Ron Geesin.

OPPOSITE TOP:
Curved line detail of Steven Harkin leather briefcase 'My Case'.

OPPOSITE BOTTOM:
Steven Harkin Design Dot family range of aluminium/leather bags, which are handmade in small quantities.

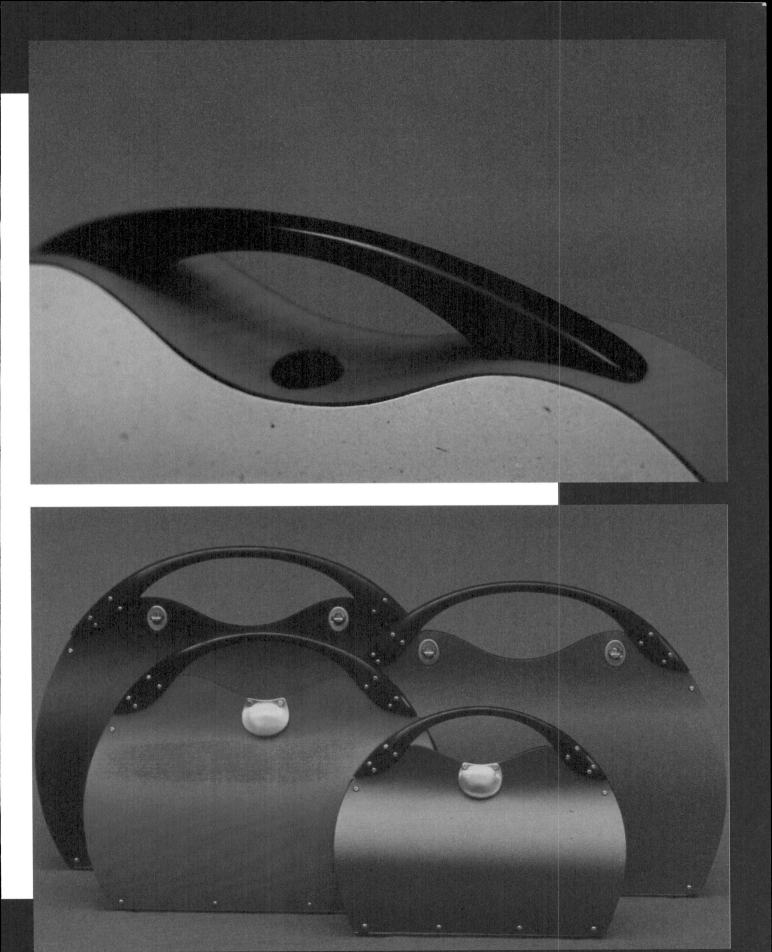

Luxury Redefined is the new
brand for the Better Thinking
unbleached, undyed t-shirt
made by John Smedley.

Bespoke and Customised Clothes

Before mass-production, people had far fewer clothes, which they valued and loved, often made themselves or had made specifically for them, which were kept and maintained for many years by repairing and remodelling. Fashion relied on individual tailors and dressmakers, as well as family and personal skills, to produce clothes from high quality materials which were fitted to the individual. These clothes were worn for a good length of time, then to be 'handed down' to lower classes or younger members of the family in poorer households.

The upper classes had made-to-order, bespoke items, such as footwear, suits, couture dresses and luggage. Many of these pieces have become current 'vintage' fashions. Now, high level designer fashion—whether or not it is bespoke—may be classed as luxury goods, including accessories such as bags, which have become the most coveted designer fashion items in recent years, much copied by cheaper brands and counterfeiters. More and more companies are branding and marketing their products with the evocative term 'luxury' (for example Viridis Luxe, the 'Luxury Redefined' t-shirt by Better thinking and John Smedley). Within the bespoke and couture traditions, a major element of their high-end specification is the hand-crafting of garments, accessories or footwear and the use of the very best materials, offering a personal service—all with the cachet of tradition and authenticity. There has been resurgence in appreciation for these finer qualities, at the same time as the aspirational desire for luxury brands spread to the wider market. Top design houses such as Chanel, Louis Vuitton, Gucci and Versace created a new democratisation of luxury fashion in the 1990s—luxury brands are no longer just for the elite, as the key names continue to expand to open stores in every major world capital. Price is still the dividing factor, but perfumes and other accessories (shoes, bags, sunglasses) provide a route to buy into the brand in a small way.

'Katy Piece Coat', in hemp blended with cashmere and knitted tunic in hemp and silk blend yarn by Viridis Luxe, Spring/Summer 2008.

In contemporary society, due to the power of exposure on the Internet, democratisation of fashion paradoxically also works in the opposite way. Small designer companies are able to have a presence in the international fashion market in the virtual world, competing with companies who have vast commercial infrastructures behind them. This allows individual designer-makers to reach a market, sell directly and avoid the mark-ups which would be added on to retail prices, enable themselves to benefit from a retail price, and gain useful direct feedback on products and lines. The consumer receives a crafted product, forms a direct relationship with the maker, and feels at once a greater connection and more personal relationship from their shopping experience. Personalisation and customisation is then an additional service that can be offered, so the customer is able to adapt or tailor the product or even commission something completely individual—a modern bespoke service.

Fashion on Demand and Markets of One

The concept of customisation in clothing has developed strongly in the last decade in order to satisfy more discerning and design-aware consumers looking for individuality in their fashion choices. Demand for more personalised products is forecast to continue rising. The market for fashion accessories has also grown continually over the same period with the new exclusivity of limited editions.

Customisation can operate on different levels. A basic level may start with a colour preference in a sweater for example, or the addition of decorative features such as embroidery on jeans. Alternatively, a standard garment may be individually adapted. At the other end of the spectrum is the handmade bespoke suit or the couture evening gown, where tailored fit, individual fabric choice and dedicated service are at a premium and exclusivity is guaranteed. These high quality luxury items are also likely to be kept and maintained longer than ready-to-wear items, and are often handed down through generations.

Increasingly, through Internet shopping, consumers are being given an opportunity to express greater individual preference, to control some of the product design choices by selection from pre-determined options—the consumer becomes, in a limited way, a co-designer of the end product. For example Nike-iD allows a customised design of its base styles of trainers, including choices of colour, fabric and logos, and different left and right feet options where "the ability to express yourself is endless". The trainers are ordered online, made up especially and delivered within four weeks. Personalised in-store service (consultation with designers) has also been added in London stores. In Japan, the knitting machine manufacturer, Shima Seiki, has opened a shop where the customer can order a personalised knitted sweater or outfit to their own choice of fabric and colour, to be delivered in two weeks. In Selfridges, London, Bodymetrics installed a virtual 'try-on' booth for denim jeans, in which you are scanned and your data stored on a card. You can then virtually try on a number of styles and order your preference to be made up to your size. A web-based service to custom build jeans is offered at Mejeans, which also require you to take and input your own measurements. These services to markets of one can eventually have a significant impact as individual preference can be catered for, while technologies can offer a more cost effective route to a personalised service—not the same as being measured for a bespoke handmade suit, but a significant improvement for many consumers over mass-produced items, especially if size and fit is normally a problem. This hybrid of personalised products and mass-production is known as 'mass-customisation'—a new holy grail for mass-manufacturing, the benefits of which can be less speculative production and therefore less waste in the clothing cycle. The result is better fitting fashions and footwear which may not be discarded so quickly, through the more rewarding relationship built up by involvement in the final product selection and aesthetics. The application of 3-D body scanning technology in a fashion context points to the potential for individualised patterns and bespoke service for a new paradigm of customised fashion on demand, bringing with it major changes in existing ways of manufacturing and experiencing fashion: a new era of digital bespoke.

An image produced by 3-D body scanning technology.

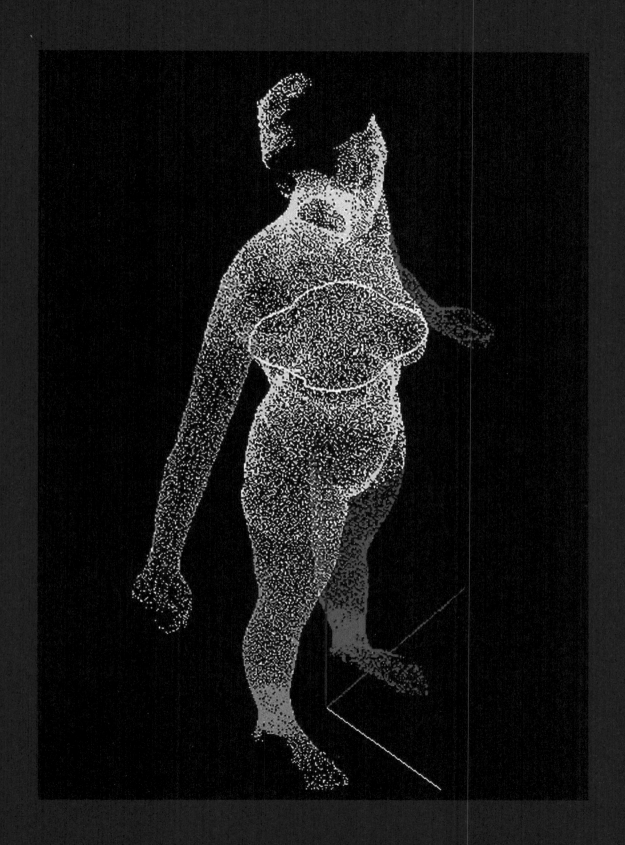

BESPOKE SERVICE

GRESHAM BLAKE

SAVILE ROW *in London is the traditional home of bespoke tailoring, steeped in tradition and luxury. There has been the occasional maverick—such as Tommy Nutter in the 1960—breaking some of the time-honoured taboos. Today another generation has taken a fresh look at gentleman's tailoring, and there has been a real resurgence in a younger client wanting the luxury and individuality of bespoke fit and service.*

GRESHAM BLAKE set up his tailoring business in Brighton, tapping into a new clientele including celebrities of the music and film businesses. In addition to his service for both men and women, he has launched an off-the-peg line, Glorious British, using fabrics woven in Huddersfield and manufactured in Crewe, consciously drawing on heritage and with full transparency.

ABOVE:
Made to measure contemporary tailoring: checked covert coat and pinstripe suit (designed for long life) by Gresham Blake. Photograph by David Ellis.

RIGHT:
Suits and jackets from Gresham Blake's latest off-the-peg range Glorious British, with traceable provenance of totally UK sourced fabrics and manufacturing. Photographs by David Ellis.

Norman Cook (aka Fat Boy
Slim) shows off the quality o
his new Gresham Blake suit
the sea at Brighton.

Craft and Mass-Production

Ixn fashion, hand-crafted work such as beading, embroidery and filigree crochet is normally associated with couture fashion, still to be seen in top fashion houses such as Dior, Christian Lacroix, and Armani, but also in emerging designers such as Manish Arora, who capitalises on the hand-craft skills of his native India. The fundamental crafts of draping, tailoring and skilful manipulation of fabrics are still embedded in contemporary fashion. Handmade goods still appear in mass-produced fashion in the high street stores, often manufactured in countries with ancient hand-crafted textile traditions. Beautiful and distinctive weaving, embroidery, dyeing, knitting and crochet are still carried out by hand where labour is cheap (by western standards), in India, Asia and Malaysia for example.

Design fuels the fashion industry and a constant stream of new ideas are vital to its continued success, in order to provide the crucial ingredient of novelty, aspiration and desire, to maintain and increase sales. These sales in turn provide employment for a multitude of workers at all levels of the industry, in all areas of the globe as seen in the fashion stories earlier. In the currently prevailing economic system, growth is the goal for businesses, although this is beginning to be challenged by theorists through issues that delve beyond the scope of this book.

Fashion design is fed by a mix of inspiration and concrete needs and constraints. However, as the machinations of the seasonal design and buying and production cycles progress, there is still an important place for individuals producing fresh ideas. These small-scale operations design with simple equipment and the craft techniques of drawing, painting, hand-printing, knitting, embroidery and hand-weaving. For example, many well known fashion collections start by buying in textile samples, either from professional studios at seasonal trade fairs such as Indigo in Paris (part of Paris Pole Mode), which are in turn fed by individual freelance designers. Company design teams also scour art colleges' end of year shows, particularly in London, which is known for showcasing UK graduates in events such as Graduate Fashion Week and New Designers, and also hosts a two week long Design Festival. In France, scouts attend the annual Hyeres fashion competition to discover new fashion talent. The design team of New York company, Donna Karan, have been such regular scouts over the years that the company became a major sponsor of the New Designers exhibition. Here is the ground level of textile and fashion design, based on the fruits of design education and individual craft practice, which is sourced by companies seeking fresh new talent and ideas, to take back to their in-house teams and inspire the more commercial results required for the mass-market. Some of these ideas, such as embroideries, may be translated directly into commercial production, utilising the large number of hand-craft workers available in Bangladesh, or China for example.

Growing awareness of malpractice, ethical and environmental issues in fashion and textiles has also led to a greater appreciation of craft traditions and indigenous skills. A number of textile-led fashion companies working across Asia, from a base in Japan, offer a more responsible and slower fashion, one that connects with the traditions and skills of Asian textile practices while remaining firmly commercial. This form of fashion exists in direct contrast to fast fashion with its creation of comfortable, apparently simple yet often very sophisticated, clothes.

A group of Lambani embroiderers, Kanataka, India. Image courtesy of Sarah Ratty.

OPPOSITE:
Vintage blouse intricately hand-crocheted, made in China, circa 1960s. Image courtesy of Sandy Black.

精工巧制
M
100% COTTON
HAND MADE
SHANGHAI CHINA
RN 58554

The garments utilise textiles of the highest quality and purest form, capitalising on the skills and knowledge of traditional weavers, embroiderers and hand-workers across many Asian countries. These clothes do not change significantly with seasonal fashion cycles, they sit alongside fashion as a parallel, not dependent on catwalks or major advertising budgets, yet quietly aspirational—an evolutionary design sensibility rather than one of radical change. The designers express through their collections a desire to utilise the best of traditional skills and influences and absorb these into multiculturally inspired ranges of clothes, thus bringing these traditions into the fashion arena.

The legacy of traditional Japanese methods of weaving, dyeing and printing for the creation of the kimono through the centuries has made the innovative fabrics developed by designers such as Issey Miyake, Jurgen Lehl, Nuno and Mina Perhonen possible. These designers build on the knowledge, experience and skills base of individual weavers, dyers and embroiderers in small craft-based production units. Utilising the country's forward-looking technological prowess, they create a hybrid approach that respects and uses craftsmanship of the highest order while designing for and capitalising on mass-production technology.

OPPOSITE:
Sharply tailored dress by Alexander McQueen, Spring/Summer 2008.

RIGHT:
Garments from Mina Perhonen's Summer 2008 Collection. The attention to the processes of weaving, dyeing and printing—processes which are part of the Japanese legacy of traditional fabric and material craft—is paramount within the industrially produced, innovative fabrics. Images courtesy of Mina Perhonen.

THE MERGING OF CUTTING-EDGE TECHNLOGY AND CRAFT

NUNO

A FINE *example of capitalising on mass-production technology can be seen in the work of Reiko Sudo and Nuno fabrics, one of the most important textile design studios, founded in 1984. Nuno (meaning functional textile) specialise in creating unique fabrics, many of which are exclusively made for fashion designers such as Comme des Garcons, Armani, Donna Karan, ATO menswear, Cerrutti Paris, Calvin Klein and many more. The relationships and collaboration built with the fabric weavers (who they refer to as engineers) is fundamental to the production of Nuno fabrics. The role of Reiko Sudo and her team is to provide the vision and the inspiration, the weaver's role is to provide technical expertise, but Sudo stresses that it is a process of mutual exchange and understanding.*

NUNO DO not produce hand-woven prototypes which are then interpreted industrially, but concentrate on the visual and tactile qualities they wish to produce, which are then developed directly on the computerised industrial looms.

ALL MANNER of materials and processes are applied, including natural and synthetic, metallic and plastic coatings. Some Nuno fabrics are hand-manipulated after weaving—hand-dyed or hand-printed. In terms of sustainability, the company has many current initiatives. Their fabrics are so unique that the garments they make are kept for many years and the studio offers a remodelling service

OPPOSITE AND LEFT:
Nuno Circle origami pleated
bag using Teijin Eco-Circle
polyester, which can be
recycled as new.

for their own line of clothing. This is in effect, slow fashion, which creates a loyal following despite not changing radically each season.

NEW ECOLOGICAL fabrics include undyed, unbleached 'brown cotton' grown in India. Brown cotton is a strong cotton variety which does not need chemicals and whose deep creamy colour develops through oxidation. The yarn is substantially twisted, so does not need mercerisation and, unlike most organic cotton fabrics, is woven into distinctive waffle textures. Nuno has worked with polyester for 25 years, creating innovative surface treatments and pleated effects. Now Nuno has begun to work closely with fibre manufacturer Teijin and their new EcoCircle recyclable polyester fabric. They are creating a Nuno Circle line, beginning with bags and working with a group of Sudo's students from Zokei University in Tokyo. In order to educate customers they are spreading the recycling message to all the department stores that sell Nuno products. A key concept is Envelope garments, which come with an addressed envelope in which to return the garments to Tiejin when no longer wanted, The garments are then recycled into new fibre, of equal quality. At the opposite extreme, Sudo created a unique fabric many years ago from banana fibre or 'basho', grown only in Okinawa island (developed originally when the crop failed in order to recycle the fallen trees), and has continued to produce it ever since. This fabric is far softer than other banana fibre fabrics made in the Philippines, and can be seen in the Armani Casa collection for interiors.

Basho banana fibre from Okinawa Japan. Image courtesy of Nuno Corporation.

OPPOSITE:
Nuno Circle' origami pleated bag (fully opened) by Nuno using Teijin Eco-Circle polyester, which can be recycled as new.

MAKIKO MINAGAWA

HAAT

FOR OVER *30 years textile designer Makiko Minagawa has worked with Issey Miyake, since the inception of Miyake's design studio. Minagawa has directed the innovative fabric developments within Miyake's collections and has been instrumental in realising Miyake's visions, designing textiles that respect the environmental resources and craftsmanship while embracing new technologies, including collaborating on the development of the pleated polyester fabric for the Pleats Please line. Minagawa is widely recognised as one of the world's leading textile designers, and her work has been exhibited in the Museum of Modern Art in New York.*

IN 2000, Minagawa launched her own label HaaT out of the Issey Miyake Inc., incorporating Indian production within Japanese production. The name HaaT is Sanskrit, literally 'village market', but more importantly an evocation of the combination of heart and hand, *haath* in Sanskrit.

THE CLOTHING is produced in Japan and India, juxtaposing advanced technology and hand-work such as decorative kabira overstitching and special fastenings. The textile-led collection is an eclectic hybrid of tradition coupled with modern fabrics and knitwear, manufactured with advanced technology, using a wide range of fibres and techniques, often in unusual combinations. Fabrics may range from cotton, silk and wool to polyester, hemp

and cupro rayon. The Autumn/Winter 2007 collection featured
a tweed-like fabric using the inventive mix of hemp and alpaca,
together with wool and polyester.

THESE UNIQUE combinations of materials, surface texture and
decoration, together with subtle tonal colours, create Minagawa's
signature. The collection represents a fusion of influences and
craft skills from its producers' heritage and is not intended to be
identified with one country—a truly borderless fashion.

Kabira hand-stitched quilted
and embroidered jacket and
scarf, Autumn/Winter 2007
collection. Images courtesy
of Issey Miyake Inc.

Techno-Eco: Future Visions

Textile developments are paradoxically looking both back to pre-industrial methods and forward to highly technological solutions to current issues of production and longevity. Fashion itself—in terms of silhouette and form—may not be too different in the immediate future. We only have to compare the futuristic styles of the 1950s and 60s science fiction films to see that clothing did not radically change, unlike some technological concepts which have now become science fact. However, fabrics will be expected to perform more in a range of ways such as by 'self cleaning' through protective nano-scale coatings and requiring less laundering. Change will also be evident through 'smart' and 'feel-good' fabrics, which can monitor environmental conditions and respond to needs by delivering therapies or even raising the alarm. Current research will no doubt make this a future reality as attention has turned to the molecular level of engineering and nano-technologies, still highly controversial and engendering much debate in academic and political arenas.

Science fiction writers have long envisaged the future filled with nanobots (tiny nano-scale robots), which will clean and repair materials and cellular tissue, form particles which can travel through our skin (already available in cosmetic products and sun screens) and create changes in form, colour and structure within materials, clothing and the built environment. The convergence of digital technologies across many platforms is already having profound effects on lifestyle and breaking down divisions between previously separate areas. Data transmission and storage, still and moving images, sound and music are all now, effectively, technically indistinguishable and can be combined at will to develop new and interactive or, increasingly, immersive experiences. Cybernetic visions of the future have everyone retreating to their digital bubble, controlling their appearance in reality much as is now seen in the virtual world such as Second Life. Here real money is made by selling virtual clothing, which has become attractive as a testing ground for both mainstream and outrageous individualised fashion concepts— hence the recent appearance of major fashion stores such as American Apparel, H&M and Nike alongside individual fashion designers and creators. This seamless integration of the virtual and the real now questions perceptions but may become the norm as public space is increasingly filled with screens, tags, sensors and high-end devices. Computers are everywhere, and they are changing their physical form to become both ubiquitous and invisibly embedded in our surroundings.

The merging of the private and public spheres is already evident from Internet blogs, social networking sites and everyday mobile phone conversations. Almost without comment, the UK has become the most widely surveyed nation in the world with speed cameras and CCTV on every corner and global positioning systems allowing our movements to be tracked without difficulty. The implications are, by turns, threatening (Big Brother controlling mechanisms) or reassuring (monitoring the whereabouts and safety of children or keeping in touch with friends). Through current research, more and more of these functionalities are being targeted on the textiles and clothing that make up our individual interface with the world.

M&S i-pod enabled suit. Designed and made by Bagir, featuring Eleksen technology.

OPPOSITE:
Skorpions is an XSLabs project by Joanna Berzowska and Diane Mainstone, consisting of kinetic electronic garments that move on the body.

Wearable computing has been under development for 25 years, but successful clothing products are proving elusive, until the various components, such as reliable conductive textile technology, power sources, performance reliability and washability are sufficiently synchronised. Estimates now range from three to 15 years for the first 'killer application' in truly wearable technology. Instead of putting computers in clothing, new developments in electronic textiles (e-textiles) focus on making textiles electronic using conductive fibres made of either semi-conductive polymers or metals, and traditional textile manufacturing methods, such as weaving or embroidery. This enables functionality in clothing and furnishings, which are less cumbersome than early wearable computing. Advances in research for the medical and healthcare sectors have recently produced wearable technology products available in the commercial market for personal wellbeing, such as the Numetrex heart monitoring sports bra, or the WarmX heated vest; both knitted using established knitting technologies.

Intelligent Textiles, a UK company combining electrical engineering with textile design, have developed integrated electronic circuitry through traditional textile weaving technology. The textiles are mass-produced industrially and cut and sewn as normal fabric. The company aims to "make electrical products soft and soft products unobtrusively electronic". Product concepts include a single layer woven keyboard and two fabrics—Heat (which warms up where needed) and Detect (which senses pressure)—both of which are resistant to abrasion and can be washed at least 30 times and feel and perform as normal textiles.

It is still early days for many of these developments, but they are definitely on their way. What are the implications of all these smart and embedded technologies for eco-fashion? If we wash clothes less, because they have nano-finishes which keep them clean (such as Nano-Tex and Nano-Sphere available now), then how will we get the fresh feeling of newly laundered clothes, which has become a pleasurable expectation and experience? Mostly, we wash our clothes to freshen them, rather than because they are really dirty. This may have to be simulated in another way—perfumes released on contact perhaps. Micro encapsulation of products in textiles has been available for some time—found commercially in lingerie and tights administering aloe vera or in socks for controlling odour. The integration of more sensory experiences into clothing is, however, a goal pursued by many researchers looking at emotional design. Jenny Tillotson of Sensory Design and Technology Ltd is pioneering research for embedding micro fluidics into textiles to create a personal 'scent bubble', with integrating sensors to provide a smart responsive environment, for stress relief and wellbeing, which she terms Scentsory Design.

Technological esearch is progressing rapidly at the nano-scale for radical new fibre and fabric properties. Fuelled by military and medical research, the fabrics will be designed at the molecular level to be more effective than anything available currently. The goal is for real interactivity, such as clothes that change colour and pattern at will (camouflage or disco delight), become cooling or insulating (mountaineering or commuting), or many other areas of wish-fulfilment. The implications for end of life of all these concepts may not yet have figured too highly on their development agenda, but will create another raft of issues if the design thinking for this new paradigm is not holistic.

Glover liner by Intelligent Textiles using Heat fabric and Numetrex heart monitoring sports top with conductive fibres.

OPPOSITE:
Skorpions is an XSLabs project by Joanna Berzowska and Diane Mainstone, consisting of kinetic electronic garments that move on the body.

New York based fashion designer Angel Chang is one of the first to create a fashion-led collection using wearable technologies with integrated sensors. Cute Circuit have developed a number of design concepts for electronic sand clothing which look at emotional lifestyles, including the Hug jacket/t-shirt which can signal an embrace remotely to your loved one!

Many technologies relevant to smart textiles are now maturing, as others continually emerge. In the near future, products will seamlessly integrate into many life situations, and will be intuitive, ever-present and almost invisible in use, and genuinely transform and improve lives for the elderly and infirm, or those with impaired mobility perhaps. However, this will take many more years to perfect in clothing. Could nano-technology help solve the fashion paradox? If our clothes do more for us in our daily lives they will become support systems, but still, fashion is relevant—will we want to forever dress in the same clothes as those found in Star Trek. Currently, fabric finishes are expected to last the normal 'lifetime' of the garment, through perhaps 30 washing cycles, but encapsulated perfumes and treatments often disappointingly fade much faster. In order for these thing not to remain just a gimmick, the research and design must address both the maintenance and end-of-life scenarios of 'invisible' technologies in clothing. Nano-scale treatments perform at the level of bonding molecules and are therefore permanent. Ecologically, there are problems of hybrid materials and disassembly, such as polymers (for coatings) and metals (nano-silver for antimicrobial treatment) used on natural fibres for example, which will need to be factored in at the end of the garment's life. Combined materials make fabrics impossible to recycle by current sorting methods, therefore incineration or landfill become the only alternative. New ways of recycling hybrid fabric have yet to be developed commercially. The excitement and value of such responsive clothing will only be translated into real lives if these problems can be addressed both at the beginning and end of the garment's life cycle.

Technological developments take time, and are not always right in first realisation. Paving the way in 2001, Levi's launched the pioneering ICD jacket (produced in collaboration with Philips technology) and there are now a number of second-generation specialist outdoor jackets on the market for use in skiing or snowboarding (O'Neill, Burton) which contain buttons integrated into the sleeve or fronts for operating an MP3 player and plugging in headphones. These products work because of their niche market, aspirational status, and long-lasting styles, but the Levi's jacket failed because of cost, battery problems and inflexibility. People like to change their clothes more often than their gadgets. M&S are trialling a business suit with similar functionalities for the non-sportswear market in collaboration with another pioneering UK technology company, Eleksen, who developed a patented electronic switching textile ElekTex and a flexible fabric keyboard, based on pressure sensitivity. Following a 2006 partnership between Eleksen and Microsoft, these can now be seen in innovative computer bags, backpacks and outdoor clothing. A key feature of this technology is its flexibility and ability to be washed—signalling a new raft of potential wash and wear applications that have not yet been thought of.

Spyder ski jacket with built-in mps player controls and WarmX, a smart conductive fabric which is built into this knitted top to heat. Image courtesy of WarmX.

There are inevitably a number of barriers to be overcome before electronic smart textiles become universally usable and acceptable. The lack of global standards is impossible to overlook due to divergent strategies and cultures of research and development, as is the pressing issue of power supply. Power sources are a key issue for smart textiles, which will only be resolved when the relevant enabling technologies converge in their development stages. What is needed is the creation of smaller, lighter, longer lasting batteries, or ideally, to eliminate batteries altogether and harvest and generate sufficient energy from an individual's motion or the environment. This will provide the true breakthrough and transform niche product prototypes into mainstream items available to all, avoiding the current dependence on finite energy resources.

Many exciting initiatives are in progress, which demonstrate radical design thinking which also have an ecological underpinning, such as the disappearing plastics of the Wonderland project by designer Helen Storey and polymer chemist Tony Ryan, or the spray-on fabric-in-a-can of Fabrican by Manel Torres. It remains to be seen which of these will truly provide solutions we must have for our techno-eco-future.

Eleksen USB cord fabric keyboard in collaboration with Microsoft.

FIBRES TO FABRIC

To many, eco-fashion means buying natural materials like cotton and wool, and avoiding synthetic, oil-based materials such as nylon and polyester. This sounds like common sense at first but, upon investigation of the ecological and environmental impact of these fibres, and the ethical issues involved in their production, the case is not so straightforward.

Much has recently been written in the press about ethical consumption and making environmentally and ethically sound choices when purchasing food or other products. But how can this be translated to clothes buying? How are consumers to

Garments from the From
Somewhere range.

know the difference between one fabric and another? How can they find out about its production? Is fair trade cotton better than organic cotton? What about the impact of dyes? How do fashion designers make their choices? To encourage a greater understanding of the complexities of textile production, this chapter gives an overview of the production methods of some of the more common fibres used in our everyday clothing choices. It looks at the arguments for and against using different natural and manmade fibres and fabrics, to help inform those choices. The chapter addresses some of the conflicting messages that can be found, by giving an outline of the technical background and processes of manufacturing fibres. Examples of textiles and fashion are used to illustrate the way different designers and companies have approached their own collections and ranges.

Considering their importance in our lives, it is surprising how little is commonly known about fabrics and their provenance, and how much inaccuracy exists, even within the fashion industry. Of course fashion does not exist without fibres and fabrics first. The Industrial Revolution of the eighteenth and nineteenth centuries was based upon textiles (particularly wool and cotton) along with the development of factory-system production, which still maintains its dominant position. In today's industrialised global economy, fibre and textile production for mass-markets is highly automated. In developed countries, such as the US, the cultivation of natural fibres has long been mechanised for maximum efficiency in production and lowest costs. However, many small farmers in developing countries around the world continue to rely on manual methods of cultivation. Manmade and synthetic fibres, developed at the end of the nineteenth century, can only be produced in factories. Their process uses either oil-based or cellulose-based starting points, such as wood pulp and cotton, for chemical processing. These fibres opened up an entirely new world of possible products, and were hailed as 'miracle fibres', which are now found everywhere—and will be for a long time to come.

As consumers begin to demand greater transparency in the provenance of their purchases, it is clear that clothing labels are currently inadequate. Until very recently there has been little or no information of the sources of fibres and textiles in clothing at the point of purchase by the consumer. At best there may be promotional swing tags about the specific qualities of fibres, like those found on Merino wool or Egyptian cotton. EU legislation stipulates that only fibre content must be given, not origin, although previously country of manufacture was also required. Significantly some companies, for example the Swedish retailer H&M have reintroduced this policy themselves, with all garments carrying prominently displayed 'Made in...' labels. Given the vast scope of the subject, this chapter cannot be totally comprehensive, therefore further information sources are given at the end of the book.

Contemporary Issues

Although warning signs have been evident over decades, the groundswell of public awareness of the issues such as climate change and depletion of natural resources has now become a torrent with high profile media campaigns and celebrity endorsement. The emerging social awareness is typified by the film *An Inconvenient Truth* by Al Gore, 2006, or the *11th Hour*.[1] A tipping point has been

Satellite image of Aral Sea in 2003 showing the shrinkage in water areas by over half in a few decades. Image courtesy of NASA.

reached in which the convergence of environmental and ethical issues has been key. There is universal recognition that time may be running out to find sustainable solutions for the future of the planet and its people. Whether these are to be based in nature or manufacture is by no means yet clear, as debate continues.

Around 26 million people worldwide are involved in the production of textiles and clothing. What is more, the clothing industry's position as one of the biggest global industries means that its environmental impact on the planet is considerable, especially when fibre, dyeing, garment manufacturing, transportation and wastage are all taken into account. A graphic illustration of this is the draining of the Aral Sea in Uzbekistan over the last four decades. The draining is largely attributed to the irrigation needs of cotton growing, highlighted in a chilling Environmental Justice Foundation study on the Uzbekistan cotton industry: *White Gold: The True Cost of Cotton*, 2005.[3] This has been called "one of the most staggering disasters of the twentieth century" by the United Nations Environmental Programme (UNEP) in which political and economic control for immediate gain have devastated natural eco-systems and ruined livelihoods.

Natural versus Synthetic

Natural fibres are based in agriculture and synthetic fibres are based in manufacturing. A high proportion of those growing the plant crops for fibres, or tending livestock are in the developing world, include some of the most impoverished countries. The inexorable rise of synthetic fibres since the mid-twentieth century has now created a significant dependency on oil-derived polymer fibres for clothing fabrics, interior textiles and technical textile products, in addition to the reliance we place on oil for energy. Manmade fibres now account for nearly 60 per cent of all textiles, compared to 40 per cent in 1990. Oil has finally been recognised as a finite resource for which alternatives must urgently be sought and much research is underway into 'bio fuels', which use annually renewable sources like maize. Like all the issues, there are arguments which can be made to the contrary. Critics suggest that bio fuels will require too much land and divert crops away from food.

Creating textile fibres from renewable and sustainable sources has been the subject of much research in the last decades, resulting in new branded fibres such as Tencel (lyocell) and Ingeo (polylacticacid (PLA)). Lyocell, the first new manmade fibre since the invention of nylon, was developed in the 1990s using fast-growing eucalyptus wood as source material in a closed loop system that is a variation of the viscose rayon process. Ingeo is a polymer of lactic acid, derived from maize, an annually renewable crop.

The Problem of Cotton

Cotton is the most universal of textile fibres, associated with purity and positive natural qualities. However its cultivation uses vast quantities of water and agro-chemicals. Recent campaigns by organisations such as the Environmental Justice

1   Directed by Nadia Conners and Leila Conners Petersen.

2   Source: UNIDO (United Nations Industrial Development Office), cited in "Well Dressed, Institute for Manufacturing", Cambridge University Press, p. 60.

3   Environmental Justice Foundation: www.ejfoundation.org

MAJOR FIBRE TYPES

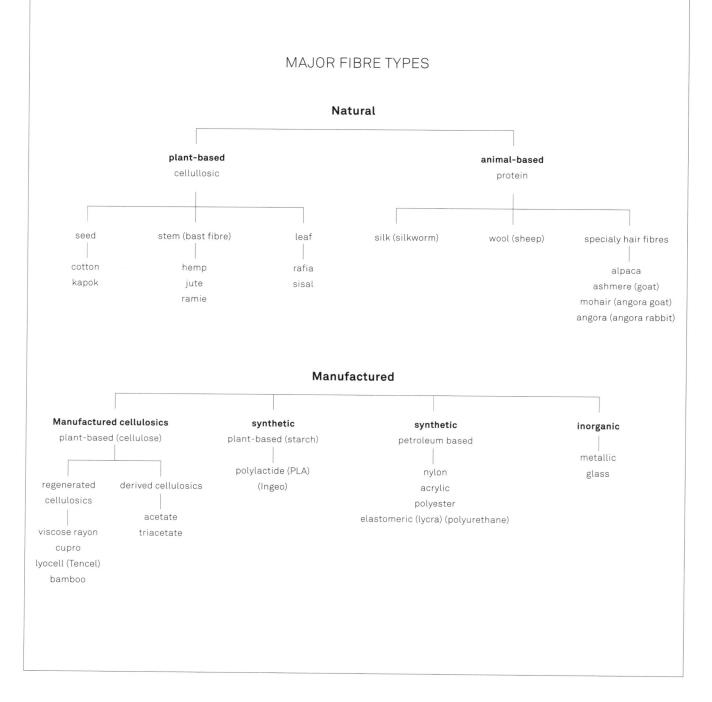

Natural

plant-based
cellullosic

- seed
  - cotton
  - kapok
- stem (bast fibre)
  - hemp
  - jute
  - ramie
- leaf
  - rafia
  - sisal

animal-based
protein

- silk (silkworm)
- wool (sheep)
- specialy hair fibres
  - alpaca
  - ashmere (goat)
  - mohair (angora goat)
  - angora (angora rabbit)

Manufactured

Manufactured cellulosics
plant-based (cellulose)

- regenerated cellulosics
  - viscose rayon
  - cupro
  - lyocell (Tencel)
  - bamboo
- derived cellulosics
  - acetate
  - triacetate

synthetic
plant-based (starch)

- polylactide (PLA)
- (Ingeo)

synthetic
petroleum based

- nylon
- acrylic
- polyester
- elastomeric (lycra) (polyurethane)

inorganic

- metallic
- glass

Foundation (EJF) and Pesticide Action Network (PAN) have raised awareness of the terrible problems associated with the use of pesticides on cotton and other crops by smallholding farmers. These problems are particularly prominent in regions of India and Africa, which rely on cotton as a cash crop. Pesticides are used in order to increase yields and to meet the demands of western fashion markets, often with dire consequences, such as illness and death. One of the biggest issues and anomalies, according to PAN, is that many of the pesticides utilised in these countries are actually banned in the US and EU. These agro-chemicals are often manufactured and exported by UK, the EU or US companies to places where they are not used safely and protective clothing is not easily available.

Chemicals and Textiles

All aspects of fabric production, both synthetic and natural, use a range of chemicals at some stage in the production cycle. From growing and cleaning the fibres, to dyeing and finishing the textiles, chemicals are employed, including common chemicals such as sodium chloride (salt) and chlorine bleach. The environmental impact of chemical usage in the textile industry is still a major concern, which only recently started to be tackled by legislation and the chemical companies and textile manufacturers themselves. The contamination of water systems by dye effluents is now being addressed in major industrialised complexes, but is still a major problem in parts of many countries such as India and Bangladesh.

Given this scenario of a polluting textile industry, the power to change and influence is in the hands of everyone—consumers, designers, buyers and responsible manufacturers as well as governments and lobbying organisations. It is our problem, not one to be solved remotely by an outside force, and individual actions count. It is no longer good enough just to buy. We must also question and, as more problems receive coverage, achieve greater awareness. Consumer power is now a force to be reckoned with and responded to by retailers and their suppliers; making informed choices can make a difference. As consumers we also have to be prepared for costs to return to more realistic levels.

The Designer's Role

One of the most important decisions a fashion designer has to make is what cloth to use in the collections. This is tempered by practical questions of cost and availability under the time constraints they are working to, which can be highly pressured in the fast fashion business. The choice for ecologically sound fabrics has always been severely limited and certainly not available in the mass-market, let alone the designer level market. It has been the pioneering companies (Katharine Hamnett, People Tree, Gossypium) that have gone right back to the source of the fibres, particularly cotton, and shown the way for ecological and ethical clothing production. The first design criterion is aesthetic, and designers' choices have, until recently, rarely been based on sustainability issues. The rapid turnaround of collections has meant that, until now, sustainability has not entered into the equation. Now there is an urgent need and growing desire for more insight into production methods to help make more informed choices which can improve the environmental impact of clothing, and meet higher ethical standards. Many of the pioneer eco-clothing companies are interested in opting out of mainstream fashion cycles, producing goods which do not follow fickle trends, but start from a passion for change, and holistic views of the consequences of western consumption. Now the two extremes of large- and small-scale production are beginning to move closer to each other, and designers can be key in influencing the agenda for greater sustainability, and creating consumer demand.

Fibre Types

Fibres are classified as either natural or manmade (manufactured). Natural fibres are derived from plant sources—for example cotton or linen—and animal sources—for example wool, cashmere or silk, which exist as fibres in their natural state and require spinning into yarns. Manufactured fibres do not occur naturally and are derived wholly or partly from chemical processing. They are further divided into cellulosic (created from processing natural cellulose) and synthetic (synthesised chemically often from petroleum-based products). These fibres are extruded and then spun into yarns. Rayon was the first manmade cellulosic fibre, invented in 1885, and nylon—the first wholly synthetic fibre—appeared in 1936. Synthetic fibres are based on manufacturing polymers as the fundamental building block of the fibre, whereas cellulose is a naturally occurring polymer found in wood and plants.

Regenerated cellulosic fibres such as rayon, are now referred to as 'first generation' manufactured fibres, whereas synthetics represent the 'second generation'. The products of recent developments in the last two decades, such as microfibres, which have refined the technology and performance of previous processes and fibres, are called 'third generation' fibres. Fibres derived from plants and animals are all intrinsically biodegradable when disposed of in the appropriate conditions, but conventional petroleum-based manufactured fibres may take up to two hundred years to begin to decompose in landfill.

Plant Fibres: Cotton

Cotton is one of the major fibres used in clothing. Cultivated continually for at least 5,000 years, cotton is the most important non-food agricultural commodity worldwide. Coming from the seed hair of the cotton plant, a fluffy white ball (a 'boll') of cellulos, cotton is grown in warm climates all over the world, using industrialised mechanical processes in countries such as the US and Australia, or small-scale manual methods in developing countries such as India and Africa. The largest volume producer of cotton is now China, producing four and a half million tonnes annually, followed by the US and India. The statistics are significant—in the EU

Cotton growing in a
smallholding in India.

RIGHT:
A Cotton Module. Large-
scale cotton cultivation in
the US uses mechanised
processes throughout.

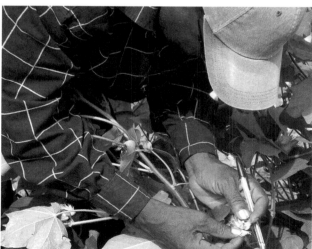

Cotton production in Africa.
The workers here are baling
the high quality hand-picked
cotton bolls for processing.

and the US alone we consume 45 per cent of the world's cotton product, despite being only 13 per cent of world population. Until very recently, cotton accounted for the largest share (over 60 per cent) of all clothing fabrics produced. This dominant position, resulting partly from the ubiquity of the t-shirt and denim jeans, has in recent decades been overturned by the rapid rise in production and consumption of polyester, which now accounts for about 75 per cent of textile production. However, as mentioned above, the environmental impact of conventional intensive cotton production is many times its economic significance. It has been calculated that, although cotton occupies only four to five per cent per cent of agricultural land, it consumes 25 per cent of all insecticides and ten per cent of pesticides used worldwide. For each t-shirt's worth of cotton, 150 grams of pesticides and fertilisers are used. Cotton also requires large amounts of water for its cultivation. In modern intensive cotton agriculture estimates vary but it is suggested that between 20,000—40,000 litres of water are used to grow each kilogram of cotton. Irrigation is a further ecological difficulty to be overcome in many places in the developing world, such as India. However, according to Damien Sanfilippo of PAN, water usage is dependent on the method of production, not just the nature of the plant.[4] In West Africa, organic cotton is often sustainably produced using rainwater, due to lack of any infrastructure for irrigation.

There are estimated to be 27 million cotton farmers worldwide, with approximately three quarters of production coming from the developing world, much of it from individual smallholdings growing cash crops. Until the 1950s, cotton was largely grown without the use of potentially hazardous agro-chemicals, but the invention of the insecticide DDT (Dichlorodiphenyltrichloroethane) was at that time seen as a boon for productivity in cotton growing, particularly in the US where cotton production was mechanised in the mid-twentieth century. Instead of picking by hand, the mechanical pickers collected bolls from two rows at once using a chemical defoliation of the bushes for easier picking. Demand for cotton fibre has continued to increase through the decades (almost doubling since the 1980s), fuelling the need for intensive farming methods. These methods impose health risks for the farmers (a significant number of deaths have occurred) and dire consequences for the environment—not to mention the recent evidence for pesticide residues in clothing made of cotton originating from Uzbekistan and the US.[5] New Zealand has reported incidences of high pesticide residues in clothes imported from China but, to put this in some perspective, it is still very uncommon for these residues to be generally found in clothing.

To further add to the issues in growing cotton, subsidised production in the US, China, and the EU has led to overproduction in these countries and a fall in prices on the world markets, adversely effecting many producers in developing countries. Attempts by the World Trade Organisation to reduce and eliminate subsidies, has so far been ineffective. However, the results of subsidised cotton maintains cheap clothing for western consumers. This is the difficult story behind the cotton we use daily. Our jeans, t-shirts, underwear, sheets and towels come at a hefty price.

In order to address some of these serious problems, the organic cotton movement has developed over the last 15 years, rapidly increasing in the last few, stimulated by the awakening of consumers to the global issues of climate change and poverty in developing countries. This has created the demand for

4 Damian Sanfilippo, PAN, speaking at the Soil Assosiation Seminar, Organic and Natural Products Fair, London, 16 April 2007.

5 Losz Environmenal Justice Foundation quoted in "Deadly Chemicals in Cotton", 2007, p. 15.

more transparency and accountability in textiles and garment production. A 2005 UK survey by the Co-operative Bank found that 61 per cent of consumers had purchased products based on a company's ethical reputation and 31 per cent had actively sought information. However, organic cotton is still a niche market, currently accounting for less than one per cent of global cotton production. There are many levels of paradox at play: small eco-aware companies and designers wanting to use organic cotton fabrics have found it difficult to source the relatively small quantities for their use, so product choices are not available. Will we, the consumers, now enjoying the financial benefits of cheap and disposable t-shirts and ten pound jeans, be able change behaviour and expectations to support the higher costs of organic cotton? Demand for organic cotton has outstripped supply, because it takes time and forward planning to meet these mounting needs but production is increasing rapidly at 50 per cent each year. Guaranteed markets are becoming evident and with major companies such as Nike and H&M now committing themselves to using an increasing proportion of organic cotton in their products over the next five years, there are now signs that this supply and demand deadlock may be opening up. With the imbalance of scale between organic and conventional cotton so extreme, it will take a consumer and manufacturing revolution for organic cotton to become mainstream but, as a significant portion of all clothing is made of cotton (around 60 per cent), this is where one of the greatest environmental and ethical impacts for change can be made. Any movement towards organic cotton will have immediate benefits.

An example of cotton growing naturally.

OPPOSITE:
Bale of industrially picked cotton in the US.

Organic Cotton versus Conventional Cotton

The main difference between organic and conventional cotton cultivation is in the use of chemical pesticides, fertilisers, insecticides and herbicides to control pests, weeds, and in soil quality—these are banned in organic agriculture. Conventional intensive cotton farming depletes the soil, necessitating increasing use of chemical fertilisers, whereas organic farming uses crop rotation to enrich the soil and employs natural predators to control unwanted pests. Aerial or hand-spraying of chemicals in conventional cotton pose hazards to people, water supplies and other crops, with harmful substances potentially entering the food chain, a risk which is virtually eliminated in organic growing. Organic cotton also uses less water than conventional cotton as the richer soil retains more moisture, but irrigation is still required in many areas. In addition to these benefits, there are the obvious health advantages for people, plus the farmers are paid a premium price for their quality cotton, and do not have to buy expensive chemicals, increasing their income. Unlike 80 per cent of US conventional cotton, organic cotton does not use genetically modified (GM) seeds. However, there are serious concerns that it will be impossible to prevent cross-contamination in the long term as the use of GM seeds spreads to other countries such as India.

One of the major problems economically for farmers is the transition period from conventional to organic, as it requires three years for soil to be replenished. The soil must have this conversion period before the organic certification to be obtained. Different companies are taking different stances on this issue, and there

Cotton being dyed, woven
and spun into yarn.

is a growing awareness of the support needed for cotton farmers undergoing this procedure. Katharine Hamnett only uses certified organic cotton grown in India or the US, but is currently working with the UN on a special certification for this 'in transition' category. Gossypium buys and uses transitional cotton to directly support the farmers in India, labelling it 'Pure and Fair' and 'Fairtrade' rather than the sometimes misleading term—organic.

As the organic sector is so new, with many producers only established in the last five years, labelling and standards for organic cotton fibres have only recently been established by the Soil Association in the UK, by Organic Exchange in the US and other such regulators. The EU established its Eco label criteria for textile products in 2002 however this is not an organic certification. There are currently almost a hundred different 'eco-labelling' schemes for textiles and clothing in existence across different countries for both environment and consumer health. Most standards are set up by private organisations with differing levels of recognition at consumer level. The issue of harmonisation of these standards is currently being to be tackled and the Global Organic Textiles Standards (GOTS) scheme has been implemented since late 2006.

Fairtrade Cotton

A deal of confusion and debate centres on the recent use of the Fairtrade label for cotton textiles, as opposed to its well established marketplace recognition in food crops such as coffee and bananas. The Fairtrade label is seeing a phenomenal growth at retail level as major brands and retail outlets (Starbucks, Sainsbury, M&S) adopt this standard, claimed to be recognised by 50 per cent of people in the UK.

Fairtrade is a label that "guarantees a better deal for third world farmers". Whatever the global market conditions, Fairtrade offers a 'fair', fixed price and longer term trading conditions, assisting small-scale producers and farmers in developing countries. It also includes a 30 per cent premium set aside for local social and environmental projects. However, in the case of cotton, Fairtrade certification is not at all the same as organic growing standards, although farmers may be minimising their use of pesticides, the certification only covers the production of the cotton fibre, and not the manufacture of the final product made from the cotton. The organic standard set by the UK Soil Association and other bodies excludes GM seeds, and since 2006, the Fairtrade standard has forbidden the use of GM seeds in all its commodities. Therefore, Fairtrade cotton is not necessarily organic. However in the UK, the Soil Association has, in summer 2007, released its standards for organic textiles production, which will address some issues for the consumer.

The best current ethical and ecological solution for purchasing cotton products may therefore be cotton which is both organic and Fairtrade, although there are debates as to whether Fairtrade always offers the best price to farmers, and some believe that the organic premium, which goes directly to the farmer, rather than through agents or intermediaries, is of more benefit. There are also different models for Fairtrade organisations and for the products themselves, and the use of the term 'fairly traded' is also confusing. However, deciding to

6   Author Interview, 17 September 2007.

buy Fairtrade cotton products over conventional cotton will usually be a more sustainable and ethical choice for consumers. There may eventually be a merging of the two standards—organic and Fairtrade—as each have their benefits, which would be of great help to the producers and consumers. One major manufacturer of t-shirts, Continental, has recently converted a small part of their Turkey-based production to organic cotton. Their president, Philip Charles believes "all organic cotton should be fairly traded but not all Fairtrade cotton should be organic" as Fairtrade certification is designed specifically for third word producers.[6] Pesticide Action Network Cotton Project are now sponsoring a campaign called WearOrganic, which will especially target younger people in education.

According to the US based organisation Organic Exchange, production of organic cotton is greatest in Turkey and India (with around 10,000 metric tonnes each for 2005) followed by China and the US (about 2,000 tonnes each). It is also grown in smaller quantities in Tanzania, Uganda, Peru, Pakistan and Mali, with other countries coming on stream.

In 1994 pioneering sustainable clothing company, Patagonia, decided to completely switch to using organic cotton in their t-shirts and other cotton products, when supplies were very difficult to find. As there is not enough capacity at present for mainstream companies to use a hundred per cent organic cotton it is being used, particularly in the US (by Nike and Timberland for example), in blends of five to 15 per cent with conventional cotton. Although this may be justifiably criticised as negligible, and 'contaminating' the organic product, it does help to increase demand and provide new markets. This strategy enables large clothing companies to join the 'green bandwagon' but is also a sign of commitment to improving the eco-credentials of their clothing. In the US, new labelling systems and certification have recently been put in place by Organic Exchange (which is part funded by the industry including Nike) to cover blended fabrics of different percentage values of organic to non-organic. Nike have committed to gradually increasing the organic cotton proportion into a hundred per cent of their production by 2010.[7] In the UK, M&S have committed to buying a third of all the available Fairtrade cotton production as part of their five year strategy: Plan A—announced in January 2007—for more environmentally and ethically sound production and clothing.

Will there ever be enough capacity for conventional cotton to be replaced by organic cotton? Again views vary on this. Given the enormous scale of the conventional cotton industry—compared to organic—critics say that organic cotton could never replace conventional cotton, as the yields are not yet comparable and there will never be enough land available for total organic production. Perhaps this is to diminish the real impact of the organic cotton movement—its lobbying to highlight the iniquities of the production of much of our standard cotton will enforce better practice everywhere for the environment and for people, in the same manner as the organic food movement has successfully exposed factory farming issues to the general public. However, in the US there is another approach pioneered by Lynda Grose of the Sustainable Cotton Project. The approach works in a similar manner to the Agrocel/Gossypium organic in conversion project in India.

7   www.organicexchange.
org/brand

Gossypium working
in partnership with
Agrocel in India.

The shocking sight of cracked earth. Image courtesy of Zack Griffin.

OPPOSITE:
Documenting soil and farming quality. Image courtesy of Lynda Grose.

8   Pecstiside Action Network, September 2005 data.

9   Lynda Grose in *View Magazine*, Issue 78, 2007.

10 *View Magazine*, Issue 78, 2007.

11 "The Men and Women Whose Shifting Power Alliences are Shaking up Indusrty", *Financial Times*, 5 March 2007.

SUSTAINABLE COTTON PROJECT

LYNDA GROSE

COTTON IS *one of the top ten crops using pesticides, with nearly six million pounds used annually in California alone.*[8] *The San Joaquim Valley, a major agricultural area, has serious environmental and health problems, with salinity and depleted soil requiring even more chemicals to sustain cotton growth. In Lynda Grose's Ecollection for Espirit, a hundred per cent organic cotton was a significant element, which helped to increase demand for production in the US, but then fell as Esprit and other companies pulled out of the market in the mid-1990s.*

NOW, WITH predominantly overseas sourcing and declining organic cotton production in the US (representing less than two per cent of world production of cotton) Lynda Grose's opinion on the position of organic cotton has shifted. She believes it is not a viable solution at present for cotton in California. Grose now champions under the Cleaner Cotton campaign, Sustainable Cotton Project (SCP), first set up in 1996, to communicate, educate and liaise between manufacturers and farmers.

    IT WAS after taking part in an SCP cotton-farm tour for manufacturers that representatives from Patagonia decided to convert their cotton production to organic. The SCP works with smaller (by US standards) conventional cotton farmers in California to improve the environmental impact of their cotton by considerably reducing their use of pesticides on a designated proportion of their land. Its programme, called BASIC, introduces the concept of biological agricultural systems and integrated pest management, which reduces the use of insecticides, herbicides and fungicides by an estimated 73 per cent, working with beneficial insects and interplanting 'trap' crops such as sunflowers or alfalfa to avoid cross contamination and reduce the need for spraying.

IMPORTANTLY, THIS programme does not use genetically modified seeds, like the majority of conventional cotton grown in the US, (which increased from 24 per cent in 2000 to 61 per cent in 2007 in California) and works towards organic principles in cotton cultivation, putting the farmers in a position to move to organic cotton later.[9] In Grose's opinion, the impact of this programme has been far greater than true organic conversion, for the simple reason that more farmers are able to get involved at low cost, providing a transitional approach and stepping stone to organic cotton cultivation, with immediate benefits.

OVER THE eight years of the BASIC programme, the project claims an average reduction in pesticides used of 1.5 kilograms per acre, with 22 farmers saving 5.7 tonnes of chemicals overall in 2006, and more joining the scheme in 2007. The BASIC programme is therefore a bridge between conventional and organic farming and, by encouraging the use of non-GM cotton, works towards 'cleaner cotton' and rebuilding the declining US organic cotton production, which dropped to 6,354 tonnes in 2006 from a high of over 24,600 tonnes in 1995. Although this is still a minute proportion of the conventional cotton crop in the US, demand for organic cotton is high, currently satisfied by importing it from overseas.

RETAILERS AND the media are now becoming involved and promoting the idea of local production with the slogan "Handmade in the US".[10] American Apparel is now discussing the conversion of 20 per cent of its business to Cleaner Cotton, the sort of result that certainly demonstrates the achievement of influence on the industry that was an original goal of this pioneer eco-activist. In 2007 the *Financial Times* identified Grose as one of its "green power" brokers.[11]

12 Author Interview,
with Abigail and Thomas
Petit, 2007.

FAIRLY TRADED, ORGANICALLY-PRODUCED COTTON

GOSSYPIUM

ABIGAIL AND THOMAS PETIT, *founders of Gossypium, are passionate about cotton and fair trade. Passionate about comfortable, long-lasting clothes which do not change every season, and about making a lasting difference for the future. They now have an established business in Lewes, Sussex, selling their 'Pure and Fair' cotton clothing—t-shirts, nightwear, yoga-wear, childrens-wear and casualwear for adults.*

THE DISTINCTIVE aspect of Gossypium is their direct relationship with the farmers in India who grow the cotton used in their clothes. They oversee the yarn production, knitting, weaving and making up of the garments, which are shipped by slow boat to the UK, and sold in their shop, via the Internet or by mail order. Their journey has been a little tortuous at times (their accountant advised them to close in 2003) but they persevered with their principles, a vision of a better deal for the cotton growers and full traceability for all products. They now find themselves on the crest of a wave of consumer awareness and demand for ethically-produced clothing. In 1998, they managed to "start a revolution and deliver a solution before people had even understood the problem".[12] Before Gossypium (the name is Latin for cotton) became an entity, Abi and Thomas, both textile technologists, spent two years working in India directly with the farmers who grew cotton on their smallholdings. The duo pursued a vision which respected hand-crafts and symbiosis with nature to produce a high

quality cotton nurtured with care. They searched for local, empathetic factories to make their initial batch of 10,000 t-shirts, which were to be sold to Oxfam in Belgium, where Thomas was based. Many of the farmers naturally used methods which conserved precious water resources (only four bathfuls per kilogram of cotton, compared to the 40,000 litres used in Australian irrigated land) and work in harmony with natural cycles. These are the key methods involved in organic cultivation. Others were using chemicals but a group agreed to join the initial organic conversion programme they had negotiated through Agrocel, a cotton broking organisation working with small-scale producers throughout India. However, believing in an integrated and non-exclusive approach to empowering farmers, Gossypium still supports farmers who use pesticides appropriately, so they can continue to have a market for their cotton. Agrocel, in partnership with Gossypium, became the first fair trade cotton broker, and now work internationally.

THE PETITS believe that fair trade organically produced cotton is a key tool for reversing the current downward price trend in fashion— from 'more, cheaper and faster' to 'less and quieter'. They formed an ongoing partnership with Agrocel, (which started up in 1988) who then went into organic cotton production in 1998, and together they pioneered a combination of the principles of both organic and fair trade systems, creating their products "without exploitation". Remarkably, each bale of Agrocel cotton is completely traceable to the actual farm that grew it.

DURING THE difficult transitional period to organic farming, when yields are lower, Gossypium promises in advance to buy the crop, thus creating financial security for the farmers, while also paying eight per cent above the market price. They started working with 42 farmers who took the risk to convert to organic, a number which had grown to 850 by 2006 (out of about 20,000 in Agrocel). Gossypium source

knitting, weaving and sewing factories as close as possible to the crops to minimise transportation and, due to their non-fashion orientated range of classically designed clothes, were able to create all round steady work. The 'classic' unseasonal designs mean no rushed orders and no cancellations which normally run rife in fast fashion.

ABIGAIL PETIT trained as a textile process engineer at Leeds University and describes herself as, "an industrialist with the heart of a craftsperson". She was diverted from an early desire to practice medicine, then psychology, by the seduction of textiles and the rediscovery of her former love of fabrics and craft. Following her degree, she worked for three years for Traidcraft, a pioneering fair trade organisation, designing their first clothing range and producing it in Bangladesh. This was a formative experience that solidified her subsequent direction and philosophy: "I left with a mission and learnt three things—one, they were right about fair trade, two, it was too early, and three, I had to go into the mainstream industry and find out how they did it. You cannot sell clothing on the back of organic food— clothing had its own rules."

PETIT IS aware of both the negative and positive histories and legacy of the Industrial Revolution, and the importance of textiles within it. However, she believes the textile industry "had the seeds of imbalance in it" from it's conception. For 220 years the industry was based on power and slavery, such that industrial (conventional) cotton was, and still is, just considered feedstock to the machines. However, all fibres have their place (each has its different qualities) and there is still a need to support the textile industry for its importance in our lives. Petit spent nine years working for The European Clothing and Textiles Trade Federation (now Euratex) in Brussels before finding herself in India. In a delightful book called *The Eye of the Needle*, she tells her own personal and allegorical story of her journey of discovery, from making things by hand for her friends as a child, to finding

a place—India—where craftsmanship was still practiced and valued. Within the book she tells of how she was inspired to realise the vision of William Morris—to make goods that are needed and appreciated.

GOSSYPIUM HAS deliberately broken and shortened the normal supply chain by working directly with the farmers. This breaks all the rules of normal trading, and creates a closed-loop production cycle. They have sought to demolish the 'smokescreen' between retail and the producer, to eliminate gatekeepers and overcome the separate languages. They have also encouraged an upward shift on prices, and can happily defend a higher price than high street stores for their Pure and Fair products. Petit says "having held the price on our yoga trousers for five years is one of our greatest achievements" in a pricing market which has declined year on year.

PETIT IS eloquent on the subject of Gossypium's cotton cloth and the value of returning to the raw material—a phase which has been taken for granted for so long, as merely a substrate for further embellishment. Petit was a consultant to M&S for many years, and during this time took their representatives to the cotton fields. This education has effected current sourcing policies of M&S, however, Petit has reservation about the mixed messages of the five pound fair trade cotton t-shirt, believing the price is still too low. Gossypium have created a new trading relationship with suppliers. Unlike other companies Gossypium are satisfied if costumers buy from them just once a year.

Linen

Linen is one of the oldest fabrics known to man. Having been recorded since antiquity and discovered in Stone Age sites and as shrouds in ancient Egyptian tombs, linen is known to have been used for textiles more than 6,000 years. Its main qualities are high strength, lustre and durability, producing a high quality fabric despite being a brittle fibre without elasticity.

Linen, like cotton, is a fibre consisting of cellulose, produced from the woody stems of the flax plant (rather than the seeds as in cotton), a category which is referred to as 'bast' fibres, and which includes hemp and ramie. Flax was once grown prolifically in the EU, and is especially associated with Ireland, although it grows in many countries with a temperate climate. Production is now concentrated in the EU, China, Egypt and former Soviet Union countries. Flax plants do not require irrigation, and can be grown with minimal or no use of fertilisers. Like the other bast fibres, the extraction of the fibre from the stems (by a process called retting) is traditionally done by manual methods which are highly labour intensive and slow, but ecologically beneficial. Retting (or soaking) slowly detaches the fibres from the rest of the stem material, and was traditionally done by natural decomposition (rotting) for several weeks in the fields to produce the best quality fibre (dew retting). Retting can also be achieved significantly faster in pools or tanks of water, using mechanical turning or by chemical means. Chemical retting, using soda ash for example, reduces the retting time to only a few days, saving time at the expense of quality. Once extracted and cleaned, the long, fine fibres are then spun into slightly uneven yarns, whose refinement depends on the different retting method used. The stronger fibres are harder to spin and weave than cotton, which contributed to the dominance of cotton once the Industrial Revolution took hold. The natural colour of linen is off white or light brown so the majority of linen yarns and fabrics are bleached (a process that at one time would have been achieved by laying it out in the fields for natural bleaching by the sun, but now is done by chemical means.)

Linen is a relatively expensive fabric to produce and is always associated with luxury, particularly in domestic textiles. Linen has a tendency to crease, but this is now more acceptable and became highly fashionable for Summer wear for men and women in the 1980s. Many linen fabrics, however, are coated with resins or formaldehyde compounds for a crease resistant finish. Linen continues to be a staple fashion fabric for every summer season due to its affinity for absorbing water and keeping the body cool.

Sophisticated style in specially designed linen fabrics by Shirin Guild. This design is from the Autumn/Winter, 2007 limited edition collection. Photograph by Richard Pireira.

Hemp

Hemp is one of the oldest forms of agricultural crop. One of mankind's earliest fibres, hemp has claims to archaeological finds in China from 10,000 BC.[13] Hemp and flax, from the same family of bast or stem fibres, were the two most important textile fibres in the EU until they were replaced by cotton. Hemp was at one time ubiquitous. Before the realisation of synthetic materials, hemp was grown all

13 Mina Hegaard in Gibson, K, *Hemp for Victory*, Whitaker Publishing, 2006, p. 87.

Hemp fields in growth before
being harvested for use in
sacking, sailcloth, canvas, rope,
building materials, paper,
soaps, clothing or food.

over the world to be used for sacking, sailcloth, canvas, rope, building materials, paper, soaps, clothing and food. It is one of the most versatile of crops, aficionados claiming many thousands of products can be made from every part of the plant: the seeds make oils and foodstuffs for animals and humans, the woody stems produce the fibres for textiles, ropes or paper and the remaining tough fibres are used for building materials and the leaves produce animal bedding.

Another well known use of course is as marijuana, but this is obtained from a different variety of *cannabis sativa L.* (Latin name for hemp) than the crop which provides all the products mentioned above. Marijuana cultivation has contributed to the continuing bans currently imposed, particularly in the US, on growing the industrial variety of hemp. The key psychoactive ingredient, Tetrahydrocannabinol (THC), is less than one per cent in the varieties of hemp grown for textile and industrial use, as compared to more than three per cent in marijuana. The varieties are not interchangeable—the fibre plant has no notable drug value and the drug plant has no fibre value.

Despite this distinction, the history of hemp cultivation in the US is completely contradictory and fraught with political conspiracy theories. Originally championed by the founding fathers and Thomas Jefferson, who held the first US patent for processing hemp, it was an important crop. In the first years of the Levi's Company, it is said that their work trousers were originally made of hemp sailcloth for its combination of ruggedness and softness.[14] However, as the growth of the synthetic fibre and chemical industry developed rapidly in the early twentieth century, hemp could have posed a threat to these new industries. Powerful lobbying in the media (for example the film *Reefer Madness*) led to the outlawing of marijuana in 1937. This was also erroneously applied to hemp cultivation which was also criminalised. Paradoxically, during the Second World War, hemp fibre imports from Russia stopped and the US government encouraged all farmers to grow hemp 'for victory'. The ban in the US still stands, however a similar 1971 UK ban was lifted in 1993, when the environmental benefits and potential of hemp were recognised. The ban's demise followed a campaign involving Hemcore, a UK company promoting hemp cultivation and products. Hemp growers are now licensed annually in the UK.

After a period in the wilderness, and due to the current receptive atmosphere, hemp is gradually returning to favour as one of the best solutions for ecologically sound cultivation. Hemp's credentials are impressive. Hemp grows very quickly—a crop can be grown in three months or less (compared to cotton which takes six months). Being a form of virulent weed, hemp grows in all conditions, needs little or no fertilisers or pesticides, and requires one fifth of the water needed to grow cotton. What is more, it is one of the limited varieties of plants that actually enrich the soil it grows in, rather than depleting it as so many crops do. Hemp can grow up to ten feet tall, is planted densely for its stems and produces higher fibre yields compared to flax plants. As such, hemp growing is already naturally close to being organic, even without any certification. The majority of hemp currently available is produced in China, followed by Romania, Russia and Poland, where it is still cultivated by hand. These commercial enterprises, such as Ecolution in Romania, have been assisted by EU subsidies which are available for growing non-food crops (such as flax and hemp), giving these countries a financial incentive and competitive advantage, in an unusual reversal of the situation with the US subsidy of cotton.

The first pure hemp fabric to be grown in the UK for generations was made into a jacket by Katharine Hamnett in 1995. Image courtesy of Bioregional.

14 Chris Conrad in Gibson, K, *Hemp for Victory*, Whitaker, p. 88.

Hemp cultivation and farming in the UK.

One barrier to its success for contemporary fashion and clothing is that hemp carries with it perhaps the archetypal 'sackcloth' image of traditional eco-clothing—heavy, lumpen and unstylish. Hemp fabric can often be confused with linen fabric but when hemp fibres are fine rather than coarse, they can be spun into yarns with a silk-like handle. With careful development, working directly with the producers in China, pioneers such as Barbara Fillipone of Earth Goods in the US have developed much higher quality, finer fibres, and encouraged innovative blending of hemp with other natural fibres. As hemp has an affinity for blending with many fibres, including renewables such as Tencel, there is now a much wider range of cloths available. In the last 15 years research and development of steam explosion retting to improve fibre extraction and processing has produced far finer fibres, which—either on their own or blended with cotton, silk or wool—can be woven or knitted into much finer fabrics than sackcloth and canvas. The quality of these fabrics is indistinguishable from other high-end fashion fabrics. Quietly, since the mid-1990s a number of clothing companies, notably The Hemp Trading Company (THTC) have begun to make basic clothes, and fashion designers such as Issey Miyake, Calvin Klein, Paul Smith, Chloe and Stella McCartney have started to use fabrics with hemp content.

Bobby Pugh is owner of The Hemp Shop in Brighton, which originally opened in the 1970s. As a passionate campaigner for hemp Pugh, for the last 15 years, has been sourcing hemp fabrics and manufacturing basic ranges of clothing. He is of the opinion that hemp is a solution to many of our current environmental problems. 90 per cent of products in use today could theoretically be substituted by hemp. Paper is a key issue as worldwide usage has increased astronomically—from 14 million tonnes in 1913 to more then 250 million tonnes annually in the 1990s. Pugh suggests that, in paper manufacturing for example, replacing wood pulp from trees by pulp derived from hemp would not only produce four or five times more pulp, but save almost all of the chemicals processing normally used. He is categoric about the role of hemp in the environmental crisis: "I believe we would not be in the current environmental disaster if hemp growing had not been banned." Others disagree that hemp is the ultimate saviour; in that the volume of land required to grow sufficient hemp would not be viable. John Roulac, author of *Hemp Horizons* refutes some of the 'hype' saying: Hemp can supplement our current fibre needs, but cannot replace trees unless we grow tens of millions of acres of hemp. Planting and harvesting new hemp fields on such a scale would require tremendous effort and energy. On the other hand we could greatly reduce timber cutting for our paper needs right now by using the vast quantities of agricultural straws that are typically burned in the field.

ECOLOGICALLY SUSTAINABLE FABRICS

LOOP FABRICS AND ELEMENT 23

SOURCING ECOLOGICALLY *sustainable fabrics is one of the most difficult tasks currently facing fashion designers. Due to demand being so small, supplies have been limited, and qualities have tended to be somewhat basic. After years of pioneering work by small companies, the inevitable constraints of supply and demand are now being influenced by consumer awareness and the buying power of the major manufacturers and retailers as they join the new wave of environmental action in the textile and fashion industries.*

JOCELYN WHIPPLE set up Loop fabrics in 2006. Loop was set up as a "distributor for envirotextiles" to help meet the needs of smaller businesses for attractive, sustainable and ecological fabrics. Whipple researched hemps viability for contemporary textiles and moved to California, where more companies were working within the Green Movement, and where there was still an infrastructure for a local textile and fashion production. In California, she became involved with the 'alternative' culture promoting eco-clothing through events. In 2005, when she returned to the UK several eco-fashion companies were making an impact, such as People Tree, Ciel, Wildlifeworks, Enamore and THTC. With the help of renowned developer Barbara Filippone, who spent 15 years working directly with Chinese fabric producers, Whipple was able to import and build a range to meet the sustainable fabric demand from these contemporary UK designers. Hemp is the core of this range, existing

Blended fabrics by Loop Fabrics, using finer hemp fibres developed in China. Such fabrics show the versatility and sophistication of contemporary hemp for fashion.

OPPOSITE:
Nahui Ollins stylish bags (made from post-industrial waste sweet wrappers) handwoven and made in Mexico by workers' cooperatives. Images courtesy of Nahui Ollins.

in traditional heavier weights as a pure fibre but also in new lighter weights and innovative, biodegradable blends with silk, Tencel and cotton. These fabrics completley banish the original sackcloth stereotype of hemp fabrics. All Loop fabrics are classified according to their eco-credentials, and use SKAL approved fabric finishes. Loop has developed its own labelling system called the Sustainable Biodegradable Product (SBP) envirotextile mark, which rates each fabric from 50–100 per cent according to its fibre and fabric finishes. Most fabrics are semi-bleached, using peroxide rather than chlorine bleaches, and prepared for dyeing. The fabrics need more care in use, as many are more unfinished than consumers and designers are used to. Whipple believes hemp has the huge potential to rebalance existing resources for textiles, paper and oil, but that more investment is needed into developing hemp-processing technology and fibre production. According to Whipple, hemp needs to be allied more closely with linen. She feels, though, that there is an expectation that ecological fashion and fabrics will look, feel and perform the same as conventional fabrics, but this is not possible due to the differences of processing and the use of minimal treatments. A shift in understanding of these quality issues is needed with designers and consumers modifying their habits, perceptions and even definition of style.

AS AN agent under the umbrella company Element 23, which represents a number of US clothing and accessories brands in the EU market (including Stewart & Brown, Del Forte Denim and Nahui Ollins bags), the collections are shown at London Fashion Week's Estethica event, and in the Pret-a-Porter Paris So Ethic pavilion. Whipple constantly contributes to the ethos of eco-chic by bringing more companies to the consumer who operate transparently throughout their supply chain. She believes strongly that the pioneer ethical brands have paved the way for many of the current brands to follow, with their huge commitment and dedication to eco-principles.

Other Plant Fibres

Many other traditional fibres produced in small quantities in different parts of the world have recently been re-examined in the context of sustainable production, especially where particular properties may be required or small-scale production becomes viable. Several other bast fibres, such as coir, sisal and jute, are used in furnishing and flooring products as well as more industrial uses, but recent attention has been given to other plant sources for deriving lightweight fabrics suitable for clothing. These include banana fibre, nettle fibre, coconut fibre and bamboo. Bamboo has recently undergone a great deal of exposure and increasing attention from fashion companies as a sustainable fibre. However, bamboo is a hybrid natural/manmade fibre, one of the fast-growing plants, cultivated in China, formed of a high percentage of cellulose which is processed as regenerated cellulosic fibres in the same manner as viscose is produced—a natural plant starting point processed by chemical means.

Natural growing Basho fibre.

All the ecologically sensitive fabrics discussed above which have been developed successfully for fashion and high quality basic clothing are a direct result of much passion, time and investment spent in working directly with the growers and textile mills around the world to achieve the highest quality fibres and fabrics. These have found a niche audience in the design-led fashion market, for relatively affluent people who can make choices to buy ethically and environmentally superior products. Importantly, though, they have paved the way for the larger manufacturers to step up to the line and follow. Ethical and ecologicalfashion is now sweeping through the mainstream industry with incredible speed, as high street retailers from M&S and H&M, to TopShop and Tesco roll out their organic, fair trade, and environmentally-aware fashion lines.

Animal Fibres

Animals provided the first source of clothing to man in the form of their pelts. All animal hairs, like human hair, consist of protein. Four important animal fibres are considered, including silk, the only natural filament fibre. Animal hair fibres are traded according to their fineness by which the different qualities of wool, alpaca or cashmere are defined. The fineness of animal hair fibre is measured in microns. An average quality for alpaca is 22 microns whereas cashmere may be as fine as 16 microns. Wool, on the other hand, is far heavier: 50–80 microns, whereas Merino can now be finer than cashmere—11 or 12 microns. The international trade associations set standards and award labels for fibres of various fineness.

Wool

The production of wool from sheep is another ancient practice dating back over 6,000 years. Originally wool was a key staple fibre alongside hemp, linen and cotton.[15] Sheep are particularly suitable for poor or rocky terrain which is difficult

15 Historically, wool was prized for its warmth, comfort and protective qualities, and dominated textiles until cotton became the principal fibre during the Industrial Revolution.

Wool and wool cloth was extremely important to the UK and EU economies from medieval times, as evidenced by the establishment of Guilds and companies such as the Worshipful Company of Weavers, dating form 1155.

In the Houses of Parliament in London, the Lord Chancellor still sits on a ceremonial 'Woolsack'—a seat stuffed with wool, first introduced in the fourteenth century by King Edward III as a reminder of the UK's traditional source of wealth (the wool trade) and as a sign of prosperity. Today the Woolsack is stuffed with wool from each of the countries of the Commonwealth.

Flocks of merino sheep in Australia. Image courtesy of Australian Wool Innovation.

for cultivation of agricultural crops. Hence we find sheep on the moorlands of England and Wales, the highlands and islands of Scotland, the mountainous wilds of New Zealand, the barren terrains in China and the dry open pastures of Australia or the US. The UK alone has over 60 breeds of sheep, known for their sturdy, fairly coarse wools, whereas the well known Merino sheep (originally bred in Spain) which produce long fine luxuriant wool of the highest quality are now mainly bred in Australia, New Zealand and South America. Wool is the fibrous hairs from the fleece of the sheep, but it is also a technical term used in the textile industry to classify and label all animal hairs such as mohair and cashmere (both from special breeds of goat), or alpaca, llama and camel hairs, and even angora, from the angora rabbit. All these animal hairs have different characteristics, but wool itself only comes from sheep.

Wool is a protein fibre with unique physical properties, such as its hollow structure, supporting the retention and transmission of heat from the body. Its microscopic scaly cell structure gives it the ability to become matted into felt, a solid fabric with many useful properties. Wool can absorb a large quantity of water, up to 30 per cent of it's own weight, without making the wearer feel cold or wet, as heat is actually generated when moisture is absorbed, enhancing comfort in significant changes of temperature. Wool fibres have crimp and are highly flexible and versatile, enabling wool to be used in many applications from clothing to furnishing and industrial uses, depending on quality or 'grade'. Different grades of wool can be obtained from one animal, and this sorting is highly skilled and still done manually by hand and eye. The fleece is removed by shearing or clipping the sheep, and though shearing became mechanised, it is still an encounter between highly skilled shearers and the individual animals. The fleece comes off as one piece, taking an expert shearer only one or two minutes, and weighs an average of 3.6 kilograms, about half of which, after cleaning, will remain to be made into yarns and fabrics. The magnificent Merino sheep have been bred specifically to produce large amounts of fine wool, up to eight kilograms per fleece. One of the useful by-products of wool is lanolin, from the natural grease in the fleece, which is removed by 'scouring' or washing the raw wool with detergent then refined for use in soaps and cosmetics.

There are about 24 million sheep in the UK, compared with almost 147 million in China, but Australia is still the largest producer of raw wool, producing 326,000 tonnes in 2005, followed by New Zealand with 175,000 tonnes, then China with 168,000 tonnes. A quarter of world wool production comes from Australia, whereas UK wool production of less than 30,000 tonnes represents only two per cent of the world's raw wool.[16] Most wool for clothing comes from flocks bred especially for their fleece, but lower grade wools are also obtained as a side product of meat production, (a third of UK wool is from this source), and is often used particularly in the UK, in carpets. It takes a year for a sheep to grow a fleece, with shearing taking place annually. Breeding of animals and the process of gathering fibre is a more arduous task than for growing and harvesting cotton or other plant crops. Consequently wool is more expensive than cotton or linen.

Merino sheep were first introduced into Australia by the settlers in 1788, with the export trade soon developed—2007 being the two hundredth anniversary of the first bale of Australian wool arriving in the UK. However, as with cotton, the previous

16 Figure from British Wool Marketing Board, 2005.

Wool and fashion merge
beautifully in this piece
made from merino wool.
Image courtesy of Australian
Wool Innovation.

importance of wool worldwide has been usurped by the growth in synthetic fibres. Now wool only accounts for three per cent of all world fibre production.

What can be more ecologically sustainable than a self-renewing fibre which grows continually and can be shorn from the animal without harm? This sounds ideal but, as is inevitable with the increase in intensive farming methods now employed around the world, there are certain issues of animal welfare and pesticides used in disease-preventative sheep-dipping which compromise the ecological credentials of wool fibre. 'Mulesing' is the greatest problem, a controversial practice widespread in Australia, in which the sheep have some of the wool-bearing skin from their tail and breech area removed to prevent 'flystrike'.[17] However, the most effective solution to this problem of animal welfare has been the lobbying of the wool industry by campaigning organisation People for Ethical Treatment of Animals (PETA). There are now agreements to terminate the mulesing practice worldwide by 2016, and in Australia by 2010. Research is in process to create alternatives to mulesing, such as the use of clips to remove skin without cutting, and selective breeding to encourage less hair growth in the affected areas. Various technological solutions to improve wool quality and reduce the need for sheep shearing are being continually researched. Some are benign, but others are questionable, such as causing the hair to fall out easily by feeding the sheep particular chemicals or growth hormones.

When the wool has been shorn from the sheep, it is prepared for spinning by scouring and 'carding'—a process of teasing the fibres out from the tangled fleece over drums of wires into a fine web, which is then gathered and formed into a loose unspun rope called a 'sliver' or 'roving'—ready for spinning. Wool spun at this stage is called 'woollen spun', and is more hairy, with shorter fibres than the more refined worsted wool, which goes through a further combing process to remove the short hairs and make the longer hairs parallel before being coiled into a 'top' for spinning. Worsted-spun yarns make smooth fine woven cloths or fine gauge knitwear, woollen-spun yarns are usually used for coarser knitwear and carpets.

Woollen fabrics have been a mainstay of both military clothing and of fashion, used for example in the tailored formal women's' outfits of the 1940s and 50s, in classic tweeds and suiting for men, and favoured by many top level designers from Chanel to Missoni, Claude Montana, Sonia Rykiel, Donna Karan and Alexander McQueen to name a few. Despite promotional campaigns, wool gradually fell out of favour due to competition from easy care synthetics and the spread of central heating. The heavy woollen layers of fashions worn in previous decades are now unthinkable in many places especially in the global warming era. Sales and production have continued to decline in world markets, but there are now moves to redress this situation and to reaffirm the qualities of wool in both performance and ecological terms, appealing to the contemporary consumer. The Australian Wool Innovation (AWI) now markets Australia's mainstream wool as "environmentally assured" to emphasise its eco-credentials. Its promotional material states: "By comparison to other fibres, Merino wool is a true green fibre—natural, renewable, sustainable, biodegradable, and the product of grassland eco-systems. On average every sheep in Australia enjoys over one hectare of rangeland on which to roam."

An Australian sheep. Image courtesy of Australian Wool Innovation.

17 Flystrike is a contamination by blowflies in which the sheep's flesh is eaten by larvae.

In the Autumn/Winter 2007 collection, Sans makes a statement with its fleecy organic wool jacket and trousers of organic cotton and wool mix.

Organic Wool

In the UK, dipping of sheep has been alternately compulsory and non-compulsory in law over the last 20 years. Production of organic wool, which does not use pesticides in sheep dipping, or harmful chemicals in any part of the production of yarn, has been developed by small-scale producers in the UK such as Garthenor Wools in Wales and Cornish Organic Wool. The latter produce natural undyed knitting yarns and fleece for the craft market from UK breeds, and claim to be the first company to gain Soil Association Organic certification for the entire process from sheep to yarn.

According to the Organic Trade Association, it is estimated that one acre of organic land produces two (one hundred gram) skeins of organic wool. On a larger scale organic wool is not yet cost effective and has not developed its market; consequently virtually all wool used in fashion today is conventionally grown. However, according to the Australian woolgrowers organisation AWi, Australia currently produces 100–200 tonnes annually of certified organic wool complying with international organic standards, which is a minute proportion of the total wool production.[18]

Speciality Fibres

If wool is the backbone of the animal hair fibres, several other animals have been bred for millennia for their fine and lustrous hair, particularly those camelids and goats native to the high mountains of the Andes in South America or the Himalayas in China and Mongolia. These include the llama, the alpaca, the cashmere goat, the mohair producing angora goat and the wild vicuña and guanaco. These fibres have been termed speciality or noble fibres due to their relatively high cost and rarity.

The romantic and nostalgic images that accompany fibres such as cashmere, mohair, alpaca and vicuña are marketing inventions of our industry to promote a sense of luxury and quality to the final consumer and give a rather delicate and fragile hangtag to the genre. The reality has been somewhat tougher where, as inhabitants of our hostile planet, fierce battles of evolution and survival have taken place—the vicuña has struggled back from near extinction this century but the same cannot be said for the chinchilla. Reawakened human awareness of Nature's global balance has given new respect to the various species that produce speciality hair as most of them live in the world's most inhospitable places and thus make use of otherwise unproductive environments. For this book alpaca and cashmere have been selected as key representatives of these luxury fibres.

Alpaca

Alpaca fibre comes from the hair of the alpaca, a domesticated animal of the camel family native to the Andes of South America. People of the high altiplano in Peru and Bolivia have depended on the hardy alpaca and llama for subsistence and fibres for textiles for millennia (some say for as long as 10,000 years). To the Incas,

TOP:
Cones of undyed alpaca yarn grown and spun in Peru. Photograph by Ben Gold.

BOTTOM LEFT:
Alpaca fleece is sorted by colour after shearing. Photograph by Ben Gold.

BOTTOM RIGHT:
Alpaca grazing near the Parinacota volcano bordering Chile and Bolivia.

cloth was currency, and the vicuña and alpaca fibre were reserved for royalty. The llama is used as a pack animal as well as for meat and fibre, whereas the smaller and gentler alpaca is kept largely for its hair and meat. According to the AIA, there are around 20,000 Peruvian families breeding alpaca and collecting the fleece, producing 120,000 quintals annually (one quintal = one hundred kilograms). The commercial alpaca trade is centred in Arequipa in Peru, which co-ordinates the marketing and sales of 4,000 tonnes of fibre per year around the world for spinning into yarns for knitting and weaving.

Alpaca fleece has evolved to cope with extreme changes in temperature found in the high plains, and is distinctive for its lustre, warmth and strength, while being extremely light. Due to its structure comprising air pockets, alpaca fibre has superior thermal qualities compared to wool or cashmere, nor does it retain water. There are two types of alpaca, the huayaca with shorter hair and the suri, with very long curly hair, which is increasingly rare—less than ten per cent of all alpacas. The alpaca fibre is obtained by shearing the animals every two years and is of similar fine quality throughout its fleece, which produces from two to four kilos of fibre. The natural colour of the fibre varies from cream through shades of light and dark brown to grey and more rarely, black, although the majority are now bred in cream, due to the ability to over-dye colours. Alpaca is well known for being knitted into 'ethnic' hats and sweaters, and woven into blankets, in its natural colours, with a strong growth in popularity during the 1970s. Many artisan groups in Bolivia and Peru produce hand-knitted goods for personal use and for export. However, fashion has recently rediscovered alpaca, which is experiencing renewed popularity.

A phenomenon of the last 20 years is the growth of so called 'hobby farming' of alpacas in North America, Australia and the UK to support the burgeoning craft knitting and weaving market. Despite their native habitat being at altitudes over 5,000 feet, alpaca animals have been successfully imported and bred in these countries to provide fully traceable yarns and products to meet the contemporary ethical consumers needs for crafted and authentic products.

Huayaca alpaca with cream coloured coat.

Cashmere

Cashmere fibres come from the extremely fine undercoat of the cashmere mountain goat which originated from Kashmir in northern India, an area now divided between Pakistan, China and India. These longhaired goats are bred in small herds in several colder parts of Central Asia including the Himalayas, China and Mongolia. The origin of cashmere as a manufactured fibre, woven and knitted, are obscure, but can be traced to the dynasty of the Grand Moguls in the sixteenth century—a time of great empires and developing trade routes between east and west. The first cashmere shawls to reach the west were highly prized rarities.

Cashmere is one of the softest, most luxurious and expensive of fibres, due to its scarcity, and the difficulty of collecting the fibre, which is obtained by frequent combing during the moulting season. Each animal produces only one to two hundred grams of this fine hair (the 'duvet') per year. It can take the cashmere hair of five goats to make one sweater, and the hair from 30 to accumulate sufficient fibre for one overcoat. The raw fibre is transported by individual herdsmen over

ABOVE AND OPPOSITE: Cashmere goats of varied colours in Mongolia. Images courtesy of Stewart and Brown.

tortuous routes to collecting points to be taken either to China, The EU or the US for processing and spinning, leaving little of the value of the fibre with its producers, thus perpetuating poverty and an unstable situation. However there are signs of change. Although attempts have been made to breed the goats in other countries including Scotland and New Zealand, the cashmere goat does not produce the soft protective duvet in any other parts of the world, increasing the rarity of cashmere compared to alpaca or mohair for example. However, quality still varies greatly, dependent on origin, length and fineness of hair and purity of the final fibre. Once an exclusive fashion fabric for only the rich, the fashion for cashmere knitwear, in particular, took off in the 1990s, and created a demand that has been met by increased Chinese and Mongolian production, resulting in more low quality cashmere now being available widely at all levels of the market. Mongolian cashmere has been the highest quality, but there are increasing worries about 'contamination' of the purest fibres by cross breeding. It is now possible to find both expensive luxury one hundred per cent cashmere knitwear, and versions sold in mass-market stores such as Uniqlo for much cheaper prices. Cashmere is also blended with wool and other fibres to lend a luxury cachet to many products, using as little as ten per cent. Given the natural and time-honoured methods practiced in the growing of alpaca and wool, these fibres exhibit many of the qualities sought by organic production methods, until they reach the industrial aspects of the spinning, dyeing and fabric production stages.

ORGANIC PIONEERS

STEWART AND BROWN

PARTNERS IN *both life and business, Karen Stewart and Howard Brown decided to start their own eco-fashion company in 2002. Karen had previously worked as a fashion and knitwear designer for Patagonia, the outdoor clothing company that has pioneered sustainable materials, and wanted to design for a younger, more fashion orientated customer. The Stewart and Brown business, based in California, has five product ranges, each focused on a different aspect of sustainable production or materials.*

THE ORGNC range uses only a hundred per cent organic cotton for t-shirts, dresses and tops in a range of fabric constructions, all manufactured locally with minimal environmental impact; the Green range of separates is made using only natural and sustainably produced fabrics such as hemp, linen and Tencel; the Surp+ range takes factory surplus fabrics to create new fashion accessories and bags which can utilise the relatively small quantities others are not interested in, saving resources and energy. The Green and Surp+ ranges are manufactured in Asia in audited factories used by other ethical brands. The Knits range is a speciality of the company, using New Zealand merino yarns. The animals are reared to strict environmental and welfare standards, creating premium knitwear that is soft and eminently wearable. Stewart works in collaboration with the manufacturers to create intricate stitches and textures inspired by her travels to the range. As a trained painter, she draws inspiration from

Stewart and Brown cashmere lacy knit cardigan, spring 2007, and 100 per cent Merino wool knitted tank dress with waist detail, made in China with fair trade. Images courtesy Stewart and Brown.

the images in her sketchbooks. These compilations of ideas, found objects and memories combine textures and colours seamlessly. The creme-de-la-creme of the five product categories is undoubtedly their Cashmr range—made from a hundred per cent Mongolian cashmere, which unusually is processed, spun and knitted entirely within Mongolia, keeping the added value of this precious commodity within the country and community that produces it. Stewart and Brown are the only US company to produce cashmere knitwear in this way and visit Mongolia regularly. The fibres come from cashmere herders co-op in the remote rugged region of northwest Mongolia. The co-op is dedicated to providing the nomadic herders the resources necessary to sustain their heritage, livelihood and ultimate survival. The fibre is hand-combed from the downy undercoat of the cashmere goats, which produces the finest and longest hair. Mongolian herders normally sell fibre to Chinese manufacturers across the border. However, the recent upsurge in the popularity of cashmere has meant that pressure has been put on the herders to pay less attention to fineness and quality, which varies according to whether the animals are bred for meat or hair. The production of Stewart and Brown cashmere knitwear is of high standard, sometimes using hand-operated machines, occasionally on automated industrial machinery, but always hand-finished under the direction of Stewart.

STEWART AND Brown call themselves "organic pioneers", creating timeless designs within a sustainable business model that has little precedent in the US. They advocate conscious consumption, and demonstrate over the long term that it is possible to be both responsible and profitable, while providing the highest quality design and ethical values. Stewart and Brown donates a percentage of all sales to non-profit, non-governmental environmental and social welfare organisations. By putting their philosophy into action, they hope to influence others by becoming the role model they were missing.

Stewart and Brown knit camisole in 100 per cent cashmere, made in Mongolia, with 100 per cent organic cotton t-shirt, made in US Image courtesy Stewart and Brown.

Silk

Silk is another of mankind's earliest fibres, cultivated in China for thousands of years, (as early as 2700 BC) and one of the most precious and sought after. The secrets of silk production were protected on pain of death for about 3,000 years, until they finally travelled from China to the Byzantine Empire. The trading of silk fibre and cloth was important to the developing international trade via the famous Silk Road of ancient history. Silk production (sericulture) eventually spread to the EU and Japan, where cultivation was refined. Silk is best known for its lustre and affinity with dyes to produce vibrant colours. However, the nature of the commercial fibre production, derived from the cocoon of the domesticated Bombyx Mori moth larva or silkworm, might preclude many looking for ethical and ecological yarns from using it. This is due to the fact that, in order to preserve the length of the fibre in the cocoon, the silkworms are stifled by heat as they transform into a chrysalis and their life cycle curtailed before they would naturally break out of the cocoon and become moths, ruining the unbroken thread.

Natural silk is a protein secreted by the silkworm and spun into its surrounding cocoon as a continuous double filament thread. This thread is carefully unreeled to produce the silk fibre. Amazingly, one cocoon can yield a mile of silk. However, production is still very labour intensive, and in some places, still done by hand. The filament thread then has to be de-gummed to produce the lustrous white fibre used in the highest quality silk, if it is not de-gummed it becomes 'raw silk'. It is then twisted or 'thrown' to create the yarns for weaving. The shorter fibres left over from filament silk production are made into 'spun silk', which is still lustrous but less smooth with fuzzier surface. This white silk is normally dyed in the familiar vibrant colours associated with silk fashions.

There exists another type of silk, wild silk, which is not intensively cultivated, and where cocoons are gathered from the moth's natural habitat of oak trees, and which produces a coarser silk of a brown colouration. The silkworm in cultivation exclusively feed on mulberry leaves, whereas wild silkworms feed on both oak and mulberry. As the moths have fully developed and escaped the cocoons, these are already broken, and the most lustrous quality long filament silk cannot be obtained from wild silk. However, one type of wild silk—Tussah silk—is grown commercially, as the Tussah silkworm leaves a neat hole when spinning its cocoon as an escape route, enabling longer filaments to be obtained. Tussah silk can therefore meet the needs of those wishing to wear silk without killing the silkworms. Colours, however, are limited to the natural brown palette. For centuries China was the only producer of silk, but now the main countries producing silk fibre are Japan, China, Russia, India and Thailand, where mulberry trees can be grown to feed the silkworms. It has been estimated that an acre of mulberry trees eventually produce 40 grams of silk. Given such an exclusive fibre, it was initially the cloth worn by emperors, royalty and aristocracy and continues to be a prized fibre, but larger volumes now produced in China have enabled it to become much more commonplace in recent years. In environmental terms, silk is biodegradable and wild silk certainly meets high ethical and environmental standards until the dyeing stage. Dependant on the dyestuffs used this stage can be environmentally compromising, hence, most tussah silk is undyed.

Wild silk moth, *Antherea assama*, which is commonly found in North-East India. Image courtesy of Samant Chauhan.

RIGHT:
Wild tussah silk cocoon in tree.
Image courtesy of Samant
Chauhan.

BOTTOM LEFT:
Clusters of tussah silkworm
cocoons hanging from trees
in Bhagalpur, Bihar, northern
India where designer Samant
Chauhan works with NGOs
and local people to produce
100 per cent wild silk fibre
and fabrics for his collections.
Tussah silk is harvested without
killing the silkworms, who
emerge naturally form the
cocoons. Image courtesy of
Samant Chauha.

BOTTOM RIGHT:
Wild tussah silkworm emerging
from cocoon. Image courtesy
of Samant Chauhan.

Manmade or Manufactured Fibres

This section focuses on some of the most significant contemporary fibres for fashion, and is not intended to be comprehensive. The section discusses cellulosic fibres such as rayon, processed from natural materials, new fibres from renewable sources, and the synthetic fibres polyester and Lycra.

Cellulosic Fibres: Rayon

In response to the impetus of increasing population and demand, the Industrial Revolution and its mechanisation of fibre and textile production, and scientific developments of the nineteenth and twentieth centuries, it was perhaps inevitable that manmade substitutes for natural fibres and new production methods would be developed in the name of technological progress, spurred by the potential for lower priced mass-produced goods and a higher standard of living. The first manmade fibre to be invented in a quest over centuries for 'artificial silk' was viscose rayon, a lustrous fibre patented in 1884 by the French Count Chardonnet, and commercially made in the UK and US by Courtaulds and then Dupont from the early twentieth century. These new fibres were highly popular in the fluid fashions of the 1920s and 30s. Once commercial production of the first manmade fibres was achieved, the race was then on to find cheaper substitutes for all natural fibres. This led to many further developments in both cellulosic and petroleum oil based yarns, such as nylon (polyamide), acrylic and polyester, and creating a symbiosis between the chemical industry, the textile industry and fashion, which continues today.

Early rayon manufacturing comprised viscose, acetate or cuprammonium processing methods, depending on types of chemical solvents used. The fibre is processed from natural cellulose in the form of either waste cotton linters or wood pulp derived from fast growing trees like pine or eucalyptus, (a renewable resource). The natural cellulose is then dissolved in a chemical solvent to make a viscous liquid and extruded like spaghetti through specially shaped holes in a 'spinneret' creating fine endless filament threads which then solidify and are processed to give different textural effects, then spun into yarn. This type of fibre is classified as 'regenerated cellulose', with different names according to the solvents used in the process. Most common rayons today are viscose rayon, using caustic soda as solvent, whereas 'cupro', uses cuprammonium hydroxide. Before the name rayon was invented, the fibre was often called 'art silk', due to its high lustre but was a lower price alternative to silk, and this avoided the negative word-associations of 'artificial' or 'substitute'. Cupro fabrics, known for their deep sheen, were popular in the US until the 1970s, and the fibre continues to be made by just two companies. Japanese manufacturer of branded Cupro, Asahi, claim that Cupro is biodegradable in both soil and landfill after two months. Manufactured viscose and cupro are still pure cellulose fibres, like cotton and linen, but acetate (cellulose acetate) fibres are made from cellulose as a starting material (using acetic acid during production) and are not pure cellulose. Acetate fabrics are light and fairly weak, familiar from their use as linings for clothing, as is cupro.

Recent Developments in Renewable Fibres

The environmental impact of the viscose process for making rayon and other fibres (air and water pollution from emissions) has recently been the subject of legislation. This enforced improvements are to be made in the manufacturing process to recover or minimise the chemicals produced which are escaping into the environment.

Exciting breakthroughs were made in the 1990s in creating new fibres based on using renewable plant materials and closed loop manufacturing systems, designed from the outset to be more sustainable and environmentally sound than existing fibre processes. In 1996 a new regenerated cellulosic fibre, lyocell, was created by Courtaulds in the UK under the trade name Tencel, (now owned by viscose manufacturers Lenzing in Austria), in the first virtually closed loop system for a manufactured fibre process. Tencel is the only fibre to be awarded the EU-based eco-label, and is biodegradable in suitable conditions. It is marketed as "the new age fibre", claiming a combination of all the benefits of natural and manmade fibres: "Soft as silk, strong as polyester, cool as linen, warm as wool and absorbent as cotton."

The Tencel process is a variation on the viscose process, called 'solvent spun' with the same starting point as in viscose, natural wood pulp extracted from renewable and sustainably certified forests of pine, beech or eucalyptus trees. Wood pulp is dissolved in a non-toxic solvent which can be recovered and re-used, making Tencel, or lyocell, the first 'green, manmade fibre. Tencel fabric is known for its drape and can be textured for surface effects such as 'peach skin' handle.

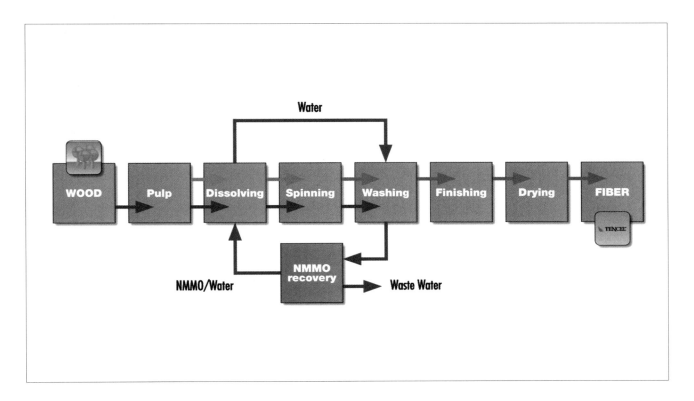

Bamboo

The classic regenerated cellulose viscose process is now being applied to other renewable cellulosic feedstock—bamboo, which is native to China, and grows extremely fast. Chinese companies developed the extraction of fibres relatively recently and now manufacture and spin the fibres for knitting and weaving. Bamboo is faster and cheaper to grow than cotton, grows up to nearly five metres and is easier to process and extract fibres compared with linen and hemp. It has attractive aesthetic qualities of softness, sheen, drape and cool handfeel, and is biodegradable (but takes less time to degrade than the other cellulose fibres).

It also has natural anti-microbial properties but this is easily lost in the manufacturing process unless the alkalinity levels are carefully controlled, as bamboo is highly sensitive to conditions. Many claims are made for this anti-microbial property, especially when bamboo is blended in underwear and sports clothing, which may well be overstated. However, as a relatively new fibre in clothing, there is a novelty value, and some sustainable credentials in the original material. Initial uses have been focused on leisure wear and knitted bamboo fibres can be found in underwear, knitwear and casual clothing, some using a hundred per cent bamboo and others in blends with cotton, wool or nylon. The demand for bamboo appears to be developing very strongly in different lvels of the market.

Bamboo t-shirt by the Continental company and bamboo yogawear.

Ingeo

Beyond the plant-based cellulosic fibres, recent research has also developed sustainable fibres from starch (such as corn or sugar cane) and from plant proteins such as soybeans. Commercially, the first fibre available which is completely derived from the annually renewable source, cornstarch, is Ingeo. Developed by the Cargill Dow chemical company in the US, Ingeo is now marketed by their subsidiary company NatureWorks. In turn, this company has now become a joint venture with one of the foremost Japanese synthetic fibre manufacturers, Teijiin. The company has two main products from the same source—either a polymer plastic, used in food packaging, car panels, carpets, or the same material formed into a fibre and then spun into yarn which is branded Ingeo for clothing and interior uses. The process of creating this synthetic polymer from cornstarch is said to be a 'cradle-to-cradle' system.[18] The plant sugars are fermented and become lactic acid molecules that then combine (polymerisation) into the polylactide polymer, known as PLA, in the form of plastic pellets. These can then be converted to fibre by the same routes as other synthetic fibres. However, this fibre is intrinsically biodegradable in specific conditions, and can therefore return to the soil to nourish another crop of corn, although the subsequent dyeing of fabric might affect the benign quality of this end of life scenario, together with the disposable method. The main impetus is currently on biodegradable supermarket bags, rather than fibres.

18 Promoted by McDonough and Braungart in their book of the same name published, 2002, North Point Press.

Oil-based Synthetic Fibres

Taborelli manufacture this woven fabric from Ingeo yarn. Image courtesy CLASS.

All of the common synthetic fibres such as nylon, acrylic, polyester and Lycra elastomeric or spandex fibre) are based on synthesised polymer structures, (ie. long chains of smaller molecules) which have highly significant properties such as elasticity, strength and durability. The chemical components for the polymer are derived from petroleum oil, and the synthetic fibres are known as the second generation of fibres, the first being natural fibres. Supply of synthetics is controlled by manufacturing rather than nature.

Nylon was the first completely synthetic, chemically manufactured, fibre. Invented in 1938 in the laboratories of the Dupont Company in the US, Nylon was promoted as a 'miracle fibre' to the public. "Better things for better living—through chemistry" was an early advertising slogan. Nylon revolutionised the manufacture of women's' hosiery, which became known as 'nylons' from their launch in the 1940s to an eagerly waiting public. Several different types of Nylon are used in clothing and industrial applications such as carpets and tyre cords. This highly popular development was followed over the next ten years by other polymer fibres: polyesters, polyacrylics and polyurethanes for example.

The raw material for manufacturing polymers is derived from petroleum oil, which is a non-sustainable source. Once created, however, many polymers can be reprocessed and re-used many times. However, most polymers end up in landfill where they do not decompose in two hundred years. There are several ways of creating the fibres and yarns, in one flowing process which always starts with the polymer chips either melted or dissolved in solvent, which is drawn through a spinneret, cooled and hardened as the multiple filament fibres are formed. These are then twisted and spun in a wet or dry system into a final yarn. The characteristics of the fibres can be determined by variations in the solutions, the spinning and finishes applied. These synthetics have gradually overtaken the early ones for clothing use and, since the 1990s, acrylic fibre is no longer produced in the US or UK. Courtaulds in the UK was a major manufacturer of acrylic fibres and yarns in the 1960s and 70s, the heyday of early manmade fibres, which mimicked the look, but not the performance of wool.

When observed microscopically, all natural fibres have specific cross-sectional shapes which help to give them their particular characteristics. For example, silk filaments are triangular in cross section with an even, smooth surface, giving lustrous quality, wool has an oval cross section, scaly surface and is crimped, giving elasticity, cotton fibres have a kidney-bean shaped cross section and are twisted along their length, giving body but appearing dull. A key feature of manmade fibres is the ability to engineer specific cross sections and apply surface texturing qualities in order to mimic natural fibres or create brand new effects not possible any other way. These processes have recently been applied at smaller and smaller scales, to fibres below one denier in diameter, known as 'micro fibres'. This engineering of structure and textured surfaces have produced far more desirable effects than the early synthetics, for example the 'peach skin' surface effect applied to viscose approaches silk in its handle.

Lycra and Elastomeric Fibres

One of the most important groups of polymers used in contemporary clothing are the elastomeric fibres made from polyurethane. First developed as a substitute for natural rubber in corsets and underwear, elastomeric fibres were pioneered again by Dupont (now Invista) in 1959 with their world-famous Lycra brand. Many other brands of elastane fibres now exist, all based on similar principles in which the long polymer chain is coiled when relaxed, allowing the fibre a high level of stretch (to at least twice its length) and recovery to its original state. It is now commonplace to find up to ten per cent elastane fibres blended with both natural fibre and other synthetics to give flexibility and greater comfort in wear.

The body-conscious decade of the 1980s and its exercise boom first stimulated stretch factors in leisurewear. 'Stretch' has now extended to become commonplace in both knitted and woven fabrics, in casual and more formal tailored clothes. Although high comfort and performance is the aim of these fabrics, there are serious problems with the end of fabric life. At present, the only fibres that can be reclaimed and recycled are monofibres without elastomeric content. The limit of manual sorting is currently into pure fibres only and the majority of blended fabrics will be dumped in landfill. Re-use, or keeping the garments for longer is one way of reducing the impact of synthetic material, but demand needs to be created for specialist recycling of such fabrics, as their volume is increasing, although trials have been run in the US.

Polyester—The Rise and Rise

Polyester is now the largest single fibre group within global textiles production—estimates being as high as 52 per cent. It has grown to this position over a mere half century, overtaking 'king cotton' as the key textile fibre, and used in lingerie, outerwear, furnishings, homewares and industry.

Polyester is a generic title covering a number of fibres with varying properties, the most important of which is polyethylene terephthalate (better known as PET). Like most manufactured polymers it can be produced both in sheet form (think of the plastic bottle) and as a fibre (think of the fleece). Dupont first produced polyester in 1951, known then by the trade name of Dacron. The fabric is known for its 'easy care' properties—light, strong, fast drying, wrinkle resistant and highly durable—and is often blended with other fibres, especially cotton. However, it does easily retain odours, so is washed often, but needs no ironing and has a very fast drying time in air.

The process of manufacturing polyester, as with most synthetic fibres, starts with molecules containing carbon, derived from petroleum oil. These molecules are then linked together by chemical process into long chains of molecules or polymers, with specific chemical compositions—in this case an 'ester'—which characterises the fibre. This staring compound is formed into pellets which are then melted into liquid form and forced through a spinneret to form fibres which are cooled and hardened in air to form filaments. This process is relatively simple compared to many others, contributing to polyester's low price and availability.

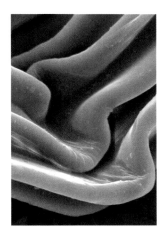

The microscopice surface of polyester.

The fibres are characteristically smooth, giving the typical unbroken surface of polyester. However, in the spinning process many surface effects can be imparted to the filaments which can eventually appear bright and shiny or dull and matt, or the cross sectional shape of the filament can be changed within the spinneret. Polyester is sensitive to heat and is 'thermoplastic'. Its relatively low melting point enables the fabric to easily be set into permanent pleats or 'crushed' effects which have now become commonplace. This quality has been exploited particularly well in Japan, where improvements to fineness and handle of polyester have been strongest. The well known collections of Pleats Please by Issey Miyake are the ultimate easy care designer clothes. They can be washed, hung to dry quickly, need no ironing and look the same as new each time. They are made of a hundred per cent polyester therefore the clothes are durable and can be worn for a long time without degrading through laundering.

So polyester in the form of clothing has undergone a remarkable change in fortunes, from a low point in 1970s design with stiff double knit fabrics, to the present day when the most respected top-level designers use the fibre by choice. Its ecological credentials are interesting, as balanced with cotton, there is lower water consumption, and in theory, once made, the fabric can be recycled may times to a product of equal value.

Blended Fibre Fabrics

The previous sections have focused on individual fibres, but a high proportion of everyday fabrics are made from blended fibres. Usually this blending occurs at the beginning of the spinning process to create 'intimately blended' yarns and fabrics. The purpose of blending fibres is to combine the most beneficial properties of each. The well known 'polycotton' sheets are a blend of cotton and polyester fibres to give the comfortable feel of cotton with the enhanced durability and easy care of polyester. Many blends used for clothing are natural/synthetic for similar reasons, more common than all natural blends.

However, expensive natural animal fibres such as cashmere or angora are often blended with cheaper wool fibres for knitwear, and with mohair and alpaca for suiting and coat materials, resulting in lower costs while still retaining their luxury cachet. Polyester has an affinity with many other fibres, and is also blended with other synthetics. Elastane fibres such as Lycra and Elite are blended with natural and synthetics to give enhanced comfort and performance in leisurewear and sportswear, and increasingly in many types of standard clothing, such as tailored jackets. Many blends also include several different fibres at once, to create speciality yarns and fabrics, and create exclusivity. While the benefits during use are clear, the difficulty with blends is apparent when garments are discarded and then become part of the disposal problem.

Recycled Fibres

More and more attention is now being given to recycling of textiles back into fibres—a practice that used to be commonplace with wool textiles. Old processes are being looked at afresh, and new schemes for returning clothes are beginning to be tested out at retail level in the UK, US and Japan for example. The process of creating fibre from textiles is one of mechanical tearing of the fabrics into smaller pieces, and repeating until the material is in a fibrous state. This has been used for about 200 years, and no new technological innovation has been applied recently. According to a 2005 report for Defra, only a quarter of textile waste is collected for recycling or re-use at present.[19]

Recycled Polyester

To many, one of the most surprising recycled fibres is recycled polyester. Obtained from the now ubiquitous clear plastic water bottles, or PET, recycled polyester is an up-cycling source of supply that would otherwise have gone into landfill. In 1993, US company Wellman were the first to introduce a polyester textile fibre, EcoSpun, made from post-consumer waste plastic bottles.

Outdoor clothing company, Patagonia, have become a champion of recycled polyester fleece, the main fabric made from recycled PET, which is a knitted pile fabric identical to one made from new polyester. They have achieved this by partnering with a Japanese company, Teijin, who have developed their own closed loop polyester recycling system. The potential for development of this process has been recognised with new initiatives: M&S have pledged to use recycled PET, to recycle their polyester and that in a few years none of their clothing will end up in landfill. A new company, Closed Loop London, is planning to divert 35,000 tonnes of waste plastic packaging from landfill or export, to be converted into new packaging materials mainly for the food and cosmetics industry.

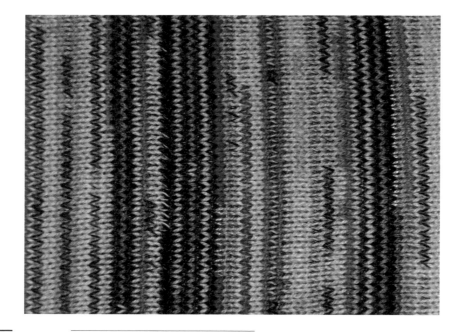

Recycled cotton from innovative design company Muji.

19 "Clothing Take-Back for Recycling and Re-use", Oakene Hollins Consultants, 2007.

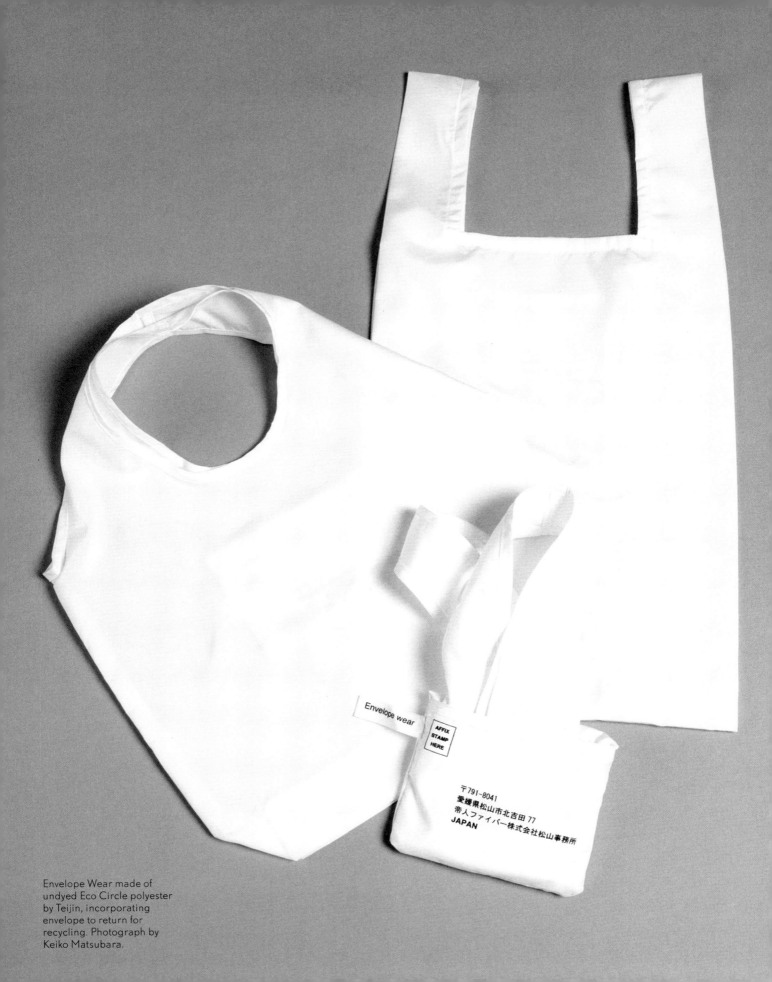

Envelope Wear made of
undyed Eco Circle polyester
by Teijin, incorporating
envelope to return for
recycling. Photograph by
Keiko Matsubara.

Envelope wear

AFFIX
STAMP
HERE

〒791-8041
愛媛県松山市北吉田77
帝人ファイバー株式会社松山事務所
JAPAN

MULTIMEDIA TEXTILES FROM RECLAIMED MATERIALS

KATE GOLDSWORTHY

KATE GOLDSWORTHY *employs both hand-crafted and digital techniques in her multimedia designs. An interest in sustainable design and a desire to override preconceptions surrounding recycling underpins her work and has encouraged an original response to choices of materials and processes. Inspired by light, transparency and movement, her textile pieces are multi-layered, sheer and dynamic. Goldsworthy is currently working on the Ever and Again research project based at the Textiles Environment Design (TED) resource centre at Chelsea College of Art and Design, focused on the concept of life cycle thinking and designing-in solutions as part of the creative design process.*

GOLDSWORTHY IS studying for her PhD entitled Material Re-creation, processing thermoplastic waste into textile products designed for disassembly and further recycling. her work particularly focuses on recycled polyester, for both interior decorative panels and garments. She describes her work thus:

Once we understand the criteria needed for efficient recycling, design can begin to assist the smooth running of these closed loops. By designing characteristics that allow for easy disassembly, product recycling can become simpler and more efficient at end of life.

For this Ever and Again project, I wanted to explore the idea of 'resurfacing' as a way to produce 'upcycled' textile products through a process of studio based experimentation. I was inspired by the traditions of lace-making, appliqué and marquetry as well as more innovative technologies to develop these samples. I began with research into new reprocessing and finishing technology for both textiles and plastics; the main concept was to use these processes to 'upgrade' otherwise low quality materials which are often resigned to out of sight applications.

During practical experimentation, I selected techniques which were particularly suitable for use with thermoplastics, and

tailored them according to the material reactions observed. The resulting work explored design strategies of 'monomateriality' and 'cradle-to-cradle' design, with the intention that products can be recycled through multiple life cycles. I hope to develop these concepts into more industrially applicable solutions for more refined and large-scale interior products. My intention is to produce textiles made from a hundred per cent post-consumer recycled waste which can be returned to the recycling system from which they came after their 'designed life' has been fulfilled.

Recycled Wool and the Shoddy Industry

Wool was one of the original fibres to be recovered, recycled and re-used. As demand used to outstrip supply, recycling was necessary in order to provide the required quantity of material. The natural quality and resilience of wool meant that this processing of 'remanufactured', 'reclaimed' or 'salvaged' wool was very successful, however its textile industry name 'shoddy' has eventually became synonymous with all poor quality materials and finished goods. The qualities of original wool vary, therefore so did shoddy. The market for recycled wool was also dealt a deathly blow by the highly successful marketing campaign launched in 1964 by the International Wool Secretariat. The campaign promoted 'Pure New Wool' or 'Virgin Wool' which was branded with the famous Woolmark logo—becoming one of the most recognised brands worldwide. This mark was a guarantee that the wool in a product had not been reprocessed. Now the shoddy factories and reclaimed wool dealers have virtually gone, but the value of this highly sustainable process has begun to be recognised once again. Currently, the increasing quantities of disused garments we throw away are dumped in landfill or shipped overseas for processing or sale. The reclaiming cycle starts by shredding, extracting unwanted materials, scouring to remove dirt and grease, re-oiling to lubricate the fibre for spinning, and dyeing. Many of these processes use either acid or alkaline solvents, which are ideally reclaimed in a closed loop system. Designer Annie Sherbourne has developed a yarn for knitting made from 50 per cent recycled London textiles and 50 per cent pure new wool.

Felts—Non-Wovens, Industrial and Craft

Felt made directly from woollen fleece requires a combination of abrasion and water, with heat and pressure speeding the felting process. The scales of the wool fibres enmesh together irreversibly to create a solid mass of hardwearing fibre with useful properties such as warmth and cushioning.

Industrial felts are the type of materials, along with wiping cloths, at the bottom of the recycling chain—the lowest grade useful products which can be made from reclaimed materials. The sorting and grading will extract first clothing which is re-usable, then textiles which can be re-processed into fibres for new textiles and finally those which cannot be used in any other ways are processed into thick coarse felts for industrial uses.

Dyeing and Finishing

As part of the normal manufacturing processes of textile production, all fabrics are finished in some way before they are ready to be used in clothing or furnishings, and most are dyed using chemical dyes (first invented by Perkins). These are the hidden aspects of fabric production—from simple processes such as washing to remove

Stuart Rose (M&S Chief Executive since 2004) promoting the M&S eco-thinking to literally "Look Behind the Label" in the campaign. In this case the effects of the dyeing process on the environment are concerned.

oils used in manufacturing, starching to stiffen, steaming or heat setting to achieve the correct proportions, cutting or singeing the surface to remove hairs and give a smooth handle—to additive processes which apply protective coatings or bond one fabric to another. Fabric finishing is an industry in itself, of which consumers are hardly aware. Fabrics straight from the weaving or knitting machines are called 'grey cloth' or 'loomstate', and are often very different from the final product. Many natural fabrics such as silk, cotton and linen will be bleached to achieve whiteness, and may then be dyed to required colours in response to fashion needs. Formaldehyde—which is known to be toxic—is used in many steaming and finishing processes.

Synthetic dyes created a revolution in colour in the nineteenth century, and quickly became the norm, replacing the precious natural dyes such as cochineal, indigo and madder. Natural and synthetic dyestuffs were developed for all the major types of fibres, including acid dyes, reactive dyes, sulphur dyes and pigment dyes. The chemical industry grew enormously, dominated by giants such as ICI, Ciba and Sandoz (now Clariant), but the textile dyeing industry's effect on the environment was severe. Water pollution was a key problem as effluent from the processes was untreated or poorly treated. In countries where textiles and dyeing are still done by manual methods, or standards have been lacking, the dyes have often directly run into rivers and streams. This problem has now been addressed from both sides, but globally the industry is still far from perfect. Attention has been paid in the EU to removing the most harmful chemical dyes from use in cloth and strict standards are now in place for industrial effluents.

Other ways of colouring fibres have been explored—utilising the natural colours of the fibre, and reviving older strains that have been bred out. Fox Fibre cotton was first launched in the 1980s and grown in the US to produce naturally tinted shades of pink and green cotton without the need for bleaching or dyeing. However shades are limited and, of course, do not adjust with changing fashions. A new company, Natural Colour Cotton, has taken up the same concept to produce coloured cotton with no dyes. Similar experiments have also been undertaken to produce coloured sheep wool by feeding particular chemicals, a practice which is ethically fraught.

After enzyme washing treatment, each pair of denim jeans is fashionably distressed manually. Image courtesy of Tejidos Royo and Clariant.

SEXY, RUGGED, ACCESSIBLE AND INIDIVIDAL

THE STORY OF DENIM

THEY'RE SEXY, *rugged, accessible and individual. They fill everyone's secret desire. Did I say sexy?*

THE ORIGINS of the—now archetypal—blue jeans that are worn worldwide are established as being from the EU. However, the accepted wisdom that the name 'denim' is a contraction of 'Serge de Nimes', a town in France, has been challenged in recent research. Confusingly, there are a number of fabrics which might have a bearing on the derivation. Serge de Nimes was known in France before the seventeenth century, and in the UK by the end of the seventeenth century, but at the same time another fabric called 'nim' was also manufactured in France. Both were a twill weave, partly made from wool, whereas Serge was always a mix of wool and silk. However, a fabric called jean, a blend of cotton or linen with wool, was known to originate from Genoa, and was imported into the UK in the sixteenth century. Mills in Lancashire started to produce jean which, by the eighteenth century, was made of cotton and used for men's clothes. The distinguishing feature between cotton denim and jean was that denim was made with coloured warp and white weft, whereas jean was made with both warp and weft in the same colour: blue.

    DENIM WAS stronger and reserved for workwear, whereas jean was used more generally, including in sailors trousers. By the late eighteenth century, denim was being manufactured in the US, in order to reduce imports from the UK and EU.

Denim dress by Gary Harvey,
made from 42 pairs of Levi
501s in various shades of
indigo, cut up to create a tiered
ballgown with corset waist.
Photograph by Robert Decelis

THE STORY of the birth of the denim jeans—or 'waist overalls' is well known. Dry goods salesman, Levi Strauss, had travelled to the mid-west of the US to sell canvas to the gold rush pioneers in 1850, but found the miners were more in need of hardwearing clothing. He supplied fabric to a tailor, Jacob Davis, who had the idea of putting copper rivets at the stress points such as pockets, which made the overalls very strong. This proved popular and Davis approached Strauss to partner him in paying for the patent for an "Improvement in Fastening Pocket Opening" which was granted to them in 1873. So began the Levi's denim empire, using fabric made at Amosteag Mill in New England, which became the biggest textile producer in the world before decline and closure in 1936. Natural indigo dye was used at first, originally grown in California, but imported by Strauss from India. Eventually natural indigo was replaced by the new synthetic dye from the early twentieth century.

FROM HUMBLE workwear, denim jeans were adopted by the cowboys of the western States, and then spread across the rest of the US. Denim jeans were adopted as a sign of rebellious youth in the 1950s and went on to become the staple casual uniform of young people everywhere—a symbol of social and sexual freedom. By the 1970s, denim was styled, decorated and customised and became so ubiquitous it no longer signified rebellion. Designer label jeans appeared at high prices and the market became saturated. In the mid-1980s, to stimulate demand, Levi's relaunched their classic 501s with a seminal advertising campaign (set in a laundrette), which increased sales eightfold. Although there was a decline in the 1990s due to the rise of combat pants, since then constant development of new concepts in fit (hi rise, low rise, baggy, skinny), finishes (stone washed, bleached, torn, embroidered) and colours (white, black, dirty) have kept the denim market buoyant and highly competitive.

A model wears APOC
(A Piece of Cloth) denim
by Issey Miyake

THE DENIM PROCESS

Cotton packed in bales ready for processing

Blending cotton fibres to give constant quality parameters

The ready made yarn on the beginning reel

The ready made yarn on the secondary reel

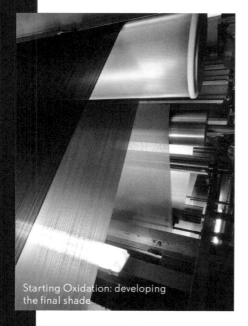
Starting Oxidation: developing the final shade

Developing the final shade

Transforming the cotton into slivers

The spinning process

Padding sulphur dyes

THE PROCESS from cotton fibre to denim fabric involves many stages—blending, spinning, fibre pre treatment, making warp beam, warp dyeing and oxidation, steaming, skying, threading dyed warp on loom, weaving, finishing treatment, curing, singeing, sewing, industrial garment washing and manual finishing.

Wrap preparatio of the dyed yarns

Wrap preparatio of the dyed yarns

Photographs by Tejidos Royo Spain. Images courtesy of Clariant International.

COMERCIALLY DEVELOPED COTTON FIBRE

NATURAL COLOUR COTTON

THE QUEST *to commercially develop a naturally-coloured cotton fibre that needed no dyeing began 25 years ago. At this time US entomologist, Sally Fox, began developing very old strains of coloured cotton, which had all but disappeared—displaced by the massive production of pure white cotton that was easy to dye in any colour the market desired. Ancient cotton was a naturally pigmented fibre that grew in shades of green, brown and beige—for example brown cotton from India produced khaki coloured fabric. For ten years Fox worked to crossbreed and develop these coloured cottons into FoxFibre a revolutionary concept in ecologically sound organic cotton fibre that needed no dyes. The cotton was coloured in soft pale shades of green and browns, but after initial success, FoxFibre faced problems in getting the fibre processed due to protectionist fears of contamination of the machinery producing mainstream white cotton.*

ONE GOAL was to produce a blue cotton—perfect for jeans, but the company struggled to survive in a relatively hostile environment. The idea was ahead of its time, and still needed further work on the colour variability and range, taking about ten years to develop a new colour. However, Fox Fibre is available to craft knitters.

THE PIONEERING work which Fox began in California was taken up in China in the 1990s. Investment in 18 years of research and development, starting with crossbreeding seeds from Peru, Turkey and China over many generations, led to improvements in the staple

A pair of baby mittens from the Perfect Start range of naturally coloured undyed baby clothing.

OPPOSITE:
Naturally coloured cotton grows in soft shades of pinks and browns.

length of the fibre, enabling the Natural Colour Cotton Company to industrialise the production of coloured cotton. A UK branch of the company, headed by John Conneely, an eco-entrepreneur and textile manufacturing specialist who has worked with China over the past four years, was charged with bringing this cotton to market in a range of baby wear and leisure clothing. Five hundred tonnes of the naturally coloured fibres are now being produced by organically certified cotton growing methods meeting GOTS standards, with this set to increase dramatically each year. Conneely predicts that in 2008 there will be more naturally coloured cotton than regular organic cotton available.

THE NATURAL Colour Cotton Company now operates across the whole supply chain from seed to fabric to finished garments, producing coloured cotton in stable shades of green, brown and beige, and also a range of sustainably produced bamboo maternity and yoga wear. Benefits of the naturally coloured cotton fibre are that no chemicals are used, no fertilisers or pesticides are used, no scouring or bleaching is necessary and of course no dyes are added which means no water pollution. The natural soft handle, the total elimination of chemicals, and the pale soft colours are ideally suited to baby wear. Released under the brand name, A Perfect Start, the baby wear is now distributed in eight different countries after just a year in business. This has won the company a prestigious Product of the Year, business award for in 2007.

THE IDEA of 'green clothing' has taken root commercially: sales of organic cotton are set to triple over the next two years to 1.3 billion pounds and Natural Colour Cotton is riding the wave. It will perhaps only be a matter of time before Fox's vision is finally achieved.

Production of Fabrics

Fibres become yarns that are then processed into fabric by one of the following manufacturing methods: weaving, weft or warp knitting, braiding, lace-making, or matting fibres into felts or industrial 'non-woven' fabrics. All production methods were originally manual which were then mechanised during the great transformation and upheaval of the Industrial Revolution. As industrialisation continues to spread globally to every corner of the developing world, there are still many places where the hand-skills of weaving fine cloth remain and can be valued, for example India, Bangladesh, and Bolivia.

Hand-knitting as a cottage industry has long disappeared in the west, but remains as a craft, and whenever fashion cycles return to handmade looks, as in recent years, the skills of Chinese hand workers are called upon to produce hand-knitted and hand-crocheted jumpers, dresses and cardigans. Handmade lace once thrived in the UK abd EU, especially when the fashion for starched lace collars was at its height in Elizabethan times, but it survives as a hobby or for the tourist trade, in Brussels for example, replaced since the nineteenth century by sophisticated warp knitting machine-made fabrics. Handmade felts survive as small designer companies make inventive new products such as shoes and quirky gifts, and long-standing traditions continue in countries such as Turkey where felted carpets for the tourist trade are made. It is beyond the scope of this book to look at fabric manufacturing in detail, but the profiles of fashion and designer companies give insight into contemporary production, and its issues, at all levels from small-scale designer-makers to handmade production and mass manufacturing.

The new paradox incorporates all that has gone before, and much contemporary design is based on the rediscovery of old techniques and technologies, integrating them with modern materials, technologies and aesthetic sensibilities. The fashion industry is one of the last major industries to be based on manual skills—almost all garments are still made by individuals working a sewing machine. The complexity of operations to convert two dimensional fabrics to three dimensional clothing, together with the sheer diversity of products and rapid changes in styles, materials, colours and trims, not to mention the inherent uncertainty and unpredictability of orders in the fickle fashion market, means that automation has not so far been possible. This however, provides employment to a vast number of people worldwide, as production moves around the globe in a constant quest for cheaper. The next chapter discusses these paradoxical issues in more detail.

Organic felted woollen pillows
in beautiful rich colours.

FABRIC TO FASHION

This chapter examines the complexity of the fashion industry and its structure and process in relation to design and maufacturing. The industry operates on many levels from elite designer and luxury brands to everyday clothing, which itself is still subject to changes in fashion—think of how the style and proportion of the basic t-shirt has evolved from long, baggy and straight to become shorter and more sculpted to the body.

Although constantly embracing the new and looking forward to 'next season's key looks' or 'the next big thing', fashion is paradoxically one of the few major industries to be heavily reliant on old fashioned manual labour and hand-skills for manufacturing the clothes themselves.

Mina Pehonen has added a fringe to this knitted cape to add an individual look. Autumn/Winter Collection 2007.

Fashion Cycles in the Fashion Industry

Although aspects of the fashion production chain, such as cutting and handling, are increasingly automated, virtually all clothing is still made manually, using craft skills and the sewing machine. Each garment is sewn individually, but usually by several different workers in a production line using updated versions of the machine first invented in 1844—which is still the backbone of the clothing industry.

The spectrum of market levels covered by the fashion industry is very broad, but with a hierarchical structure which correlates price to both exclusivity and production methods. The UK fashion industry comprises a number of major areas and retail models, with many other niche markets between.

Starting at the pinnacle of expense and exclusivity with haute couture, which is dominated by such legendary names as Dior, Chanel and Balenciaga, or Norman Hartnell in the UK, this level of fashion comprises hand-crafted complexity and unique *tour-de-force* pieces completely constructed by hand. The renowned *petits mains* (seamstresses and embroiderers) who work within the workshop atelier of a design house still hand-embellish fabric with lavish amounts of beaded and embroidered decoration. However, the genuine couture customer has now dwindled to around 2,000 clients worldwide who attend salon shows by invitation and actually buy the couture dresses. Despite this, in 1987 designer Christian Lacroix opened the first new couture house for nearly 30 years (also selling ready-to-wear) and in 1997 Jean-Paul Gaultier added a couture line to his collections. This activity is equivalent to a 'loss leader' as the majority of the income of these couture houses is now derived from subsidiary products such as accessories, perfumes and sunglasses. The male equivalent of *haute couture* is bespoke, made-to-measure tailoring. Totally handmade suits, individually crafted with several fittings along the way, are epitomised by the traditions of Savile Row. Bespoke tailoring has also undergone something of a renaissance in recent years, with and a new generation of tailors springing up, such as Gresham Blake. Several fashion designers have undergone some of their early training and experience in these establishments— notably the, world reknowned, UK-based designer Alexander McQueen.

One stage down from these dizzy heights is the elite designer-brand level of fashion, often owned by the luxury conglomerates, where emphasis is on recognisable signature style, strong silhouette, innovation in cut, design and detail, highest quality fabric and manufacturing standards, and exclusivity through relatively limited production at substantial retail prices. These are the major fashion leaders, doyens of the catwalk shows, with their own retail stores, and who often produce several lines—their main line and cheaper 'diffusion' lines (for example Prada and Miu Miu, Donna Karan and DKNY, Yohji Yamamoto with Y's and Y3 designer sportswear). Other design houses, such as Comme des Garcons, Dries van Noten and Paul Smith are still independently owned, with significant retail presence and flagship stores.

On a much smaller scale are innovative independent labels or emerging designers, who are highly directional in fashion terms and trade under their own personal names, often in partnership, for example Clements Ribeiro, Emma Cook, Eley Kishimoto, Christopher Kane, Proenza Schouler or Veronique Branquinho. This category of labels stage catwalk shows or unusual salon presentations and are very closely watched by the press and buyers for 'the next big thing'.

Y's and Y3 designer menswear on the catwalk by designer Yohji Yamamoto.

Primark (pictured) are one of the biggest players in the value mass-market retail fashion market arena

Intricately hand-crafted
stitched bodice Spring/
Summer 2008.

Edun Spring/Summer 2007.
Edun aim for sustainable
and socially responsible
production through trade
with African businesses.
Image courtesy of Edun.

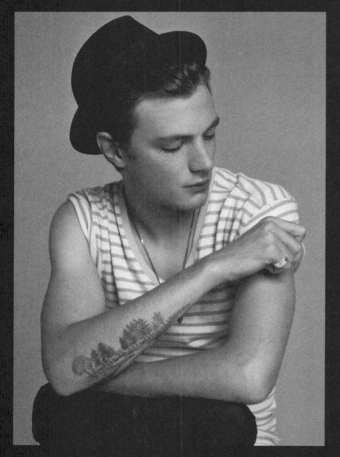

Mens' and womens' casual
fashions, Spring/Summer
2007, from socially
responsible clothing label
Edun, who work with African
businesses to encourage
sustainable production and
trade. Image courtesy of Edun.

1   In response to public pressure, Gap Inc is taking steps to address its impact on workers. Its 2005–2006 CSR report states:

We've come to see that some of the everyday business practices in our industry—from decisions about where to source products to last-minute changes to product orders, to poor production planning on the part of factories—can have a significant impact on working conditions in factories.
    In 2003 Women Working Worldwide (an NGO) published a research report entitled 'Bridging the Gap' which showed that inefficient purchasing practices are endemic throughout the garment industry, and that the situation is not unique to Gap Inc.... Decision-making in our supply chain is complex, and some aspects of global garment production will always be unpredictable. Nevertheless, we are committed to taking ongoing steps to improve our performance.

2   Carruthers, R, and Santi, A, "What Price a Conscience?", *Drapers*, 4 August 2007.

Another design-conscious level, but priced towards the top end of the high street, are so-called 'bridge' retailers who manufacture their own labels for their own store chains—Jigsaw, Karen Millen, Whistles, Monsoon etc. These are multiple outlets supplying vast quantities of repeated designs but with a boutique feel and clear fashion offering. Next in the hierarchy come the mid-market stores (John Lewis or Galerie Lafayette), department stores and also independent retailers catering for a more local than global clientele. These shops often feature less widely known international brand names of high quality but which are not so press worthy or fashion forward. These outlets have traditionally catered to the older age group, but this demographic is now breaking down.

Selling at lower prices on the high street are the branded chain stores making their own mass-produced goods for the mainstream market. They aim to be right on trend with fashion by commercialising strong ideas, and getting them in store at exactly the right time for the trend to be strongest. Here, quality is maintained at a level appropriate to price points and market segmentation. This includes multiple stores from M&S, and Oasis, to Gap[1] and Zara for example.

Finally there is the newest addition to the fashion pecking order, the 'value' mass-market in which high volume at the lowest price is the driving factor. These include discount stores and supermarkets, such as Primark, Matelan and the supermarket labels, for example George at Asda and F&F at Tesco. These stores offer the cheapest quality, but which is perceived as very good value at the price, in fashion basics such as jeans for as little as six pounds (or even three pounds) and white one pound t-shirts. Some of this clothing follows major fashion trends but the rest is basic clothing that bypasses fashion, made in bulk as commodity clothing. This market segment has developed only in the last decade or so, spurred by the major changes in international trade agreements which allow imports from cheaper labour countries.

Right at the bottom of the fashion heap are the clothes which are 'knock offs'. Counterfeit designer labels sold on market stalls or similar outlets represent a sizeable amount of business globally. In general the retail prices of fashion reflect volume and economies of scale of production—the price falls in direct proportion to the amount of units produced per style. At the higher ends of the business, production volumes decrease, and the proportion of design, marketing and service cost, as well as direct manufacturing costs, rises dramatically, directly impacting the retail price.

There are many price differential anomalies in the marketplace. A garment such as a t-shirt may be a very low priced commodity item in a discount store, or sold at designer level at a much expensive price point, with higher and more costly production values (such as better quality fabrics) and often higher aesthetic design values. Each of these garments is the product of a very different supply chain route, such as country of manufacture and labour costs, which helps to account for the differential in prices. When sustainability issues are factored in on top of this pricing structure, it results in an inevitable rise in fabric and manufacturing costs, which creates barriers for companies who do not want to see their prices rise. However, often in practice, these costs will balance out over time through efficiencies. Dan Rees of the Ethical Trading Initiative suggests companies are now asking "how can I turn this into a business opportunity?" instead of "how much is this going to cost?".[2]

Recently, there has been an interesting spate of high profile cross-sector linking via top designer and high street fashion collaborations—for example Karl Lagerfeld, Viktor & Rolf and Roberto Cavalli with H&M, Yohji Yamamoto with Adidas, Julien Macdonald for M&S and so on. However, many designers now consider the clothes 'inspired by' their work, (which are sold in high street chains often in the same season), too close for comfort—and unfair competition, hence a steadily increasing number of court cases taking place. Ironically, many designer labels have consulted for high street stores for a long time (Paul Smith and Betty Jackson for M&S, Jasper Conran and John Rocha for Debenhams) and will continue to do so. Another recent phenomenon is for celebrities such as Kate Moss and Madonna to lend their names to high street fashion lines (TopShop and H&M respectively), initiatives which have received mixed press reactions, but created the desired marketing hype and sales.

One of the most interesting new types of partnership is the co-opting of the credibility of eco-fashion labels to the mass-market—notably the collaboration between People Tree and TopShop which resulted in a dedicated concession space within the London store, and the short-lived venture between Tesco and Katharine Hamnett to produce an ethical clothing line Choose Love made from organic cotton. This groundbreaking partnership required a change in Tesco's entire sourcing procedures for the Choose Love line, with Tesco having to commit to buying a crop of cotton in advance, but Katharine Hamnett was said to be 'disappointed' with the supermarket giant's overall commitment, including lack of marketing and plans for shop-within-shops.[3] The mismatch may also be that the value retailer with low margins is not used to developing a product from scratch and therefore has a lot further to go to become an ethical brand.

The industry has polarised in recent years between the two extremes of luxury and value fashion. As the consumer has become more demanding, design-aware, and fickle with their loyalty in an overcrowded marketplace the traditional UK middle market is seeing a large decline. In order to remain as competitive as possible, manufacturing sourcing has continually moved around the world for decades, but abolition of worldwide trading quotas in January 2005, opened up previously restricted countries to possibilities of export, particularly China, with its massive workforce and aggressive expansion of manufacturing capacity. The repercussions of this major shift in the power balances in the fashion industry are still emerging, with manufacturing continuing to migrate from West to East. This fundamental change and its challenges means that new ideas and paradigms for an ethical future for the fashion and clothing industries are now required.

Kate Moss for Top Shop 2007. Image courtesy of TopShop.

3   Santi, A, "Katharine Hamnett to Sever Tesco Tie-Up", *Drapers*, 29 September 2007, and author interview, 25 July 2007.

Design using leather, silk and certified fair trade cotton, from the Noir Autumn/ Winter 2007 Collection Noir aims to "turn corporate social responsibility sexy" by combining luxury fashion with meaningful enterprise for trade not aid.

Designs from Noir Spring/
Summer, 2007 Collection
entitled "Cotton Couture";
created to make cotton
luxurious and sexy, using
certified African cotton.
Image courtesy of Noir.

The Role of the Fashion Buyer

Fashion is a truly global business, in which the different functions such as design, fibre and fabric production, manufacturing and selling are physically separated and carried out in many different parts of the world, with companies often subcontracting several levels and in several geographical places along the stages of the supply chain. This is one of the key complexities making traceability very difficult, often as much for buyers as for consumers. Fashion is also international in its influence, with many new centres around the world now developing their fashion industries and profiles, in addition to the traditional key fashion hubs of Paris, New York, Milan and London. In the established fashion buying system, buyers travel between these worldwide centres to conduct their business and make buying decisions first-hand, seeing catwalk and showroom presentations over the 'season' of three or four weeks, twice a year. Despite the communication revolution, travel and transportation is still embedded in the operation of the industry. One of the effects of the Internet has been to facilitate and speed up fashion dissemination, increasing demand from more countries, rather than reduce travel on buying and sourcing trips. Face-to-face communication with garment producing factories around the world is still essential for companies to ensure production accuracy and quality. Fashion therefore has an undetermined but possibly significant cost to the environment. Considering the transportation of people and goods around the globe, dependent on modes of transport for those all-important face-to-face meetings, it is clear that further studies are needed in this area.

The traditional seasonal fashion cycles pivoted around two main selling seasons a year—Autumn/Winter and Spring/Summer. These cycles have gradually been eroded, although they are still the focus for the major designer catwalk and ready-to-wear shows in the fashion capitals. These new seasonal designs once remained fairly hidden, except to industry insiders, until they appeared in the shops, and ideas gradually 'trickled down' to the mass-market for their more commercially oriented and lower priced ranges, with up to a season's time lag. However, now that images are beamed around the world in a matter of minutes following a catwalk show, 'inspiration' from these shows is used at the mass-market levels to inform immediate directions in the same season—sometimes even before the original designers' range hits the stores. The catwalk shows are considered the start of the fashion-cycle in terms of the top store retailers, whose buyers place their orders four to five months in advance of the season in which the clothes will be sold, allowing time for ordering fabrics, manufacturing and deliveries throughout the supply chain. In reality this time is often squeezed. Each part of the fashion-cycle has its own timetable: the textiles which make up the collection are sourced by design teams from clothing companies at least a year ahead of the selling season, and in order for these to be available, the fibres and yarns must be developed by the mills and sold to the textile weavers and knitters between 18 months to two years before the selling season. Feeding all of this, in the major the EU and US markets, are the crucial decisions on colour which are determined by colour meetings of industry professionals which informs the seasonal stories at least two years before the selling season. This then might be said to be the true start of a seasonal cycle. Of course all these cycles overlap with each other, therefore in a large retailer's annual cycle, designs may be in progress for one season while fabrics are sourced for another and the current season's collection is being delivered in store. This still sounds fairly orderly, but this long established fashion system was, in the 1990s, severely disrupted by the development of 'fast fashion', typified by Zara. This Spanish owned company not only manufactures its own clothing, but also makes its own fabrics, and controls all aspects of the supply chain, drastically cutting the manufacturing cycle down to six weeks or less.[4] During this period, TopShop became more design-led and offered constantly changing styles at prices affordable by the majority of people, including celebrities. Although important new trend directions are still launched by the major design houses at the twice-yearly shows, fast fashion now introduces new styles to the high street every month. Re-orders are not a feature of fast fashion and if you miss a style—it's gone. This keeps customers coming back regularly for a new fashion 'fix', perpetuating the faster system and increasing expectations and competition. Thus fast fashion works in seemingly decreasing circles, squeezing the production loops tighter. However, the mid-market and designer market have also played their part in stimulating demand and driving down prices as competition is fierce at all levels. According to David Shaw in *The Fashion Handbook*, 2006:

The 20 to 30 per cent price decrease in selected clothing categories over the past five years now puts all but the most luxurious designer brands within the reach of a majority of the population.[5]

Despite being a highly specialist, powerful and responsible role in the fashion system, little attention has been paid until very recently to the crucial part played by the fashion buyer in the cycle of events within the system, especially from the point of view of sustainability. The fashions which are available for consumers to buy in the shops are there as a result of the buying decisions made and the orders placed in advance of the season. The buyers have to predict which of the season's proliferation of looks offered by the design houses will resonate with their customer profile and be within their budget. Prior internal discussions will have been held to analyse the trends seen in catwalk and showroom presentations. The buyer filters these through their own critical sensibilities, knowledge and experience and instinct—arguably one of their key assets. Once the directions and key looks have been analysed, a brief is agreed within the company and designer ranges are picked over and individual pieces selected as appropriate. A range is built—colours, sizes, details and prices are often changed to suit the buyer and secure the orders, sometimes with exclusivity deals, and the all-important delivery dates are agreed. As timeliness and punctuality are key to fashion, most orders have a very limited delivery window, after which the store has the right to cancel—passing pressures

4   Due to a unique business model based in its culture and organisation, Zara (part of the Spanish group Inditex) is the inventor and paragon of fast fashion. The key to its continued success is an integrated structure controlling design, manufacture and distribution in-house or in close proximity—approximately two thirds of the manufacturing is within the EU creating maximum flexibility and minimising time from design to shop floor. There is a tight feedback loop from store sales back to design and Zara can respond very quickly to this on-trend information—unlike other companies, 85 per cent of its manufacturing is done within the season, not ahead of it. Data from store sales is collected daily to inform planning, and indicate customers' needs and wants, and new stock deliveries are made several times a week, often with different styles. The Zara customer knows that if they sees a garment they like, they have to buy it, as it may not be there again. Inditex controls 20 production companies specialising in different products, and Zara now has over 1,110 stores in 68 countries and over 400 key cities around the world, and is the largest fashion and clothing retailer in the EU.

5   Shaw, D, "Fashion Clothing Manufacture", p. 84.

6   "How Buying Practices Impact Workers' Rights", www.just-style.com, 4 October 2007.

Colourclash dresses designed by Lousie Goldin for TopShop, 2008. Image courtesy of TopShop.

on to manufacturing. Continuity is not a feature of fashion buying. New designers and suppliers emerge, and the buyers have many options for spending their precious budgets. The infrastructure of fashion can be as volatile as fashion itself. The store sales and profits depend directly on these buying decisions, as only a proportion of items will 'sell through' at the full price at the beginning of the season, the rest will be progressively 'marked down' in sales during the season, and the final remainder will be disposed of, before the new season's lines are brought in. One of the most unpredictable factors in the entire fashion-cycle (especially for the UK) is the weather—a rainy summer or warm winter can have a major effect on sales and therefore profits. Here then is the crux of the matter. So that the buyer can be as accurate as possible in seasonal predictions and trends, buying decisions may be delayed until the last possible moment, putting more pressure on the fashion label and, in turn, on their suppliers through the chain. If delivery dates are not strictly met, or for other more dubious reasons, orders are cancelled, and the supplier is left with costly stock to dispose of. The consequences is an immense lack of security for manufacturers—they undertake seasonal work with no continuity or guarantees and grapple with the constant time-pressure of delivering goods quickly. That pressure can only be passed down to those at the base level of manufacturing—the machinists, cutters and others who physically produce the goods, and in turn their suppliers of fabric and fibre.

Until very recently, a fashion buyer or buying team would rarely engage directly with downstream suppliers—neither fabric manufacturers nor the front line farmers producing fibres. This wall has now been breached, and barriers are coming down. The take up of Fairtrade practices in the food and cotton growing industries as a tool for working directly with farmers has now brought the beginning and end of the supply chain in close contact. Campaign groups and organisations such as Environmental Justice Foundation and Labour Behind the Label have recently lobbied on behalf of farmers in developing countries and garment workers in remote factories. Accompanied by the actions of smaller, committed pioneer businesses, like Gossypium and People Tree, this has created a sea change. Major fashion companies, for example Gap, and Nike, have had to re-examine their buying and sourcing practices, and most companies have taken up the torch of corporate social responsibility. In an article on buying practices UK chain, New Look, acknowledges there is a "total disconnect of reality between the purchasing function and what happens on the factory floor" and that there needs to be closer dialogue between the buying teams and the ethical trade teams within the business. Generally buyers are not always aware of the impact of their decisions.[6]

Garment-Manufacturing
Labour, Sweatshops and Livelihoods

There is a saying that of the three desirable qualities—'fast', 'cheap' and 'good'—it is only ever possible to have two out of the three in any one project: fast and cheap but not good; good and cheap, but not fast; good and fast, but not cheap. This could also be said to apply to fashion, except that paradoxically, it appears at first sight that fast fashion had managed to deliver all three: fast, cheap and good—a supposed win-win. It has now become clear that what fast fashion has really delivered is fast and cheap, but not good overall—what may be good for the consumer and for retail, has been bad for the garment workers and small farmers in the formerly hidden supply base.

The fashion industry has a uniquely complex set of requirements for manufacturing its goods. A product such as an iron, for example, is designed according to specific needs and optimised for materials, production and costs, then tooled up and manufactured in identical units, the more the better for economy of scale. In contrast, the range of variables in the production of both basic clothing and seasonal fashion is still very high compared to mass-production in other industries. The same garment design, say a sweatshirt, will be manufactured in a number of different colourways and across a range of sizes as a matter of course in each production run, the actual volume and spread of which depends on the level of the market concerned. Supermarkets and high street brands may manufacture perhaps a thousand per style variation; a designer label in hundreds or even dozens; a start-up design company may work in very small batch production of say 50 or a hundred, whereas a bespoke service of handmade pieces works to a market of one. This fragmented production spectrum for ready-to-wear fashion, and with fast changing styles, has contributed to the difficulty in finding automated solutions and maintained the clothing industry as one of manual labour production.

Although in many modern factories there is bulk cutting, preparation and automatic handling of fabric in apparel production lines, the final product is an assembly process using skilled labour with each garment sewn individually, by several workers in the line, each sewing a number of seams, applying zips, buttons, trims or finishing processes. Although in parts of China and Cambodia for example, new model factories have been built, many factories in developing countries are much less automated, if at all, and batches of partial garments are physically moved from station to station.

A typical garment factory employs mostly female labour, with workers in many countries, for example in Cambodia or China, being economic migrants as the main breadwinner for their family. The International Labour Organisation and several international NGOs have teamed with the Trades Union organisations to campaign for equitable and fair working conditions, but conditions vary throughout the world and within countries. There are varying views on this. Designer, Katharine Hamnett, refuses to source at all in China due to the government's human rights record and banning of trade associations, whereas others such as Dru Lawson of THTC and Galahad Clark of Terra Plana have personally sourced factories they feel comfortable to work with. Michael Flanagan of Clothesource who advises clothing

Sports industry manufacturing unit, Sialkot, Pakistan. Image courtesy of International Labour Organisation.

LEFT: Women in dressmaking workshop, Syria. Image courtesy of International Labour Organisation.

Factory workers,
Exprot Prcoessing Zone,
Dar Es Saalam. Image
courtesy of International
Labour Organisation.

companies on sourcing production believes it is not the country that is important but the particular factory, as there are good and bad everywhere.

In 2001 the seminal book *No Logo* by Naomi Klein exposed to the mass-market in the US the labour issues behind many of the well known US global fashion brands, targeting Gap and Nike for example. At the time this negative exposure created a consumer backlash against the companies and served as a consciousness-raising rallying cry. During the mid-1990s, the problems of exploitation for garment and footwear workers worldwide were suddenly brought into sharp focus in the affluent consumer markets—low wages, long hours, child labour, no unionisation allowed, poor or non-existent welfare benefits and so on. Nor were EU companies exempt from criticism. In a television expose, even the venerable M&S was found to be indirectly using child labour in its suppliers' production lines, although as the company was unaware of it, they won the subsequent court case. Since then, the power of the Internet in tracking and monitoring corporate activities has been well demonstrated, and many anti-corporate websites exist, constantly lobbying for change.

The fashion industry in all countries has traditionally been rife with 'sweat shops' where (often immigrant or migrant) workers are exploited to toil in poor working conditions without basic rights. People do, however, need these jobs for survival and are trapped by their financial circumstances—a complex situation which is ethically unacceptable. More recently, campaigning organisations such as the Clean Clothes Campaign in the EU and Labour behind the Label in the UK—through their Fashioning an Ethical Industry project—have raised a voice specifically addressing the long-standing problems in the garment industry. These campaigns have proved very effective and become essential in the fight for ethical practices in fashion. It would be wrong to think that all sweatshops were in distant countries—the UK has had its share (in immigrant areas such as the East End) and there are still areas where conditions are less than ideal.

These labour issues in the garment trade are now well rehearsed and have become a constant topic of media attention which has, through this pressure, culminated in programmes of action—corporate social responsibility policies and mission statements, regular factory audits and active marketing campaigns are now well established. The International Labour Organisation, comprising governments and workers' organisations, was originally set up in 1919 and now, under the auspices of the United Nations, established fundamental conventions for workers' rights, and still governs international labour and environmental protocols. Manufacturers are bound in law to respect the International Labour Organisation rights but constant monitoring of overseas suppliers is difficult and expensive, and takes strategic planning and commitment. Over recent decades, the bulk of manufacturing has now moved out of the UK, US and other developed nations around the globe to developing countries such as China, India and Cambodia. It is fitting that, at the time when clothes are cheapest for consumers and with the growing demand for transparency throughout the entire supply chain, the era of sweatshops being endemic to the fashion industry is beginning to come to an end. However, the consequence of implementing better working conditions may well be that clothes return to their true relative value in Western markets, and stop being the disposable commodity they have become.

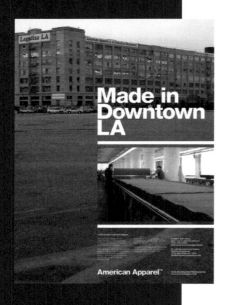

MADE IN DOWNTOWN LA

AMERICAN APPAREL

IN 2006 *American Apparel was the first fashion retailer to open a store in Second Life—the virtual world where clothing your avatar is important, and real money can be made or new ideas tested out. American Apparel is built on selling a range of basic, non-branded, well cut t-shirts for the youth market and now has 181 styles of casual separates in many colours, including hooded tops, underwear, swimwear, leggings, trousers and dresses as well as t-shirts in cotton and blended cotton and polyester.*

AMERICAN APPAREL, based in LA, is now a publicly quoted company, founded by controversial entrepreneur Dov Charney in 2000. It is a product of the Californian free-wheeling sensibility, priding itself on being sweatshop free, completely vertically integrated and "Made in Downtown LA". Almost all the fabrics are made in the US, all the manufacturing is done in one large factory and the company has committed to converting to 80 per cent organic cotton by 2010.

BY THE end of 2006 there were over 150 American Apparel stores (including overseas), and sales of 250 million dollars in 2005. Charney is said to be aiming for one billion dollars in turnover and one thousand stores worldwide. The labour policies are 'worker positive', with the mainly Latino workforce of 4,500 paid double the minimum wage, according to *Business Week*. A significant number of worker benefits are also available including a subsidised canteen, health benefits, massages and language provision. With its mix of local

ABOVE AND OPPOSITE:
Advertising images from
American Apparel.

The|Slim|Slack

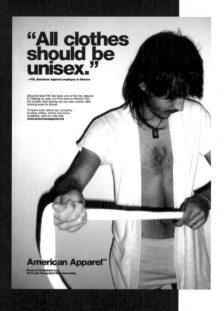

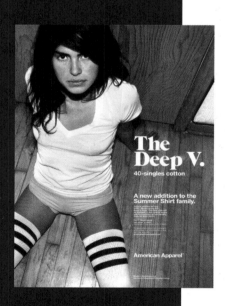

Advertising images from
American Apparel

RIGHT:
American Apparel advert
highlighting the vertical
business structure and
"Made in LA" philosophy
of the company.

Vertical Integration by American Apparel, now involving 5,000 people.

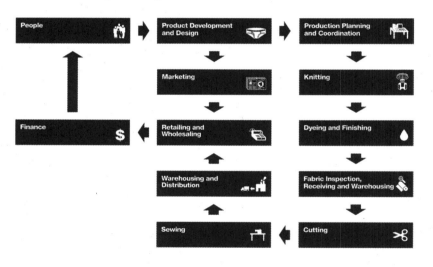

American Apparel®

Made in Downtown LA
Vertically Integrated Manufacturing
www.americanapparel.net

American Apparel®

production and pro-labour policies, American Apparel has become
a cool brand amongst its target market, also known for its upfront
and sexually charged advertising using company employees—often
photographed by Charney, which commentators have seen as
contradictory to the rest of its philosophy. A team of six workers, paid
on piecework, can make a t-shirt in 11 seconds. With over 1.3 million
garments made annually American Apparel is now the biggest clothing
manufacturer in the US.

American Apparel adverts,
such as the one above, often
feature unstyled candid shots
of employees.

The Ethical Trading Initiative

Since the 1990s, media and public pressure has been put on fashion manufacturers to address some of the major issues of labour rights for many garment workers at the end of the fragmented and complex fashion supply chains, much of which is a consequence of the fundamental structure of the industry. In the UK, this resulted in the setting up of a tripartite association in 1998, the Ethical Trading Initiative or ETI, comprising food and fashion retail companies, trade unions and NGOs. A nine-point base code of international minimum standards has been created, governing ethical trade and labour practices, which members sign up to. Many well known names are now part of this initiative including Asda, Debenhams, Gap, M&S, Primark (joined in 2007), Tesco (a founding member), Inditex (Zara), Jaeger, Next, Monsoon and New Look. It is interesting to note that the Arcadia Group (TopShop, BhS, Dorothy Perkins) were not members at time of writing, and that Levi's resigned from ETI in February 2007 following their suspension for "refusing to adopt the Living Wage provision of the ETI base code". The Levi's position was that it "cannot responsibly commit to the Living Wage provision because it does not believe it can implement it with its suppliers" within the specified time scale. These opposing positions indicate the complexity of ensuring complete implementation of and compliance with an ethical code.

The formation of the ETI responded to increasing pressure from the media and campaign groups to act on behalf of garment workers' rights globally. The UK campaign group, Labour Behind the Label—not one of the NGOs in the Ethical Trading Initiative—has highlighted issues in the fashion industry, and written two reports: "Wearing Thin: The State of Pay in the Fashion Industry", 2000, and "Lets Clean up Fashion: The State of Pay Behind the UK High Street", 2006, to check progress. Much of the debate rests on definitions and local interpretations of the Living Wage (legal minimum wage) and industry benchmark standards for pay, but there is no doubt serious problems still exist although the report acknowledges "a few glimmers of hope". In particular, Labour Behind the Label highlights the fact that too much reliance is placed on audits which are "not the panacea that many companies believe them to be, frequently failing to pick up serious problems". They also found that a company's good intentions cannot be guaranteed to translate into action on the ground. The major retailers and members of the Ethical Trading Initiative were invited to respond to points for the second report, and these responses were graded on their own scale by Labour Behind the Label. From the non-responders, and those who were "dragging their feet", "resting on their laurels", or "could do better", two companies stood out. Gap and Next were considered to be "pulling ahead" and seriously engaging with the issues.

A report which has had great impact was produced by War on Want in December 2006: "Fashion Victims: The True Cost of cheap Clothes at Primark, Asda and Tesco". This hard hitting report was based on interviews with 60 workers in six garment factories in Bangladesh, and criticised working conditions and actual wages paid as below minimums, despite the Ethical Trading Initiative base code, calling for immediate action. These reports and continued media exposes demonstrate the gap still to be bridged between good intention and practice on the factory floor of the garment industry.

"Lets Clean up Fashion: The State of Pay Behind the UK High Street" Ethical Trading Initiative Report.

What Happens to Unsold Fashion?
The Clothing Life Cycle

In chapter two, we looked at the creation of a piece of clothing—how the garment comes together and its journey from fibre to garment. As the retail selling seasons progress there is another inexorable cycle: new merchandise bought several months ahead comes in, sells at full price for a while and then it is no longer 'new', and is gradually sold at discounted prices as the season progresses in order to clear the rails for the next season's new fashions. Some high fashion goods are bought by sale shops which sell previous season's lines, many designer labels hold their own sample sales for clients, or send their surplus to public designer sales, such as London Fashion Weekend where designer labels sell previous seasons' surplus after every fashion week. If not routed this way in direct selling, then the merchandise is often incinerated. Many retailers and designers prefer to do this than let their branded goods be bought up to find their way onto the market stalls and devalue their brand equity—although some goods are certainly sold this way with the identifying labels cut out.

Secondhand Clothing

TRAID recycling bin for unwanted clothes.

Once clothes have been worn, they enter a different loop. When we no longer want our clothes (long before they are worn out) we might pass them on to the charity shops selling secondhand clothing in local areas—this makes us feel good, but it is only the tip of another iceberg of selling. Only a small fraction (ten to 20 per cent) of used clothing is resold in the UK charity shops, who sell on the majority to commercial sector merchants. The clothes are then sorted and better quality items baled in bulk and sent to developing countries, where it is sold on in local markets by specialist traders (this is known as 'salaula' in Africa). This is partly how t-shirts and jeans have infiltrated all over the globe and the discarded clothing becomes fashionable again in a new market. The remainder of the used clothing is sorted into fibre types for reclamation and recycling into yarns for upholstery or fillings; the rest, which is mixed fibres or of poor quality or damaged, becomes textile waste, to be dumped in landfill, where it takes several years to decompose. One of the issues now for the secondhand clothes trade is that, because new clothing is much cheaper, the secondhand value has been eroded, therefore it is not worth the effort of sorting for re-use or recycling. It has even been known for secondhand clothes to be more expensive than new. Many textile recyclers in the UK have closed in recent years due to these economic shifts.

As we are buying more and more clothes, and our disposable income increases, so does our waste. The entire UK textile recycling industry handles approximately 300,000 tonnes of fabric for reprocessing and recycling each year. The Salvation Army Trading Company (SATCo) is one of the biggest players in the UK used clothing industry; handling 25,000 tonnes a year. It collects clothes through clothing banks, 500,000 door-to-door collections and through a national network of shops. According to Garth Ward of SATCo, "society throws away over a million tonnes of clothing and textiles into the rubbish bins annually" which could be re-used or recycled instead of becoming landfill. He estimates that of the clothes which are collected in the UK, the sorting process produces 60 per cent re-usable, 30 per cent recycling grade and ten per cent waste. In contrast, when UK clothes are sorted in the EU 52 per cent are re-used, 40 per cent recycled and eight per cent go to waste, showing signs of decline in quality. However, in the Ukraine where UK clothes are prized, 83 per cent is re-used, 14 per cent goes to wiping cloths and only three per cent is waste. This he attributes to "different cultures, different needs, different affluence, different access to fashion".[7] The SATCo UK sorting operation in Wellingborough sorts into 99 wearable grades (by item) and 19 recycling grades. Re-usable clothes are sold to India, Africa, Baltic countries and the EU, but recycling grades are "sold into a declining market generally at a loss'"

The charity TRAID (Textiles Recycling for Aid and International Development) takes a different approach to working with used clothes, claiming to divert 200,000 tonnes annually from landfill, with 900 clothing banks throughout the country, their own sorting operations and a clever 'up-cycling' approach called TRAID Re-made to appeal to younger fashion-conscious customers looking for individual outfits. Teams of young designer volunteers are given bags of used clothes and are free to cut them up to re-design and recreate them into new, individual, customised items, which go back into the shops for sale as much trendier one-off fashions. TRAID keep their stock refreshed by circulating clothing around amongst their shops, each one responding differently to its local area. At the moment, shops are concentrated in the London area and in Brighton. A percentage of all the profits are ploughed back into projects in the developing countries and work with schools in the UK. One project funded by TRAID in 2006 worked through a local charity with communities in Madagascar, one of the word's poorest countries where 70 per cent live below the poverty line, to improve health services and sanitation.

Oxfam and Secondhand Clothing in Africa

Oxfam handles 10,000–12,000 tonnes of used clothing per year, of which ten per cent is sold in the UK (a figure which is increasing) and 90 per cent goes to commercial sector merchants. After roughly two weeks in an Oxfam shop, stock is culled from the shelves and sent to their central operation, Wastesavers in Huddersfield. Wastesavers also take in a small amount of 'frustrated stock' direct from fashion manufacturers.

There have been criticisms of the export trade in Western clothing, for stifling local garment industries and culture, as Western clothing has gradually replaced or is favoured over indigenous styles. In answer to these arguments, Oxfam conducted their own detailed study of the secondhand clothing industry in West Africa, concluding that secondhand clothing imports are "likely to have played a role in undermining industrial textiles/clothing production and employment in West Africa" which declined in the 1980s and 90s, but that "such imports have not been the only cause".[8] The report cites "unreliable and expensive infrastructure" such as lack of available materials, high costs and lack of training and access to credit, plus cheap imports from Asia which also compete with local

7   Green Solutions and Sustainability in Textiles and Fashion Conference, Leeds University November 2006. See also "The Secondhand Clothing Market" a report by SATCo and Kettering Textiles, 2003.

8   Baden, Sally, and Catherine Barber "The Impact of the Secondhand Clothing Trade on Developing Countries", Oxfam, September 2005.

production. On the other hand, the secondhand clothes trade creates substantial employment in sorting, cleaning, altering and selling the clothes. Oxfam has now set up its own project, Fripethique, in Senegal employing 30 people. It has been questioned whether this re-use of clothing is effective environmentally, given the costs. However, the benefits of recycling clothing have been shown in a study conducted by Environmental Resource Management and published in the academic journal Resources, Conservation and Recycling which found that:

Collection, processing and distribution of post consumer clothing consumes 1.7 kWh of extracted energy per kg of secondhand clothing recycled. This is insignificant in comparison with the energy associated with production of new clothing. For every kilogram of new cotton clothing displaced by secondhand clothing, approximately 65 kWh is saved. For every kilogram of new polyester clothing displaced by secondhand clothing, approximately 90 kWh is saved.[9]

The Journey of a Blouse

9   Collins, Michael, and Simon Gandy "Strealined Life Cycle Analysis of Textile Recycling", Environmental Resource Management Ltd for Salvation Army Trading Co Ltd, February 2002.

10   Durham, Michael, "Clothes Line" *The Guardian* 25 February 2004.

In February 2004 an intrepid journalist, Michael Durham, followed the trail of a colourful viscose blouse which had been deposited in a clothes bank in Ashby de la Zouche, Leicestershire to its new home in Zambia, a journey which took well over two months.[10] The blouse, which had cost 50 pounds, was collected by the clothing merchants Ragtex Ltd, who operate 200 banks and collect 95 tons of clothing per week. The blouse was graded as high quality and baled with 45 kilograms of other similar items to be shipped in a container to Africa. After seven weeks the ship arrived in a port in Mozambique and, after two weeks in customs, the container load of bales travelled overland across Africa into Zambia to a town called Chipata. An interesting transformation had taken place, as the container load was worth over £26,000 in the local trade, which is significant when most Zambians live on less than one pound per day and cannot afford new clothes.

A prosperous middle merchant trader bought a hundred bales, which he then sold on individually to other smaller traders with their own market stalls. Finally, the numbered bale containing the blouse was bought by a female stallholder and the brightly coloured blouse was purchased immediately by a 27 year old teacher, who was very pleased with it, for the equivalent of a day's salary (approximately 75p). She is quoted saying: "I'll wear it to parties. I don't buy clothes very often, just once in a while, but after paying all the bills, its nice to have a bit of money left over for something smart." Critics question this trade, and that donated goods are eventually sold, but a senior UK charity executive comments in the article "It's not aid or trade—it's trade for aid", the middle merchant is clear that "there is charity and there is business". Therefore the secondhand clothing trade turns, touching people, making businesses and raising money for charities.

Past, Present and Future

In the past, detergent foam and coloured rivers were the two of the hallmarks of a polluting textile industry which were evident in the textile producing areas of the UK. During the 1990s, improved environmental legislation covering waste and effluent began to be put in place in the UK and the EU which has changed this polluted landscape for the better. The EU has recently banned the use of certain chemicals such as azo dyes used in dyeing textiles and, in 2004, the World Health Organisation created classifications and guidelines on the hazards of pesticides commonly used in agriculture and cotton growing. Dye systems which use far less water and have better take up have also been developed.

The retail landscape was much slower to take action on environmental issues although, in the UK, M&S has been implementing an environmental policy at all stages of production for many years which, according to a spokesman quoted in the UK fashion industry weekly 'bible' *Drapers Record*, was "driven essentially by economics and being ahead of legislation rather than public demand".[11] Long before M&S started outsourcing to overseas production, it used its team of textile technologists to investigate and reduce the use of harmful chemicals, including banning formaldehyde in finishings, and sent buyers out to producer countries to examine and analyse local conditions. The article went on to say: "The effect of M&S' pressure is that other retailers may have no choice but to follow because they use the same manufacturers"—a benchmarking of standards which has proved to be realised in the launch of the company's Plan A.

Esprit in the US first created its Ecollection for retail in 1992. When this closed in 1995 it was intended that the lessons learnt from this small range would be applied across the high volume main collection—an ambitious target. Recognising that consumers were reluctant to pay higher premiums for ethical and environmentally produced clothing, the company maintained (at an initial loss) the same prices as the rest of its lines, but this type of commitment would not make long-term economic sense for any business. With changes in senior management, and Esprit now a global company, the impetus of this groundbreaking approach appears to have been lost, or at least diminished. The company's history featured on its website makes no mention of Ecollection.

11 "Greener than Thou?", Drapers, 11 June 1994.

Many eco-pioneers such as Lynda Grose (who developed Ecollection for Esprit), Katharine Hamnett (a tireless campaigner for organic cotton in fashion), and Barabara Fillipone (who has worked to develop hemp production) have passionately campaigned for change for nearly two decades, working with both fibre producers and the garment factories which supply the clothing. Their uncompromising beliefs have now clearly been vindicated, as action for change comes to the top of the global economic and environmental agenda. Ethical and sustainable principles are of such importance that they now unquestionably have to become a fundamental part of everyday living—necessitating massive changes in behaviour which will be very difficult to achieve in Western consumer societies, as people do not want to reduce their standard of living or become ascetics. Therefore strategies need to be adopted at a deep level of design and production, in order that consumers can, without necessarily a conscious decision, make a difference in their purchasing— because the research and innovative thinking for sustainability has already been built-in, by design, to the majority of products.

These strategies include not only the post-manufacture and post-purchase doctrines of reduce, re-use and recycle, but also pre-manufacture design and production for high quality longer lasting goods and lower replacement turnover of goods, (getting rid of built-in obsolescence). Design for end-of-life and disposal or better still, for re-use is part of this new process in the 'cradle to cradle' approach. As a consequence, higher prices in mainstream clothing may be needed to reflect the true value of production, which will in turn encourage less consumption.

The qualities and longevity of the highest level designer fashion (couture and bespoke) may paradoxically embody these ideas, sometimes to excess, but always with high aesthetic and creative values. Enhanced design values are important to create a longer lasting relationship with fashionable clothes and, after they go out of fashion, well designed and cherished items often acquire a wonderful patina of age, a secondhand value and respect as vintage fashion—which, after an appropriate number of years, become desirable again in fashion cycles. The costume historian, James Laver, famously quipped that over a period of roughly 150 years, a fashion goes through cycles of being—at its first inception—indecent, then shameless, smart, dowdy, hideous, amusing, quaint, charming, romantic and finally beautiful. This may be borne out (but with a postmodern accelerated timeline) by 'vintage' fashion, which became popular again in the 1990s and was truly accepted as current fashion when celebrities on the red carpet, who were looking for complete individuality, began to wear unique pieces form previous eras. Shops that had been a secret of fashion stylists and designers, such as Steinberg and Tolkien in London (now closed), gained a new lease of life and even high street shops like TopShop developed their own vintage section. In this way, the life of fashionable clothes has been extended. Other systems and strategies for future operation of fashion have been proposed—such as the extension of clothes hire, which is used currently for formal occasion wear, or sharing and borrowing of high fashion items through websites such as Bag Borrow or Steal or Keep and Share.[12]

12 www.bagborroworsteal.com

Juste dresses design by
Jhye Yang hand-woven and
produced in Bangladesh by
fair trade co-operatives..

How Design Can Impact the Life Cycle of a Fashion Garment

Design is what draws us to fashion. The combination of colour, texture and the feel of the fabric, styling and silhouette makes up the visual experience coupled with how it makes us feel and look when we put it on is attractive. Often all we see at first is a sleeve on a hanger—but something, attracts our attention. Eco-fashion must have the same qualities, to meet our desires, and then delight us with both aesthetics and its eco-credentials. For eco to become chic, design must lead the way, and the clothes must deliver all the great qualities we are looking for, while almost incidentally being well thought out and meeting one or several criteria for ecologically sustainable and ethical fashion. The designers and companies featured in *Eco-Chic* have approached eco-fashion in a number of diverse ways, each of which represents one or more positive strategies for change, often used in tandem. These can include one or several of the following:

RE-USE AND RE-DESIGN
Designers such as Jessica Ogden, Junky Styling, Ciel, From Somewhere, and those working with TRAID Remade, take used clothing which would otherwise have gone into landfill and create something new from old—cutting up and restyling suits, knitwear, skirts and other pieces. Because the clothes are non-standard, there is added creativity and individuality in each outfit—you will not see someone else wearing the exact same piece.

Junky Styling are one of the many companies who reclaim and recycle unused garments to create fresh and edgy design-conscious fashion.

REWORKED FABRICS: UNIQUE FABRICATION

JUNKY STYLING

IN THE *late 1990s, a small business was born in a run down part of London's East End. Annika Sanders and Kerry Seager refashion and transform old clothes—suits, shirts, dresses found in charity shops and surplus sales—into funky outfits stylish enough to wear clubbing. In time-honoured fashion, their restyled, self-made fashions created quite a following. Sold at first from a stall in the now defunct Kensington Market, this year, their company Junky Styling celebrated ten years in business in east London.*

DURING THE intervening years, Brick Lane and its former Trumans Brewery has become a mecca for 'alternative' fashion and an uber-cool, multi-cultural location for young, edgy fashion labels. The labels occupy the old brewery spaces and the workshops and houses, which were once home to the traditional East End rag-trade—an industry that still manages to hang on by a thread.

JUNKY STYLING is an example of a new breed of micro companies—there is a team of five and a half people (one part time) currently working for the company—which punch a great deal above their weight, influencing others and reaching a major audience through their Internet presence. On their Myspace page they style themselves as "London's Premier Recycled Clothing Company". The 'Community' fashion show marking their ten year anniversary was styled by David Holah of Body Map, the seminal design company which created new fashion waves in the 1980s, integrating the music and fashion scenes of the time.

THIS PAGE AND OPPOSITE: Outfits by Junky Styling turning old clothes into new fashion.

FOLLOWING PAGES: Parkour images advertising clothes from Junky Styling 2007. Photograph by Marian Sell.

— 198 —

A similar spirit pervades the East End fashion community today—creative individuals mix and match fashion, music, art, design and digital creativity in the raw surroundings of old warehouses.

THE SIGNATURE look for Junky Styling is the deconstructing and reworking of classic men's pinstripe suits, shirts and ties into surprisingly sexy and glamorous dresses, bustier tops, skirts and trousers. Even the invitation for their Community show was a real shirt cuff. Other reworked fabrics include tweed suits, knitwear and silk scarves, all combined with freshness and attention to detail. Everything is produced in the Brick Lane shop. Each piece is individual, and although patterns and styles are repeated, the unique fabrication means no two are alike. As well as an evolving and timeless collection of pieces for sale in the shop, taking "old/worn/dated/shameful clothing" and giving it a new life, Junky Styling also operate a Wardrobe Surgery where customers can bring in fabrics or clothes with fond memories, or handed down, and have them made contemporary again. The biggest volume of clothing brought in this category is denim—a fabric imbued with a person's life, which they are clearly loathe to part with.

JUNKY STYLING previously showed their work 'off-schedule' during London Fashion Week and in the Ethical Fashion Show in Paris. They now also take part in Estethica, the ethical-fashion section of the official London Fashion Week, and have started to gain profile and other retail accounts in the UK and overseas. The creative energy they constantly channel into diverting the textile waste stream can be a force for positive change as part of the bigger picture. As part of the wider ethical and environmental fashion movement, the influence of companies such as Junky Styling is beginning to pervade and impact the textile recycling industries and the charity sector to increase the value of waste by design and 'upcycling'.

RECYCLED ICONS

GARY HARVEY

Too many garments are deemed aesthetically redundant and discarded at the end of a season, when there are still many years of wear left. By sourcing fabrics and raw materials that have literally been thrown away, you can look good and be good too.

VOTED ONE *of the hundred most powerful people in fashion by The Face magazine in 2004, Gary Harvey is one of the hidden talents of the fashion industry. Working as the creative director behind the Levi's and Dockers Europe brand-advertising images for nearly ten years, in 2005 he broke free from the world of corporate branding to return to his own creative spirit. Advertising concepts, casting and styling are his key contribution to the lexicon of fashion imagery, having worked for Levi's on their RED, girls, anti-fit and Type 1 jean campaigns among others.*

AS AN independent creative consultant and designer Harvey produces his one-off 'recycled icons' in the same manner as couture pieces. These have become a commentary on contemporary fashion and to show that recycled can be beautiful and fun. For Harvey, fashion is about image, drama, excitement and transformation, about challenging

ABOVE AND OPPOSITE: Gary's Harveys second Collection of recycled couture gowns includes more icons of clothing such as the Funeral Dress, made of black lace, satin dresses, and everyday items such as the University Scarf Dress and the Spotty Dress— always in fashion. Photograph by Robert Decelis

perceptions with the unexpected. The recycling element is almost incidental, or it certainly started that way—the first icon dress using 42 pairs of Levi's 501s evolved when sourcing a dramatic garment in one of his photo shoots. His first collection of dresses were each made from fashion garment icons: in addition to the Levi's jeabs, he created a trench coat dress from 18 Burberry macs, a fishtail dress from 28 army camouflage jackets and the newspaper party dress using 30 copies of the *Financial Times*.

HARVEY TRAINED in fashion at Ravensbourne College and the Royal College of Art, and has now returned to the roots of craftsmanship in fashion. Having grown cynical about the greed he perceived in parts of the fashion industry, he is happy to be making pieces himself, partly by hand-stitching, partly with the sewing machine, taking a week to build each couture dress around its corset bodice. With their dramatic silhouettes, the dresses are perfect subjects for photography, although some are clearly rather difficult to wear! For his second group, shown in Autumn 2007 at fashion events in London and Los Angeles, Harvey based the pieces on recognisable classics such as rugby shirts, the wedding dress, polka dot dresses, university scarves and black Victorian mourning dresses. He visualises his ideas and finds the secondhand clothing from a variety of sources—markets, antique dealers and warehouses of surplus stock, or occasionally responds to an unexpected find. Interestingly, the publicity his pieces have attracted crosses the divide—they have been featured in both fashion magazines such as *Vogue* and *Vanity Fair* and a number of eco-magazines, such as *The New Consumer*, and been exhibited in high fashion shop displays in Paris, Hong Kong and Berlin. Harvey is challenging the accepted role of fashion and using its incredible powers of communication (and the catalyst of surprise and humour) to convey a new message that confronts society's over-consumption—the heart of the fashion paradox.

Richard Nicoll has recently collaborated with People Tree using organic textile to create this dress.

The Company Secco create household objects out of recycles everyday waste.

ORGANIC TEXTILES

As outlined in Chapter Three, the major problems with agro-chemicals and the increasing importance of small-scale farming to supply the world's cotton have led a number of companies back to the source of the fibre themselves, and to the construction of a completely traceable lineage for every piece of clothing. Examples include Gossypium, Katharine Hamnett, and The Natural Colour Cotton Company. Organic wool is less widely available as yet, but Sans and Hamnett have included several organic natural fibres in their collections.

NEW THINKING

Fashion innovators such as Issey Miyake and Martin Margiela regularly question the premise and basic systems by which fashion is made and presented. Issey Miyake's Making Things presented many new techniques for clothing including the groundbreaking APOC concept. Martin Margiela questions the notion of fashion and values process through innovative designs and presentations which have deconstructed the garment making process. Designer-turned-artist Lucy Orta integrates fashion with social responsibility and connectedness in art installation around the world, also using waste in food as symbolic enactments. Rebecca Earley created new prototypes and fashion from efficient use of processes and materials and experiments with new ways of relating to clothes. Howies think through every aspect of the life of their clothes, and road test them in reality for performance and to encourage people to wear things out. In the commercial fashion sector, choice of appropriate materials and awareness of the implications of design on the number of processes can make a radical shift in the market.

RECYCLED MATERIALS

Although a surprising number of materials can be successfully recycled and converted back into quality products, the amount of textile recycling carried out is still very limited overall. Wool, polyester, and cotton textiles and clothing provide excellent source material for recycling, but demand must be recreated in the market through well designed new products using recycled materials, and designers need to have recycled materials available. Calamai is a company that has been reprocessing fibres for a hundred years, now used by Patagonia for recycled cotton—in addition to their recycled polyester fleece. Kate Goldsworthy has focused her attention on polyester as an infinitely recyclable material for which she is developing innovative and aesthetic texture treatments for fashion and interiors. Muji produce a range of attractive recycled cotton t-shirts, using the random colours to strong effect, and Eco-Annie creates woollen yarn made with recycled textiles. Alison Willoughby is a craft-based designer who creates unique skirts which are as much works of art as clothing, recycling existing materials.

SHAPING THE FUTURE OF SUSTAINABLE TEXTILE DESIGN

REBECCA EARLEY

REBECCA EARLEY, *since graduating from a Central St Martins MA course in 1994 with an award-winning 'heat-photogram' transfer printing process, has gradually developed a design practice which puts re-thinking materials and processes at the heart of her work. The heat-photogram technique uses an idiosyncratic selection of object imagery directly transfer printed onto the material.*

AS THIS material has to be a synthetic, Earley started to use recycled polyester fleece as a base cloth. After several seasons selling and making her distinctive scarves and clothes, she became more interested in researching the textiles and printing methods she employed. Earley refers to this period as "beginning to think differently". She began these explorations of her textile process at Chelsea College of Art and Design where she is now a researcher and practitioner. Aesthetic considerations were always at the forefront of Earley's work process—one notable commission was to re-design hospital gowns for breast cancer patients, using her prints. This signified a real departure in the field of design for healthcare. Her projects were often in collaboration with other designers, from other fields—footwear, fashion, graphics or artists. From 1999 she collaborated with theorist Kate Fletcher, who had just completed her PhD in sustainability at Chelsea. Together they discussed ideas about textile and fashion life cycles and developed two projects on eco-design Materials and Fiveways. These projects explored new ways

The Top 100 project remodels and reshapes 100 blouses using different processes, and the results of exhaust printing, which show the gradual fading of dyes in a garment. Image courtesy of Rebecca Earley.

Rebecca Earley's
graduation collection,
1994, using the heat
photogram printing
technique. Photograph
by Gavin Fernandes.

This image is from the second collection under the B.Earley label using heat photogram technique 1995. Photograph by Gavin Fernandes.

of designing, addressing many ecological design issues such as waste, end-of-life, re-use and laundering. Together, Earley and Fletcher evolved a new method of collaborative idea-generation, with students and designers by facilitating creative workshops, which produced concept and product prototypes which Earley now calls "sketches". Having been introduced to a whole new language and theoretical background by Fletcher, this was Earley's suggested period of "beginning to talk differently".

FROM THIS collaboration came a strong desire to communicate the new concepts and approaches to eco-fashion and Earley went on to curate the exhibition, Well Fashioned-Eco Style in the UK, with the Crafts Council, which toured in 2006. This exhibition was important in raising awareness and bringing to the general public's attention the way in which creative new thinking can start to solve the problems of the fashion paradox, and how individuals can participate and contribute by their own choices and actions in relation to their clothes. This turned out to be the most visited Crafts Council exhibition in ten years, and its legacy is now in the informative website: www.craftscouncil.org.uk/wellfashioned. Earley worked for two years with a number of designers featured in the show to create sketchbooks of inspiration and concepts for new designs especially for the exhibition

EARLEY IDENTIFIES the current phase of her work as "beginning to make differently". She is now working on a research project with professional designers, called Ever and Again, and continues to run the Textiles, Environment, Design (TED) resource at Chelsea. The projects and ideas of the last few years have now crystallised into seven design strategies which Earley is in the process of testing out through new projects. Eventually, she hopes, this will materialise into her own book, a manual of new thinking for designers.

Rebecca Earley's 1994 graduation collection, using heat photogram printing technique. Photograph by Gavin Fernandes.

MAKING PEOPLE THINK
AS WELL AS BUY

HOWIES

WHEN SOMEONE *buys a Howies product, chances are they will already have made an emotional connection to the garment and the company because Howies tells stories—why and how the garment has been made, all its well thought through features, it's life expectancy and other information. Their catalogues are little masterpieces of emotional marketing—down-to-earth, sincere, heart warming tales of everyday life and adventures in the Howies' enlarged family. The company is clearly on a mission to connect people back to the important things of life while creating high quality clothes which have been designed by taking all lifestyle aspects into account, not least how they look and feel. The choices of fabric are explained in terms of their effective performance and functionality with great conviction and also humour.*

HOWIES PEOPLE are active, testing themselves against the elements and enjoying life. Increasingly, this core customer-base is widening its appeal to anyone who shares their values. Howies was founded in 1995 by David and Claire Hieatt, based in Wales where David had grown up selling outdoor sports-clothing. They explain their philosophy thus: "We wanted to see if we could find another way to do business, to see if a company could do well while it did some good. To create a brand that we believe in, to make people think as well as buy." The business was built on the product first, with the aim to produce high quality, affordable, well designed and long-lasting products. The couple are aware that we, as consumers, are 'hard-wired to consume' and it is

As the image above demonstrates, Howies clothes are thoroughly tested in the field.

hard to change this behaviour, but they believe in action for change. One of the company's first and most successful products was a backpack for cyclists, designed with a road sign on the back as a deterrent to motorists who instinctively reacted to it by slowing down; an example of how clever design can change behaviour with positive effect. Design is vital. In an echo of the evolution of fashionability suggested by historian, James Laver, David Hieatt believes that new ideas move through being fringe, edgy, cool, next-big-thing, mainstream, cliché, icon, archetype and, over time, into oblivion. This trajectory is evident within the organic cotton market—having started as fringe and reached 'next-big-thing' status. However, as major companies like Nike and Walmart get involved, oblivion may no longer be feasible.

HOWIES SOURCE cotton from Turkey, merino wool from New Zealand (certified by Zque to be humanely grown to high standards) and organic cotton and denim from Portugal, targeting complete transparency throughout the production chain, which includes both local and international production. The aim is to close the loop on the garment life cycle, to wear stuff out and design clothes so they can be taken apart for recycling. The Born Again jacket uses Eco Circle polyester from Teijin, which will be returned for recycling, and some of the t-shirts are made from recycled post-industrial waste cotton.

EVEN THE denim jean finishing is ecological, using a German system called eco-ball wash, rather than chemicals or stone washing. Recognising the company's lack of perfection in environmental terms, such as clothing miles, and the need to trade off benefits, Howies has subscribed since its inception to the One per cent for the Planet scheme in which a company contributes one per cent of its turnover or ten per cent of its pre-tax profit (whichever is greater) into social and environmental causes.

WHY DID HOWIES CHOOSE TIMBERLAND? AN ANSWER TO THIS QUESTION FROM HOWIES, FOR THEIR CUSTOMERS, STAFF AND FRIENDS POSTED ON DAVID HIEATT'S BLOG IN DECEMBER 2006:

We had to pick our partner very carefully indeed. Like any important decision in life, it comes down to does this feel right. If it does, then go do it. They understood why we do business our way. It's their way too.

Although they don't like shouting about it, [Timberland] have made commitment for carbon neutrality by 2010. 60 per cent of the energy for their distribution centre in California comes from solar power, and their European distribution centre is powered by one hundred per cent renewable energy.

They are one of the first companies in the world to have developed ingredients labels on every box of shoes to increase environmental transparency to help customers make more informed choices.

They will be the first shoe company to give an environmental Green Index hangtag to provide a product-specific rating of select environmental factors on five shoes this coming spring. They give employees 40 hours of paid time-off to serve in their communities. They were voted one of the One Hundred Best Companies to Work For by Working Mother magazine. They have pledged to plant a million trees around the world. They issue a CSR Report and recently launched their first facility-level sustainability report for their Dominican Republic Factory. This is stuff to be proud of. And stuff for Howies to strive for. We have a long way to go on our journey.

Made form recycled polyester
and filled with down jacket,
this jacket protects against
the elements.

AN EDUCATION in itself, featuring projects and booklists, the Howies catalogue accounts for 95 per cent of the company's business, comprising stylish casual separates: t-shirts, jeans, hooded tops, shorts, trousers, shirts, skirts and jackets in predominantly natural fabrics. Most is sold by mail order with an increasing amount of business via the Internet, but the first Howies shop opened on Carnaby Street, London, in Autumn 2007. Howies' philosophy and its fantastic recent growth (growing threefold each year) meant that after 12 years in business, new horizons and financial infrastructure were needed. After some soul-searching, Howies researched possibilities and agreed a take over by Timberland at the end of 2006—a major company but with great synergy in its own approach and products. Significantly Howies has been left intact (including the One per cent for the Planet scheme) and *in situ* in Wales, doing what it does best on a grander scale. According to David Hieatt, "by 2009 the company is set to fly".

Born Again jacket, Winter 2007 Collection, which is made from recycled polyester filled with down.

Droog collaborator, Connie
Groenewegen, designs
from the Rupture Collection
Autumn/Winter 2006, which
feature slashed leather to
create 3-D from 2-D.

SUSTAINABLE FOOTWEAR

TERRA PLANA

THE NAME *of Clarks Shoes still has resonance for anyone over the age of 30; synonymous with the children's shoe ritual of measuring the width and length of the foot to get the correct fit. Admittedly, this is not quite customisation, but a personalised service in footwear that has just started to be appreciated once more. Terra Plana is the company now run by Galahad Clark, a seventh generation shoemaker of the Clarks Shoes family, who grew up trying to avoid going into the family business, but who nevertheless learnt how to make shoes at an early age.*

IT WAS while studying Chinese anthropology in the US that Galahad Clark launched his first range of shoes, Wu shoes, inspired by an unlikely reference to the classic Clarks Wallaby shoe (a shoe so uncool it became cool) in a rap song by the WuTang Clan who were also his first business partners. Having spent some time working in Asia, Clark returned to the UK in 2002 and started to revive the existing Terra Plana brand that had been started by Charles Bergman—a Dutch friend of his father's. It was the ethos of its traditional men's shoes which first attracted Clark (the artisan techniques, the use of vegetable tanned leather) and its natural concept, pure in its foundations but needing input of modern design. Now the company has developed four footwear lines, all sustainable in different ways—Terra Plana, Vivo Barefoot, Dopie and Worn Again. The latter were created in collaboration with Anti-Apathy, a UK NGO campaigning for young people to get involved in the debates, and feature a wide range

Inventive and stylish
advertising campaign
for Terra Plana (in association
with Junky Styling).

of re-used and recycled materials such as postal sacks. For Clark, the principles of sustainable design are fundamentally about good design, considering the whole life cycle of the shoe. A typical shoe style, Boi, uses a new recycled E-leather material (which Terra Plana were the first to use) and incorporates old bike tyres for soles. The shoe lining is made from recycled shirts and denim and at the end-of-life the soles can be ground down to make surfacing material for playgrounds. All the shoes minimise toxins and are moving to water-based glues. Other re-used materials include hand-stitched quilts, overcoats and parachutes. The Dopie shoe is a more recent concept, a type of flip-flop, simplifying the production to one moulded piece (made from a combination of EVA and rubber). Despite the inclusion of eco-materials, a shoe itself is complex to make, with many parts and even the re-used materials have to be gathered. In the interests of transparency, the company has developed an innovative matrix of symbols which give the consumer clear information about each product's ecological principles and manufacture, such as lighter weight, recycled materials, locally sourced, or using minimum glue.

ALL OF Terra Plana's shoes are manufactured in China, where 75 per cent of the world's shoes are now made in one area, and which has highly efficient systems and locally sourced components (including plenty of old bike tyres). As a Chinese speaker Clark is unusual in being able to talk directly with the factories, which are also independently audited. The company has offices and staff based in the local area, pays more than the local minimum wage and is small enough to have intimate knowledge of the standards of operation.

BILLIONS OF pairs of shoes are consumed each year and waste is a huge international problem. Currently, incineration is the route usually taken for disposal, which if this produced clean energy, would be some mitigation. One of Clark's concerns is designing for reparability and investigating new recycling methods, and he is currently collaborating

The iconic Dopie shoe.

OPPOSITE:
Part of the Terre Plana
promotional material.

with research projects at Loughborough University. In response to journalists' stories tracking the provenance of Terra Plana shoes after politician David Cameron famously wore them, another initiative is looking at travel miles in the supply chain, by testing the consumer market for response to different price levels according to the location of manufacture. The same shoe design is being made in three different locations: China, the EU and Africa and will retail at three different prices, reflecting wages costs in each area, as the proportion of labour in a shoe is relatively high compared to other fashion and products. Interestingly for this project, some components will have to be shipped from China to Africa, as they are unavailable in the local market. How people will make their choices, given totally transparent information, remains to be seen, as currently the shoes are sold at a price level which is about £10 more than the mainstream ranges—a relatively modest ethical premium.

SUSTAINABILITY IS inherent to Terra Plana philosophy, but has not necessarily been a strong commercial benefit—the shoes have to sell on design first and on their artisan manufacture, which the company prides. Longevity is also important in achieving emotionally durable design that the user can respond to personally. Although transparency is key to the company operations, Clark is emphatic that new internationally recognised standards are urgently needed, managed by an independent body to set and monitor environmental performance and grading of products for an eco-label.

AS THE Vivo Barefoot range indicates, Clark is not altogether sure that we, as a race, should be wearing shoes at all. If we do, he suggests we should buy Terra Plana to help conserve the planet.

ABOVE AND OPPOSITE:
Julia Smith's Master Degree
Collection, 2006, made in
organic cotton, challenged
stereotypes and prolonged life
by being reversible. Patterns
were designed to eliminate all
waste fabric.

ELIMINATE WASTE

There are a myriad of ways to approach this concept. Julia Smith planned her fashion collection so it can be worn in different ways to prolong the interest, and also uses every piece of fabric in the cutting as part of the design concept. Others designers create clothes from only one pattern piece, avoid cutting into the fabric, or create seamless clothing.

DESIGN FOR LONGER LIFE AND RE-USE

Unlike many contemporary technological or electronic objects which we prefer to remain in new condition, hand-crafted objects grow old gracefully, taking on our own personality and shapes, acquiring the memories of use. Such items can become future heirlooms. If the design of products focuses on single material or fibres rather than mixed fibre blends, or is designed for disassembly, then the elements which go to make up the clothes can easily be recycled and gain an extra life as a different item, saving energy in making new materials. Patagonia already offer a take-back-and-recycle service for their organic cotton and polyester clothes, which created new from old.

NEW DESIGN AND MANUFACTURING PROCESSES

There are several new technologies emerging which take a different approach to creating clothes seamlessly, thereby eliminating the need for almost all of the garment sewing processes, including 3-D knitting, and laser welding. Examples are already available and range from automatic glove and stocking knitting to the revolutionary APOC concept by Issey Miyake which uses 3-D knitting and weaving. Digital and virtual technologies are in development linking body scan data to pattern making and manufacturing which will enable design and visualisation of clothes in 3-D before they are then constructed to personal size and preference— a new paradigm of fashion on demand, which could reduce the amount of clothing made overall to what is actually needed.

MAKE LESS BUT SMARTER CLOTHING

We already have clothing impregnated with perfumes or lotions, or with anti-UV or anti-microbial properties. In the not-too-distant future we may be able to create multifunctional fabrics and garments, which will do more for us for longer, like a true second skin, or make textiles which can change colour and pattern as we wish—just for fun, so we don't need so many different clothes in our wardrobes to keep us satisfied.

GATHERING THE FASHION INDUSTRYS TREASURE

FROM SOMEWHERE

ORSOLA DI CASTRO'S *label From Somewhere immediately signals the mysterious provenance of her fashions, which are made from pre- and post-consumer surplus fabric and garments produced by factories in Italy and the UK. Di Castro tells the story of her original entry into the fashion industry; when she was loathe to throw away a favourite, but incredibly stained, jumper given to her by her grandmother. She decided to give it a new life by customising it. Cutting it open to create a simple cardigan which she decoratively edged it in punto basso (double crochet).*

THIS SIMPLE, yet effective, idea launched a label in 1997. Each day she made pieces herself, recycling used cashmere knitwear (an ingenious re-use of an expensive commodity) and giving rubbish high value again after rescuing it from landfill or incineration. Di Castro took seconds from companies like BP Studio and Jigsaw, which she customised, recuperating waste as she calls it, encompassing both pre-consumer and post-consumer. The clothes were dresses, cardigans, tops created using patchworks of fabric pieces, knitted and woven prints, including reclaimed lining fabrics, with signature crochet edgings and no two ever exactly the same. From Somewhere has become a magpie of the hugely wasteful fashion industry, gathering the industry treasures, and never using new textile products. In the early days di Castro originally travelled round Italian factories to collect the otherwise wasted pieces from the factory floor which, in more recent times, are especially saved for her by factory staff or willingly donated. She takes in damaged goods and finds use for a forgotten waste with surplus fabric colour swatches now used to sell commercial collections. Not all excess fabrics in factories are thrown away, some of the more valuable (like jersey and silk) are accumulated for the stockmen and markets and sold in bulk, but di Castro rescues three to four tonnes of waste each season. Now that companies donate fabrics, cost savings are passed on.

FROM SOMEWHERE clothes are made in Italy and in the UK in relatively small quantities: perhaps only one thousand pieces annually. Production is situated close to the source of the fabrics and each piece is unique. Due to the many seams uniting the numerous, eclectic fabrics (everything from cashmere to tweed) size is not always predictable and dresses are sold by colourway rather than exact size. The designs are unique, effortlessly aesthetic and eye-catching due to their rainbow like quality of patchwork of panels. However, there are sometimes issues of repeatability. Fashion is normally sold as a series of differently sized version of a repeated design, and over time, it is the fashion buyers who have had to be educated and persuaded to accept the variations.

AFTER TEN years, as the company looks to expand its operations, di Castro and her partner Filippo Ricci have played a major role in promoting the new wave of ecological fashions and sustainability in the fashion industry. In 2006, following discussions with Anna Orsini and Hilary Riva of the British Fashion Council, it was agreed at the last minute that London Fashion Week in September would have an 'eco-space' for selling high-end, ecologically sound fashion. This is the moment Estethica was conceived. In its three seasons to date Estethica has become an important raiser of consciousness for ethical and environmental issues in fashion with its residence situated at the heart of the influential designer level of the fashion industry. For its third incarnation Estethica attracted sponsorship from high street

ABOVE AND OPPOSITE:
The From Somewhere Spring/
Summer 2007 Collection.
Image courtesy of
From Somewhere.

giants Monsoon. Around 25 designers, having met the strict criteria, are featured in a mini catalogue produced by *The Ecologist* magazine. With a growing number of designers wanting to take part, momentum is building fast and the concept of repositioning eco-fashion from niche to luxury is gaining its foothold. Di Castro and Ricci reiterated the positioning eco-fashion has recently found itself in when they stated:

One year ago, the concept of creating a serious ethical space within a mainstream high fashion fair seems almost a little subversive. A year on, and the sustainable fashion panorama is virtually unrecognisable.

Filippo and di Castro have also been instrumental in setting up a similar eco-fashion exhibition Slowhite, staged within White, the designer fashion trade fair in Milan. The mini-revolution has taken seed and born fruit. For di Castro and Ricci the Milan event is crucial. As a platform through which awareness of sustainability issues is raised for the major industrial companies and businesses at the core of fashion. Di Castro feels compelled to act for smaller environmentally-aware design companies. She believes that the large fashion brands have encouraged cheaper copies of their products to flood the market. Their diffusion lines have been problematic for smaller designers as the large brands now also saturate the second level of the market.

REFLECTING ON the success of Estethica, di Castro is most proud of the fact that after three seasons, her greatest achievement is "getting recycling bins into London Fashion Week". Long may the influence of Orsola di Castro and Fillipo Ricci continue.

ABOVE AND OPPOSITE:
The From Somewhere Spring/
Summer 2007 Collection.
Image courtesy of
From Somewhere.

SLOW FASHION

MINA PERHONEN

JAPANESE DESIGNER *Akira Minagawa designs under his fashion label, Mina Perhonen. Minagawa, after graduating from the famous Bunka Fashion College, worked as a pattern cutter and textile designer for a made-to-order clothing company. Minagawa then left to set up his own business: Mina Perhonen (literally meaning 'I, butterfly' in the original Finnish).*

WHAT MAKES the Mina Perhonen distinctive and hugely appealing is not only the whimsical visual poetry of the prints and embroideries, but the labels integrity and production values, which respect time in manufacture to capture the nuances of Minagawa's hand-drawn imagery and the specific charm of each design: so refreshing in these times of cheaper and faster mass-manufacturing. The clothing silhouette does not radically change each season, but evolves in design with each new collection, with fabrics re-used and elements reworked, perhaps in a different scale. The clothes are not presented in the usual fashion catwalk format. Instead Minagawa invites buyers and customers to touch and feel the clothes in his seasonal presentations, engaging with their charm. Minagawa sees the production cycle from the concept through to fabric production and finished product as incomplete until the customer adds their own personal story and investment into the products, developing their own long term relationship with the clothes and other items including fabric and leather bags, jewellery and shoes.

Summer 2008 Collection.

THE CLOTHES become narratives through their completion by the wearer, telling their stories. Time is inbuilt into the concept—it is hoped that you will grow older together with your mina perhonen products, adapting a dress say into a blouse as your body size and shape changes, and that mina perhonen will have a meaning and life in many years to come.

FUSING WESTERN AND EASTERN

JURGEN LEHL

ALTHOUGH BORN *in Poland and of Germany nationality, Lehl long ago found his spiritual home in Japan. Having first travelled there in the late 1960s to work for a textile company, he set up his ready-to-wear clothing business in 1972. He has fused western and eastern sensibilities in a rare movement against the fashion tide usually flowing from Japan to the west. His clothes, although sold in over 40 stores throughout Japan, are little known outside the country, as there are no fashion shows and no publicity campaigns to attract attention. There are only a handful of shops selling Jurgen Lehl in the EU and US. He is happy for things to remain that way, preferring a local-scale operation over global-scale.*

JURGEN LEHL is a consummate master of textile design, exhibiting a refined aestheticism more in tune with nature's cycles than with any fashion trend. He is an exemplar of slow fashion: high quality, intricately designed long-lasting clothes to give pleasure for many years. His textiles reflect the earthiness of his inspiration which he finds largely in the natural landscape—collecting shells, stones and pebbles from his island travels, many of which become fastenings for the clothes and accessories, and most recently have become a new range of jewellery. He has travelled extensively in India, Laos, Vietnam and China, as well as remote areas of Japan, taking photographs of the land (such as patterns in mud and sand, falling leaves and snow) and sourcing special techniques for his textiles. Lehl is a champion of

A vegetable-dyed wool jacket from the Babaghuri Winter Collection, 2007. Photograph by Asami Kikuchi. Image courtesy of Jurgen Lehl.

OPPOSITE:
Natural colour wool jacket from the Babaghuri Winter 2006. Photograph by Yuriko Tagaki. Image courtesy of Jurgen Lehl.

the hand-craft skills that create textiles and other artefacts in these regions. He also designs and makes ceramics and commission's hand-carved furniture and always prefers irregularity to uniformity.

LEHL'S FABRICS are increasingly complex—often developing several processes in one fabric, to achieve the effects he is seeking. A single length of cloth may have undergone each stage of production in a different country according to their indigenous skills—perhaps woven in India, hand-stitched in China and shibori dyed in Japan, where the majority of fabrics are manufactured into garments. The fabrics are all created from natural fibres, a principle established 25 years ago for the business, and some are dyed with vegetable-based natural dyes, after much research into making these sufficiently fast and reliable. Subtle colourings impart a depth to the textured surfaces and deliciously soft, rich palettes of browns, purples and greens.

SINCE 2006, a new range, Babaghuri has been developed to complement the main collection. The collection consists not only of clothes, but also hand-crafted furniture, ceramics, homewares and bed linen. The clothing and products are planned to be as ecological as possible, using only natural dyes or the natural colour of the material, and reducing waste in cutting and production. The clothes comprise coats and jackets, dresses, casual tops and scarves with a more down-to-earth quality that is less formal than the main Jurgen Lehl collection. Because of the limitations of natural dye colours, fabrics may be dyed and overdyed in different colours to obtain a range of shades. Some of the textiles are made using hand-spun yarn or hand-stitching and application techniques, and produced in India, Laos, China and Japan.

THE FABRICS have enormous depth and are used to their full aesthetic extent in flowing lines. One of the most unusual fabrics is made in a remote area of China, near Hong Kong, using fermented sweet potato and mud in multiple processes of coating and drying to

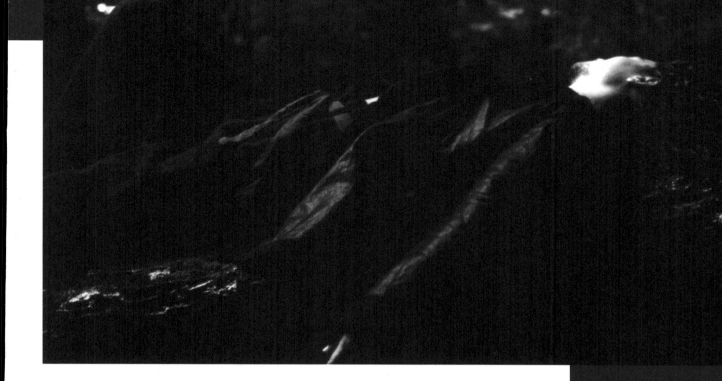

achieve a burnished indigo-like dark blue. Due to the natural dyeing process, handmade manufacturing and the small production quantities, Babaghuri clothes are more expensive and therefore have a limited market, especially as the department stores impose strict standards for colourfastness that cannot easily be matched with natural dyes. Jurgen Lehl says in Japan "only a very few people care about the environment". The company has therefore opened its own shop and and hopes to appeal to a wider market for its elegant ranges.

THERE IS universal quality in Jurgen Lehl's clothes—a pure aesthetic that can be recognised across cultures. Lehl has said, "the people who buy from us are not that interested in fashion, they are impressed by colour and good craftsmanship, and share our values of quality". Lehl continues to be true to the philosophy outlined in the mid-1980s foregrounding textile design over silhouette, and maintaining both ethically and environmentally sensitive production values on a moderate scale.

Babaghuri, Winter 2006. The mud-dyed cotton jacket is reversible to felted natural colour wool. Photograph by Yuriko Tagaki. Image courtesy of Jurgen Lehl.

The Viridis Luxe, Spring/
Summer Collection, 2008.

REDUCING THE IMPACT OF WASHING AND AFTERCARE

With most clothes we wear close to the body, the environmental impact of washing, drying and ironing is far greater than the manufacture of the items themselves, so any reduction in washing needs can be very significant in terms of carbon footprint. With nano-coatings and treatments, clothes can be made stain and dirt repellent and reduce their need for frequent washing. This potential longer life using less energy needs to be balanced with the fact that they will not be able to be recycled after use. Earley and Fletcher experimented with designing no-wash clothes in their 5 Ways project, and Martin Margiela previously sandwiched clothes in plastic creating a wipe-down side effect.

REPAIR AND REMODELLING SERVICES

At one time, alterations to clothing were commonplace, especially when a local dressmaker or tailor would have made the clothes originally. Women in wartime and beyond made many of their own and their family's clothes, handing down and remodelling good clothes for younger children. Repairing skills such as darning and mending now seem old fashioned and not worth the time, but with some creativity, old or torn clothes can be refreshed with embroidery or appliqué for a fashionable handmade effect. Customisation of jeans or tops is now a creative way to express yourself. Bespoke services are becoming more widely available which include an ongoing after sales service of remodelling as you change your life and perhaps your body size.

An example of bespoke tailoring by Gresham Blake. Many bespoke services include ongoing aftercare remodeling.

EASY-TO-WEAR LUXURY

STELLA MCCARTNEY

STELLA MCCARTNEY *is not perfect—she is happy to acknowledge that there are bound to be contradictions in trying to live and work ethically and sustainably, especially when you happen to be working in fashion. "I'm not going to stand here and claim to be one hundred per cent green or one hundred per cent perfect all the time", she told the* Evening Standard *at the time of launching her Care by Stella McCartney range of organic cosmetics in May 2007.*

WELL KNOWN for being a fashion designer with a conscience—refusing to use fur or leather when designing for Chloe and now for her own-name Gucci-backed label, McCartney does, however, admit to having worn vintage leather shoes: "I just think something's better than nothing. I'm not going to lie and I don't want to preach." This is indicative of the quick and critical judgements now being made by an increasingly aware media and public—think of the backlash after the Anya Hindmarsh 'I'm Not a Plastic Bag' promotion with Sainsbury's, which was criticised for having been made in China. The demand for total transparency is perhaps one reason for fashion companies' resistance to 'going green'.

    DAUGHTER OF famous Beatle member, Paul McCartney, Stella McCartney has followed in the family footsteps of vegetarianism and her mother's campaigning for animal rights; a torch which the designer has strongly taken up, particularly since Linda McCartney's death in 1998, by supporting PETA in their anti-fur campaign. McCartney had

OPPOSITE:
Gold duster coat from the
Spring/Summer Collection,
2008. Photograph by
Chris Moore.

an early apprenticeship in fashion, having worked for Christian Lacroix and in Savile Row, before graduating from Central St Martins with a high profile show featuring supermodels (and friends) Kate Moss and Naomi Campbell. She soon became the design director for the French house Chloe, unenviably stepping into the footsteps of Karl Lagerfeld, and achieved commercial success while there with her feminine but modern style which has been called 'rock chick meets vintage-chic', initially inspired by her mother's bohemian style in the hippie era.

DESPITE INITIALLY resisting offers to work for the luxury Gucci group conglomerate (purportedly over their use of fur and leather), McCartney signed up in 2001, with her eco-principles intact. She has continued to establish her signature easy-to-wear but luxurious clothes, an investment to create a new global luxury brand that has reported a profit in 2007 for the first time. Collaborations have been a mark of this phase, especially the collection designed for H&M in November 2005, which sold out in an hour—designer style at a fraction of the price, made in China, and accessible to a much wider range of sizes than usual. There is now a sportswear collaboration—adidas by Stella McCartney—and a range of non-leather bags with Le SportSac. The use or—more importantly for McCartney—the non-use of leather is a major issue she is attempting to deal with in the luxury fashion industry; spurred on by the continuing cult of designer bags and shoes. Even where designers use canvas there will usually be a leather trim. In her recent collections, McCartney has revived the use of 'leatherette'. However, the arguments remain to be had about the better ecological choice: leather or leatherette.

GIVEN HER credentials, it is not surprising that McCartney is one of the first big name designers to create a new, completely 'green', fashion collection for Autumn 2007, exclusive to Barneys in New York. Selling from 250–750 pounds, the collection is "one hundred per cent organic, ethical and sustainable" but small. There are only 18 pieces,

Stella McCartney knitted oversize sweater Autumn/ Winter 2007. Photograph by Chris Moore.

consisting of an oversize jacket, coat knits, shorts and other pieces that also recycle fabrics and trims from previous seasons' collections. According to *Womens Wear Daily* in the US, 19 October 2007, McCartney had to "source differently, do new designs and add an extra expense". Although other designers express interest, there is a much bigger learning curve for them than for a label which has been built on green philosophy from the start—the success of this collection could well start the tide turning in designer fashion, especially given her accolade of Designer of the Year at the 2007 British Fashion Awards. Back in 2006, McCartney stated that "we address these [ethical and ecological] questions in every other part of our lives except fashion. Mindsets are changing". Let us hope that she is proved right for the longer term.

1 *ES Magazine,* 18 May 2007.

2 *ES Magazine,* 18 May 2007.

Eco-Labelling

Traceability in the supply chain is now becoming increasingly important to the consumer of clothing, in the same manner as seen in the food industry with the growth of the organic market—some food companies have now begun to label the environmental impact of their products, and it will remain to be seen how this initiative spreads.

How is the customer buying clothes to know which is the best ecologically or ethically sound purchase? In order to become more ethical in their purchases and complete the desired virtuous circle, consumers need to be educated about the provenance of their clothing, in much the same way as food is now labelled with detailed contents, nutrition and origins. However, as with food—where words such as 'natural', 'fresh', and 'wholesome' are used constantly without definition, and even 'organic' has been applied to non-certified goods—much eco-jargon has arisen when applied to fashion. The term 'eco' is a key culprit, together with 'green', 'environmentally friendly', 'sustainable', 'bio' and also 'organic'. No internationally agreed standards exist for these terms as yet, although work has now begun, and each country has adopted different private standards. The EU developed the criteria for its Eco Label to be applied to textiles in 2002, which is mainly concerned with freedom from harmful toxins, and setting maximum limits on potentially harmful chemical residues, as is the Oeko Tex 100 certification. After much debate, in January 2007 the UK Soil Association announced guidelines for organically produced cotton to also include the basic manufacturing of the garment it is made into (several more processes for certification than the growing of bananas for example) and something of a breakthrough for organic certification of clothing rather than fibre only.

The concept of 'shades of green' is an idea which could identify a product's eco-credentials and also incremental levels of changes in manufacturing or operational processes. Could this be turned into a marketing labelling system for easy recognition by consumers? It is, though, fraught with problems, in the same way that 'traffic light' labels for food have been controversial—too simplistic, too patronising, too difficult to implement—and which manufacturers would own up to not being particularly green? The bigger questions raised by this idea are whether a little change at a time in the direction of eco-design is enough. Where does a fashion company draw the line in responsibility? Is it better to get a 'light green' product out on the market than to wait for a 'dark green' one which may take substantially longer? Industry debates are now in progress, but it is clear than some form of standardised information about origins of fibre and place of manufacture on garment labels, in addition to the current fibre content and aftercare labelling would be a good start, coupled with general independent information available in a form easy to understand by everyday shoppers. The majority of the work has been done on growing food and fibres but, when considering fashion garments, there is a raft of other areas for which green credentials are needed. Michael Flanagan of Clothesource (a market intelligence company) believes that in a few years' time, labels on clothes which give their carbon emissions will be as common as nutritional labelling on food. However, companies alone will not be the ones to implement this; it will require government legislation on an international basis.

Designs from the Noir
Spring/Summer, 2007, Cotton
Couture Collection. Certified
African cotton is used to make
luxurious, sexy sillouettes

Conclusion

As the examples given here show, the greening of the fashion industry is undoubtedly taking place, and a great deal of work is well underway on all fronts: fibre production, textile dyeing, minimising waste of energy and resources, and addressing labour rights. However, the complexity and global reach of all the aspects behind fashion can be daunting to contemplate. From a design or a consumer point of view, it is all too easy to feel helpless in the face of such enormous issues as ethical working practices and environmental problems throughout the manufacturing chain. After all, most people just want to buy something nice and not too expensive, and fashion designers want the freedom of choice to express their ideas and creativity. If *Eco-Chic: The Fashion Paradox* has helped to deconstruct some of the complexity, helped identify areas where individuals can make a difference, and to present different aspects of fashion all together, then it will have succeeded in its aims. One message is clear, there is not one 'right' answer to the seemingly insurmountable contradictions within fashion but multiple solutions to issues can be proposed which are appropriate to each level of action—by individuals, design teams, buying teams, corporate management, lobby groups, charities, education and government departments, nationally and internationally. If everyone feels more empowered, then reconciling the interests of fashion as business, fashion for fun and individuality, decent livelihoods and the future of the planet may no longer be a paradox.

Fine merino wool knitwear
from John Smedley's Autumn/
Winter 2007 Collection.

RESOURCE SECTION

THE LABELLING JUNGLE

There has been a proliferation of standards and individual labels set up to certify fibres, dyes and fabrics in different countries around the world. Most of these are by private organisations, some long established and well recognised (for example the Soil Association) and others more recently established. Some are organic standards; others are safety standards against hazardous chemicals. The EU and other governments have recently collaborated on setting some internationally recognised standards, although much is still in development, there will soon be a great deal more harmonisation. Consumer labelling for fabrics and clothing is currently also being tackled by organisations such as the recently formed group: RITE (Reducing the Impact of Textiles on the Environment). Organic Certification can be very costly to small farmers. There is some support now including PAN for merging of Fairtrade and organic standards in cotton.

The following is a brief list of resources, followed by a more detailed information summary on each, plus further useful organisations.

FIBRE, TEXTILE AND PRODUCT CERTIFICATION

Bluesign (Switzerland)
www.bluesign-tech.com

British Standards Institute (BSI)
www.bsi-global.com

Control Union (formerly Skal International)
www.controlunion.com

ECOFLOWER (EU) Sustainable Products Label
ec.europa.eu/environment/ecolabel/index_en.htm

Global Organic Textile Standard (GOTS)
www.global-standard.org

Oeko-tex Standard
www.oeko-tex.com

Institute for Ethical and Environmental Certification (ICEA) (Italy)
www.icea.info

International Association Natural Textile Industry (IVN) (Germany)
www.naturtextil.com

Japan Organic Cotton Association (JOCA)
www.joca.gr.jp

Institute for Marketecology (IMO) (Switzerland)
www.imo.ch

AGRICULTURE

Agrocel (India)
www.agrocel.cotton.com

International Federation of Organic Agriculture Movements (IFOAM)
www.ifoam.org

Organic Exchange (US)
www.organicexchange.org

Pesticide Action Network (PAN) (UK)
www.pan-uk.org/Projects/Cotton/index.htm

Soil Association
www.soilassociation.org

Sustainable Cotton Project (SCP) (US)
www.sustainablecotton.org

The Organic Trade Association (OTA)
www.ota.com

Bioregional
www.bioregional.com

ETHICAL TRADING AND LABOUR ORGANISATIONS

Clean Clothes Campaign
www.cleanclothes.org

European Fair Trade Association (EFTA)
www.european-fair-trade-association.org

Environmental Justice Foundation (EJF)
www.ejfoundation.org

Ethical Trading Initiative (ETI)
www.ethicaltrade.org

Ethical Company Organisation Accreditation
www.ethical-company-organisation.org

Fair Trade Foundation
www.fairtrade.org.uk

Fair Labour Association (US)
www.fairlabor.org

Fair Trade Certified (US)
www.transfairusa.org

International Fair Trade Association (IFAT)
www.ifat.org

International Labour Organisation
www.ilo.org

Labour Behind the Label
www.labourbehindthelabel.org

No Sweat
www.nosweat.org.uk
Oxfam
www.oxfam.org.uk

ADVISORY ORGANISATIONS AND GOVERNMENT AGENCIES

The Association of Suppliers to the British Clothing Industry (ASBCI)
www.asbci.co.uk/

Defra
www.defra.gov.uk

The Organic Exchange
www.organicexchange.org

Reducing the Impact of Textiles on the Environment (RITE) Group
www.ritegroup.org

EPEA
www.epea.com

Envirowise
www.envirowise.gov.uk/textiles

Forum for the Future
www.forumforthefuture.org.uk

Futerra
www.futerra.org

The Performance Textiles Association
www.performancetextiles.org.uk

The Textile Institute
www.texi.org

WASTE AND RECYCLING

WRAP UK Government Waste Recycling Programme
www.wrap.org.uk/

Salvation Army Trading Co Ltd.
www.satradingco.org

Oxfam Wastesavers
www.oxfam.org.uk

Textile Recycling for Aid and International Development (TRAID)
www.traid.org.uk

CHEMICALS, DYEING AND FINISHING

Chemical Industries
Association (CIA)
www.cia.org.uk

CSIRO
www.csiro.au

Registration, Evaluation and
Authorisation of Chemicals
(REACH READY) (EU
programme)
ec.europa.eu/environment/
chemicals/reach.htm

Society of Dyers and Colourists
(SDC) (UK)
www.sdc.org.uk

American Association
Of Textile Chemists and
Colourists (AATCC) (US)
www.aatcc.org

SUPPORT FOR SUSTAINABLE DESIGN

Ethical Fashion Forum
www.ethicalfashionforum.com

Fashioning an Ethical
Industry Project
www.fashioning
anethicalindustry.com

The Centre for Sustainable
Design, University College of
the Creative Arts (Surrey)
www.cfsd.org.uk/

Textiles, Environment, Design
(TED), Chelsea College of Art
and Design, University of the
Arts London
www.chelsea.arts.ac.uk

Kate Fletcher Consultancy
www.katefletcher.com

Sustainable Design Network,
Loughborough University www.
sustainabledesignnet.org.uk/

Centre for Sustainable Fashion,
London College of Fashion,
University of the Arts London
www.fashion.arts.ac.uk

The Slow Design Group
www.slowdesign.org

Better thinking Consultancy
www.betterthinking.co.uk

FIBRE AND TEXTILE ASSOCIATIONS

British Wool Marketing
Board (BWMB)
www.britishwool.org.uk

Cotton Incorporated
www.cottoninc.com

Cotton USA
www.cotton.org

Creative Lifestyle and
Sustainable Strategies (CLASS)
Textile Manufacturers Group
www.c-l-a-s-s.org/
index_eng.html

International Alpaca
Association (Peru)
www.aia.org.pe

International Wool Textile
Organisation (IWTO)
hwww.iwto.org

Masters of Linen
www.mastersoflinen.com/en/

Silk Association of Great
Britain. Conventional
silk resources
www.silk.org.uk

Organic Exchange (cotton and
other crops)
www.organicexchange.org

MANUFACTURERS OF SUSTAINABLE FIBRES, YARNS AND FABRICS

Avanti (Organic fabrics)
www.avantijapan.co.jp/
english/index.html

Bamboo
www.bamboo-fibre.net
www.moral-fibre.net

Calamai Eco-Fabrics
(recycled wool, cotton,
polyester, polypropylene)
www.calamai.it

Cupro-Bemberg
www.bembergitalia.com/
gbcupro00.html

Cupro–Asahi Kasei
www.asahi-kasei.co.jp/fibers/
en/bemberg/what_01.html

Ecolution (Romania) (naturally
processed hemp and cotton
fibres and clothing)
www.ecolution,com

Ingeo
www.ingeofibers.com/
Natureworks

Invista
www.invista.com/

i-cotton
www.continuumtextiles.com/
i-cotton.htm

i-merino
www.i-merino.com/

Hemcore (UK) Grown Hemp
for Industrial Uses
www.hemcore.co.uk/

Lenzing Fibres (Tencel)
www.lenzing.com/fibers/en/
textiles

Natural Colour Cotton
Company (UK) (organic
coloured cotton and bamboo
fibres and clothing)
www.naturalcolourcotton.com
www.bamboo-yoga.com
Peru Naturtex Partners (cotton
and alpaca)
www.perunaturtex.com/
index.htm

Seacell
www.seacell.de/en/home

Teijin
www.teijin.co.jp/english/
index.html

INFORMATION AND EVENTS

Anti-Apathy
www.anit-apathy.org

Ecotextile News
www.ecotextile.com

www.inhabitat.com

www.just-style.com/

www.textileworld.com/

www.wgsn.com

The Textile Institute
www.texi.org

FIBRES AND FABRICS

Organic Certification:
An agricultural crop can
now be certified organic
by numerous certification
agencies globally. The textile
processing and clothing
manufacturing stage is more
complex as only a handful
of accepted standards have
been created to denote
that, although not actually
'organic' in the same way that
as agricultural products are
classified, they are adopting
alternative chemicals and
processing practices that
minimise the impact on the
environment, and protect the
health of consumers, while
insuring textiles of high quality
that are economically viable.

Health and Safety Certification:
The demands and performance
expectations of modern
textile products, such as easy
care properties, fashionable
colours, multi –purpose
functionalities can only be
achieved with the use of
specific chemicals. In some
areas these are essential
requirements, depending
on the intended use (eg. for
protective workwear). EU
legislation is now in place

to register all chemical substances over a ten year period, including those found in textiles.

The following are some of the accreditation organisations that offer confidence to producers, manufacturers, and consumers through their testing and certification, with their country of origin:

Oeko-Tex Standard

Germany (global presence)
www.oeko-tex.com
www.hohenstein.de/en

The Oeko-Tex Standard was set up in 1992 developed by Hohenstein Institute, an independent research organisation. The standard was created in response to concerns about textiles posing health risks, for example from pesticide or dye residues. Headlines such as "Poison In Textiles" raised concerns with consumers, especially in products for babies and children. Most of the criteria for residues in the baby clothes category are comparable to health criteria of the organic textile standards. 12 institutes throughout the EU and worldwide test textile products and award the labels, which are applied to both natural and manmade fabrics.

Oeko-Tex Standard 100

Tests for all known harmful chemicals and substances that are prohibited by law. The following are potential ways chemicals can be absorbed into the body from textiles and for which Oeko-tex carry out stringent tests: absorption via perspiration the skin; ingestion (important in baby products); inhalation of harmful substances.

Oeko-Tex Standard 1000

This standard extends the above parameters to also examine the total environmental impact of textiles throughout the supply chain—eg. energy, water, waster, workplace conditions, noise levels etc. Only articles meeting the strict criteria for all their components are awarded the 'Confidence in Textiles' label. All companies involved in the manufacturing of a specific product, not only the textiles, must comply with the requirements of the Oeko-Tex Standard 1000 without exception.

Oeko-Tex claims: In some cases the standards to be met go far beyond legal requirements and therefore offer the consumer the greatest possible peace of mind.

SKAL - EKO QUALITY SYMBOL (Netherlands)

Skal is the inspection body for organic production in the Netherlands and legal holder of the EKO Quality symbol. This symbol stands for organic production certified by Skal that meets the requirements of EU regulations for organic production, and is becoming more widely used.

CONTROL UNION

(global presence)
www.controlunion.com
Privately owned group Control Union Certifications, formerly known as Skal International, offers a wide range of globally recognised and accepted certification programs. The company also offers two certification programmes for sustainable textile production:

• Sustainable Textile certification – (under the GOTS standards)
• Organic Exchange certification

Sustainable Textile Certification

• All fibres should be natural and have to be grown in an 'organic' way, based on the production standards that are laid down in the EEC-Regulation 2092/91, or NOP regulations.
• The whole production process should be taken into account. The criteria for the production process are laid down in the 'Skal International standards for sustainable textile production'. They encompass every process step of textile production (spinning, weaving, washing, etc) and for every step clear guidelines are given as to which processing aids (eg. chemicals) may or may not be used, in order to gain as much environmental benefit as possible.

Global Organic Textile Standard (GOTS)

(global presence)
www.global-standard.org/
the international working group on global organic textile standards was set up to develop the GOTS standard which was adopted in 2006

Founded to meet the need to reassure the customer—with one recognised label—that the product they are purchasing is organic and has been tested, monitored and checked from harvest through to processing and manufacturing to the final garment labelling.

GOTS has brought together several accreditation routes and standards under one mark for a Global Organic Textile Standard. This has begun to simplify and harmonise the various regional approaches for different stages of production so that the range of standards and legal requirements placed on the processors

and manufacturers are encompassed under one universally recognised standard allowing them to export their organic fabrics and garments with one certification accepted in all major markets. GOTS Founding bodies are:

International Association Natural Textile Idustry (IVN) (Germany)
Soil Association (SA) (UK)
Organic Trade Association (OTA) (US)
Japan Organic Cotton (JOCA) (Japan)

The key criteria are:
• Two label system: the first requires at least 95 per cent, and the second a minimum 70 per cent organic fibres in plain fabric.
• All inputs have to meet basic requirements on toxicity and biodegradability.
• No toxic heavy metals, no formaldehyde, no GM organisms.
• Environmental policy required in the manufacturing sites.
• Social criteria (based on ILO key criteria) are compulsory.
• Dual system of quality assurance consisting of on-site inspection and residue testing.

THE ORGANIC EXCHANGE

(US) (global presence)
Non-profit
business organisation
www.organicexchange.org

Facilitating the growth of organic agriculture, with a specific focus on increasing the production and use of organically-grown fibres such as cotton.

Working globally, this standard encompasses all the criteria set out by GOTS but strongly emphasises and practices its responsibility not only to offer a quality certification, but also to support and educate each participant in the supply chain from the farmer through to the retailer and consumer. It also prides itself in developing a strong voice and social equity for the farmers, while realising the benefits of treating and nurturing the land, which is their main source of revenue.

Organic Exchange offers opportunities to experience firsthand the issues which farmers face globally by organising field trips for manufacturers and retailers. These issues include: regional climate change; pressure from crop buyers; urgent need to sell crop to pay land rent at end of year; pressure to use pesticides and insecticides bysuppliers without any clear guidelines of use; rise in health problems in the region.

The Organic Exchange implement a transparent and traceable computerised process from the fibre to the consumer.

Organic Exchange long term goal is to increase the amount of certified organic land farmed for fibre production by 50 per cent per year. Key Activities are:
Brand Outreach:
Working with brands and retailers to develop and implement short, medium and long term goals to transition some or all of their cotton use to organic cotton
Farm Development:
Working with existing organic farming projects, as well as new producer groups, to help secure contracts for their existing cotton and rotation crop production and develop sound and supportable expansion plans. A new focus is increasing the visibility of farmers worldwide. Regional farming coordinators are currently located in Africa, India and South America.
Tool Development:

Supporting businesses in the development and implementation of an organic cotton program with information, tools and consulting. Tools include a quarterly newsletter, website, on-line tracking service, sourcing directory, annual conference and marketplace and regional trainings.

BLUESIGN

(Switzerland and global presence)
www.bluesign-tech.com
The Bluesign standard is textile specific, and ensures compliance with strict legislations without compromising functionality, quality or design.

Bluesign has made implementing sustainable awareness and practice for textiles organisations easy, creative and practical, making it one of the most favoured standards to date in the clothing textile industry. Many large international brands have embraced the effective and efficient tool-based service offered by Bluesign as it maintains functionality, quality and design as building blocks and ensures products do not compromise or pose any risks for Health and Safety or the Environment by defining clear routes from the start of the product concept forming and decision-making processes. Legislations and restrictions posed by standard and accreditation bodies or by government are not treated as constraints but offers create solutions in pioneering new products and ways if thinking.

EU ECOFLOWER

ec.europa.eu/environment/ecolabel/index_en.htm
An EU ecomark, set-up in 1992, awarded to recognise a wide range of products and services. Textile products

(both natural and synthetic) have been included since 1999, particularly with respect to standards protecting water pollution. Criteria for Textiles are undergoing revisions to co-ordinate with the Oeko-tex label, and extend the scope. A small number of textile companies have so far been awarded the mark.

The EU ecomarking system is a voluntary system that can be granted to goods and services that treat the environment favourably throughout its life cycle compared to other products and services in the same product group. The scheme excludes food products, beverages, pharmaceutical goods, and medical products. One of the first textile companies to be awarded this label in 2002 was Lenzing fibres for their Tencel fibre, and recently the AWI and i-merino.

ICEA–Istituto per la Certificazione Etica ed Ambientale (Institute for Ethical and Environmental Certification) (Italy)

www.icea.info
Ethical and environmental certification: a requirement that grows and makes enterprises grow.

ICEA is the most prominent body in Italy certifying products obtained using organic farming methods or having a great ethical, social and environmental relevance. It has applied for approval to verify textiles according to GOTS standards.
Key Activities:
• Inspection and Certification (independent and impartial)
• Research and Development
• Training
• International Cooperation

INSTITUTE OF MARKETECOLOGY (IMO)

(Switzerland)
www.imo.ch
Since 1992, IMO has been acting as an international inspection and certification organisation for textiles representing the greatest ecological quality.

The International Association Natural Textile Industry (IVN) has entrusted IMO and the testing lab eco-Umweltinstitut exclusively with quality assurance. IMO performs ecological quality assurance on basis of the standards of the Organic Trade Association (OTA), Demeter International, on behalf of the Soil Association and others.

IMO was significantly involved in developing the Global Organic Textile Standard (GOTS) and has been officially approved as the first certification body to offer certification according to this worldwide accepted standard for ecological textiles.

BRITISH STANDARDS INSTITUTE (BSI)

www.bsi-global.com
Operating globally, providing organisations with independent assessment and certification of their products and management systems.
For example:
Quality ISO 9001: Help implement and certify an effective management system across a broad range of business areas and standards.
Environmental ISO 14001: The international standard that specifies a process for controlling and improving an organisation's environmental performance, setting up an effective Environmental Management System.
Ethical Fashion Community of Practice: In 2006 the BSI developed an initiative to create a Community of

Practices to support all types of stakeholders (individuals, retail, manufacturers, NGOs) to devise solutions to the ethical and social challenges faced throughout the fashion industry, through a collaborative approach.

AGRICULTURAL STANDARDS

Cotton is the most important textile crop, categorised as a food crop, found in the most unlikely places in addition to textiles, utilising the cotton seed left over from the ginning process, including cattle feed, paper money and even crisps and candy bars.

Cotton is popular and has been perceived as a 'pure and natural' fibre, but these organisations have brought to the fore the reality of its production and campaign for changes which are now having a commercial impact.

Pesticide Action Network (PAN UK)
Non-profit organisation, part of a global network, working closely with partners in developing countries eg. Benin, West Africa
www.pan-uk.org/Projects/Cotton/index.htm
One of the most prominent pesticide organisations that campaign and actively work to reduce the dependence on pesticides and encourage the positive ecological, safe and sustainable alternatives. They promote the close link between food, agriculture and textiles to enable areas to become healthier and considerably more fertile.

Key areas of activity are: information, research, policy advocacy, networking and capacity building, and also support for field work. PAN has been instrumental in raising awareness of the serious health and environmental issues of growing cotton, particularly for developing countries

The Wear Organic campaign from PAN UK aims to reduce the problems from pesticides used in cotton, particularly by promoting organic and fair alternatives and working with educational establishments
www.wearorganic.com

PAN have produced a wide range of resources and reports, particularly about cotton growing, including the film White Gold (in collaboration with the EJF) about small farmers in Benin, also featuring Katharine Hamnett, a key part of their successful campaigning. A typical quote:
Organic farming...saves lives from not using pesticides. We no longer have debt problems. Income is all profit at the end of season. Land and soil are preserved.' Gera Paul, a Béninese farmer.

THE SOIL ASSOCIATION (UK)
Non-profit organisation
www.soilassociation.org
The Soil Association is now one of the most widely recognised standard that has raised awareness, supported and promoted organic farming and shown the values relating to human health. It diversified its scope, starting in 2003, in offering accreditation to cover the processing and manufacture of organic textiles, and has launched new and revised guidelines for Textiles in 2007. The standards cover the processing and manufacturing of all natural textiles, with the production of the raw materials for leather and skins being covered under existing standards for organic farming methods.

SUSTAINABLE COTTON PROJECT (SCP) (US)
Non-profit business organisation
Set Up: 1994
One of the pioneers in addressing disparity throughout the cotton textile supply chain. The core purpose of SCP has been to support and work with farmers in mainly the Californian and Mexican regions, to improve their land, livelihoods, health and families and living conditions while also sending the message of how and why consumers' and manufacturers' decisions have a major impact on them. Collaborative programmes are also being instigated for farmers in Africa.

Three key programmes are run by SCP:
BASIC: educating and working with the farmers on the dangers of pesticides and insecticides and the economical and health benefits of organic alternatives.
Cleaner Cotton: to educate manufacturers
Care What You Wear: educating consumers and encouraging the purchasing of sustainable products

THE ORGANIC TRADE ASSOCIATION (OTA)
(US and Canada)
Membership-based business association for the organic industry in North America
Set Up: 1985
OTA represents businesses across the organic supply chain and addresses all things organic, including food, fibre/textiles, personal care products, and new sectors as they develop. Over 60 per cent of OTA trade members are relitively small-scale businesses. Its mission: To promote and protect organic trade to benefit the environment, farmers, the public, and the economy. OTA envisions organic products becoming a significant part of everyday life, enhancing people's lives and the environment.

AGROCEL
Ensuring a long term future for Indian cotton farmers. To meet the demand for a reliable Organic and fair trade cotton fibre, Agrocel Industries Limited, in conjunction with Vericott Ltd. and Traidcraft Exchange, have defined and branded a cotton fibre. Agrocel Pure and Fair Indian Organic Cotton.

Agrocel, from its 12 rural service centres across India, co-ordinates organic fibre cultivation with a selected group of local farmers and acts as a broker. A team of agronomists is based at each Agrocel service centre, and monitors growing to International Organic Standards. Agrocel is one of the world's largest direct suppliers of Organic, Fairtrade and other speciality cottons. It co-ordinates the production, certification, procurement, and storage of a range of cotton fibre types. Agrocel has mobilised 20,000 farmers in the last ten years and has the capacity to reach more.

ETHICAL STANDARDS

International Fair Trade Association (IFAT)
www.ifat.org
A global network of fair trade organisations: IFAT aims to be the global umbrella and advocate for FairTrade ensuring producer voices are heard at all levels throughout a product supply chain. IFAT encompasses all product types including food, clothing and textiles.

FTO Mark
Set Up: 2004
Since 2004, the FTO Mark

above identifies registered FairTrade Organizations Worldwide through a tiered accreditation system. Over 150 organisations have already registered including Oxfam, PeopleTree and the Network of European World Shops. The mark recognises that standards are being adhered to globally in relation to working conditions, wages, child labour and the environment. These standards are regulated by self-assessment, continuous mutual reviews and external verification.

FAIR TRADE FOUNDATION
www.fairtrade.org.uk
Fairtrade—name for the trading certification and labelling system in the UK by the Fair Trade Foundation.

The FairTrade Mark for seed cotton (raw cotton before ginning) was first launched in the UK in November 2005.
• It ensures that cotton producers have received a fair price for their produce.
• Ensures that the farmer is protected against price fluctuations and is guaranteed a fixed price at the beginning of the season. (Organic cotton price still depends on world market prices).
• Facilitating the developing communities to support themselves through a premium scheme which is reserved towards instigating their own development projects. So each village/community vote on where and in what they invest back their money – eg. health centres, schools etc.
• Fairtrade cotton mark guarantees that the fibre was grown in a developing country such as India or Africa, where it had the greatest positive impacts on very poor producers. FairTrade Mark covers the seed-cotton.

Flo Cert continues the work of The Fairtrade Mark by accrediting the processing and manufacturing at each stage of the process.

FLO CERT GMBH
www.flo-cert.net

FLO - Fairtrade Labelling
Organisation
www.fairtrade.net
As well as giving assurance to the customer that producers have received a fair price The Fairtrade certification process, is also enabling a more transparent supply chain while educating the customer of the varying supply chain stages involved in the production of their product, how their decision-making process can affect their livelihood, why there had been maltreatment and unbalance of labour standards and why time restraints, late adjustments on confirmed orders and pressure on lead times can have a negative impact on the actual producers.

Each participant of the product supply chain is required to complete quarterly forms verifying from where, how much and from whom their product came from and to whom it will be supplied. FLO is currently researching the feasibility of a fair trade standard for textiles and certification at a garment making level. The efficient and traceable system instigated by fair trade and its fundamental requirement of a price premium is paving the way to enable cotton producers to slowly convert to organic agriculture. Fairtrade must be written as one word and accompanied by its logo. Other wording labelled such as Fair Trade may not be genuine certified.

Fair Trade Certified
(US scheme)
www.transfairusa.org

Ethical Trading Initiative
www.ethicaltrade.org
An alliance of companies, non-governmental organisations (NGOs) and trade union organisations.
Set up: 1998
Set up to encourage and give direction to UK companies to support their supply chain by encouraging them to meet and exceed basic international labour standards by promoting and encouraging implementation of regumented corporate codes of practice.
Key Activities:
• Their NGO, trade union and corporate members work together to identify what constitutes 'good practice' in code implementation, and then promote and share this good practice.
• Encourages companies to adopt the ETI Base Code and implement it in their supply chains. Getting new companies to join ETI.
• Requiring all corporate members to submit annual progress reports on their code implementation activities.
• Evoking, ETI's procedure for disengaging the poor performers.

Environmental Justice Foundation (EJF)
www.ejfoundation.org
Non-profit organisation
Set Up: 2000
Protecting People and Planet
EJF makes a direct link between the need for environmental security and the defence of all basic human rights.

EJF works towards: Empowering people who suffer most from environmental abuses and to find peaceful ways of preventing them.

EJF provides film and advocacy training to

individuals and grassroots organisations in the global south, enabling them to document, expose and create long term solutions to environmental abuses. EJF campaigns internationally to raise awareness of the issues our grassroots partners are working to solve locally. Today EJF has a team of campaigners and filmmakers based in London, and works internationally with partners in Brazil, Vietnam, Mali, Uzbekistan and Indonesia.

Clean Clothes Campaign
(Netherlands)
www.cleanclothes.org/
Improving the working conditions in the global garment industry.

The Clean Clothes Campaign is an EU organisation launched in 1985, to actively support garment and sports shoe workers globally. To date there have been more than 300 cases across 30 countries, seeking justice for violation of rights, through their urgent action programme. The CCC also disseminates information and organises events.

Labour Behind The Label
www.labourbehindthe label.org
Labour Behind the Label is the UK platform of the international Clean Clothes Campaign that supports garment workers' efforts worldwide to improve their working conditions. Members include: Oxfam, *Ethical Consumer Magazine* and Women Working Worldwide (who have contributed to a corporate social responsibility project with high street chain: Gap).

Fashioning an Ethical Industry project
www.fashioninganethicalindustry.org
Labour Behind the Label has supported a three year

project working with UK fashion colleges to raise awareness of the issues of working conditions in garment factories and inspire fashion students to get involved in improving standards overall. The FEI website has a wealth of resources and information for students, tutors and designers, including electronic versions of all key reports.

Fair Wear Foundation
(Netherlands)
The FWF promotes fair labour and enhanced working conditions in the garment industry world wide; this means it's member companies have undersigned to FWF's Code of Labour practices, and thereby the company has committed itself to monitor the factories of its suppliers and The Fair Wear Foundation verifies that the Code of Labour Practices is actually implemented and respected at the factories.

The FWF promotes fair labour and enhanced working conditions in the garment industry world wide; this means it's member companies have signed up to FWF's Code of Labour practices, and thereby the company has committed itself to monitor the factories of its suppliers. The Fair Wear Foundation verifies that the Code of Labour Practices is actually implemented and respected at the factories.

Ethical Company Organisation Accreditation (UK)
www.ethical-company-organisation.org
The Ethical Company Organisation runs the UK's only corporate-level Ethical Accreditation Scheme. This certifies that the Company or Brand in question has scored highly in an overall analysis of its Corporate Social Responsibility record—and such independent certification and endorsement is thought to significantly strengthen ethical brands, clearly positioning them in the premier league of ethical companies. Members relating to the fashion/textile field include: Green Fibres, The Natural Collection, Terramar Organic, Plain Lazy, Seasalt, T-shirt and Sons, Bishopston Trading Company.

Other Organisations:
Clean Clothes Campaign
www.cleanclothes.org/

No Sweat
www.nosweat.org.uk

The Fair Labour Association (US)
www.fairlabor.org/

EFTA - European Fair Trade Association
www.eftafairtrade.org

International Labour Organisation
www.ilo.org

ORGANISATIONS

The RITE GROUP (Reducing The Impact of Textiles on The Environment) (UK)
A new industry association which aims to provide advice and fact based information to minimise the negative environmental impact of the production, use and disposal of textiles and apparel. The Group's ultimate goal is to drive forward the sustainable and ethical production of textiles and clothing throughout the global supply chain through a number of innovative initiatives.

The founder members of the RITE GROUP are M&S, University of Leeds, and *Ecotextile News*. A steering committee and advisory panel of senior industry executives from fibres through to brands is now being assembled.

EPEA (Germany)
www.epea.com
EPEA is an international scientific research and consultancy institute that improves product quality, utility and environmental performance via eco-effectiveness. One of the first organisations to address the impact the whole life cycle of a product has on the environment and where the term 'Up-Cycle' has evolved.

McDonough Braungart Design Chemistry (MBDC) (US)
www.mbdc.com
Consultancy founded by William McDonough and Professor Michael Braungart in 1995 to promote and shape what they call the 'Next Industrial Revolution' through the introduction of a new design paradigm called Cradle-to-Cradle Design, and the implementation of eco-effective design principles. MBDC has developed a Cradle-to-Cradle certification mark for products and services.

IFOAM
www.ifoam.org
IFOAM is the worldwide umbrella organisation for the organic movement, uniting more than 750 organisations in 108 countries.

Organic trade is a rapidly growing all over the world. The growth rates of the organic sector demonstrate that organic products are moving from the 'niche' and entering mainstream markets. The total land under certified organic production worldwide has reached over 26 million hectares. IFOAM is at the heart of this development.

IFOAM's Organic Guarantee System (OGS) is designed to a) facilitate the development of organic standards and third-party certification worldwide, and to b) provide an international guarantee of these standards and organic certification. The IFOAM Basic Standards and the Accreditation Criteria are two of the main components of the OGS.

Defra
www.defra.gov.uk
Enabling everyone to live within our environmental means. Ten product roadmaps, of which Clothing is one, are being developed to reduce the environmental and social impacts across the life cycle of a range of priority products. This is part of Defra's work on Sustainable Consumption and Production (SCP)

Thinksustainable was developed in Defra as a package to communicate sustainable development (SD). It was created to raise awareness and understanding of SD and to help policy makers embed SD into their work.
www.defra.gov.uk/sustainable/think/index.htm
Defra has commissioned Environmental Resources Management (ERM) to undertake a study to map the evidence on the sustainability impacts across the clothing life cycle and supply chain.
www.defra.gov.uk/environment/consumerprod/products/clothing.htm#impact

BioRegional Development Group
An entrepreneurial, independent environmental organisation.

Working locally and regionally with international presence offering products, services and project driven solutions towards environmental considerations that affect everyday needs and requirements. Areas covered are: wood products, paper, textiles, food, transport and housing. Within the textile sector, BioRegional are running the Fibre Programme and The Hemp Project. The Association of Suppliers to the British Clothing Industry (ASBCI) www.asbci.co.uk/

Envirowise

www.envirowise.gov.uk/textiles Envirowise offers a wide range of free textile-specific publications providing practical advice and information to help companies reduce their environmental impact and increase their bottom line.

EURATEX (The European Apparel and Textile Organisation)

www.euratex.org
Membership based organisation
• Promoting expansion of the EU exports of textiles and clothing.
• Legislation and its application in the field of intellectual property.
• Supporting measures that enhance environmental protection and are acceptable to the industry.
• Participate in research, development, innovation and other educational projects.
• Engage in a constructive social dialogue at EU level.

FUTERRA

www.futerra.org
Futerra is a consultancy working with large and small organisations to find innovative, creative and strategic ways to promote sustainable development. They are currently working with Anti-Apathy, The Ethical Fashion Forum and the Fashioning an Ethical

Industry project to promote the new ReFashion awards, to communicate ethical fashion to both public and fashion industry executives.
Futerra is working with the Ethical Fashion Forum and the Fashioning an Ethical Industry project and starting a Textiles programme.

ETHICAL FASHION FORUM

The Ethical Fashion Forum (EFF) is a network of fashion designers, businesses and organisations focusing upon social and environmental sustainability in the fashion industry.
The EFF aims to reduce poverty and create sustainable livelihoods by supporting, promoting and facilitating innovative values-led business practices within the garment industry. It also aims to help minimise the impact of the industry on the environment by supporting sustainable standards, regulations, and labelling initiatives.
EFF is a not-for-profit organisation formed in 2004 and co-ordinated by Tamsin Lejeune and Elizabeth Laskar. It collaborates on projects such as Design4Life Ghana, and events such as the Ethical Fashion Show in Paris.

CHEMICALS, DYEING AND FINISHING

Major new EU legislation regarding the registration and use of chemicals REACH has now come into force (June 2007), aiming to give a greater consumer security and industrial knowledge base for thousands of chemicals over a ten year period for this potentially hazardous area.

REACH

www.reachready.co.uk
Registration, Evaluation,

Authorisation and Restriction of Chemical substances.
The aim of REACH is to make early identification of the basic properties of chemical substances while still supporting new developments and competitiveness of the EU chemicals industry. The regulation gives greater responsibility to industry to manage the risks from chemicals and to provide safety information on the substances.
Manufacturers and importers will be required to gather information on the properties of their chemical substances, which will allow their safe handling, and to register the information in a central database run by the European Chemicals Agency (ECHA) in Helsinki.

Chemicals Industries Association (CIA)

www.cia.org.uk
A non-profit organisation set-up in 1965, mainly funded by corporate membership subscriptions.
The CIA is the UK's leading trade association for the chemical and chemistry-using industries, representing members both nationally and internationally with involvement in manufacturing, processing, importing, consulting of diverse products and substances including the textile sector.
Part of the CIA (Chemicals industries Association) organisation advising, regulating, monitoring whether chemical substances are complying to new legislative industry standards, how much it would cost to comply, offers a match making service to match the most appropriate service providers to each others requirements.

CSIRO (Australia)

The Commonwealth Scientific and Industrial Research Organisation, is Australia's national science agency and one of the largest and most diverse research agencies in the world. Research is applied to very diverse textile sectors—clothing, upholstery, to filters, insulation and bandages. Examples of areas of research and projects include: better and more consistent crop growth, effectiveness of machinery, medical and electronic applications. CSIRO has the best equipped textile testing laboratory in Australia for investigating the properties of fibres, yarns, textiles and related materials:
• CSIRO is working with the European Union Eco-label body to have a validated declaration scheme written into the Eco-label criteria.
• ISO 14,000 is involved in assistance and auditing
• CSIRO's textile testing laboratory is National Association of Testing Authorities (NATA) accredited.

DYE COMPANIES

CLARIANT

www.clariant
www.huntsman.com/

DYSTAR

www.dystar.com

FURTHER READING

BOOKS

Sustainability and Fashion

Blanchard, Tamsin, *Green is the New Black*: Hodder and Stoughton, 2007
Black, Sandy, *"Interrogating Fashion"*, Insights and Questions: Designing for the 21st Century, Inns, Tom (ed): Gower Ashgate, 2007
Fletcher, Kate, *Sustainable Fashion and Textiles*: Earthscan, 2008

Design and Sustainability

Braungart, Michael and McDonough, William, *Cradle-to-Cradle: Remaking the Way We Make Things*: North Point Press, 2002
Chapman, Jonathan and Gant, Nick, Designers, *Visionaries and Other Stories*: Earthscan, 2007
Chapman, Jonathan, *Emotionally Durable Design: Objects, Experience and Empathy*: Earthscan, 2005
Fuad-Luke, Alastair, *The Eco Design Handbook*, (2nd ed): Thames and Hudson, 2004
Mackenzie, Dorothy, *Green Design*: Laurence King, 1991
Manzini, Ezio, *Materials of Invention*: Design Council, 1989
Manzini, Ezio, *Sustainable Everyday: Scenarios of Urban Life*: Ambiente, 2003
Papanek, Victor, *Design for the Real World*, Thames and Hudson: 1972
Papanek, Victor, *The Green Imperative: Ecology and Ethics in Design and Architecture*: Thames and Hudson, 1995
Rheingold, H, (ed) Millennial *Whole Earth Catalogue*: Harper Collins, 1995
Whitely, Nigel, *Design for Society*: Reaktion Books, 1992

Economics and Fashion Industry Management

Bio thinking Edwin Datschefski
Bruce, Margaret and Hines, Tony, *Fashion Marketing: Contemporary Issues*, 2nd ed., 2007
Gale, Colin and Kaur, Jasbir, *The Textile Book*: Berg, 2002
Hansen, Karen, Salaula: *The World of Secondhand Clothing and Zambia*: Chicago University Press, 2000
Hawken, Paul, *Ecology of Commerce: How Business Can Save the Planet*: Weidenfeld and Nicholson, 2006
Hawken, Paul, *Natural Capitalism: The Next Industrial Revolution*: Earthscan, 1999
Jackson, Tim and Shaw, David, *The Fashion Handbook*: Palgrave, 2006
Klein, Naomi, *No Logo*: Flamingo, 2000
Porritt, Jonathon, *Capitalism: As if the World Matters*: Earthscan, 2007
Steffen, Alex (ed), *Worldchanging: A Users Guide for the 21st Century*: Abrams, 2006
Whitely, Nigel, *Design for Society*, Reaktion Books: 1992

Cultural Studies

Craik, Jennifer, *The Face of Fashion*: 1993
Entwistle, Joanne, *The Fashioned Body*: Polity Press, 2000
Finkelstein, Joanne, *After A Fashion*, Melbourne University Press, 1996
Kuchler, Susanne and Miller, Daniel (eds), *Clothing as Material Culture*: Berg, 2005
Simmel, Georg, 'Fashion' in *On Individuality and Social Forms*: University of Chicago Press, 1971

Textiles and Technology

Corbmann, Bernard, *Textiles: Fibre to Fabric*: Gregg, 1983
Elsasser, Virginia, *Textiles: Concepts and Principles*: Fairchild Publications, 2005
Fereday, Gwen, *Natural Dyes*: British Museum Press, 2003
Gale, Colin and Kaur, Jasbir, *The Textile Book*: Berg, 2002
Gibson, Kenyon (ed), *Hemp for Victory*: Whitaker Publishing, 2006
Handley, Susannah, *Nylon: The Story of a Fashion Revolution*: John Hopkins University Press, 1999
Hatch, Kathryn, *Textile Science*: West Publishing Company, 1993
Hibbert, Ros, *Textile Innovation*, 2nd ed: Line, 2004
Roulac, John, *Hemp Horizons*: Chelsea Green Publishing, 1997
Slater, Kieth, *Environmental Impact of Textiles*: Woodhead Publishing, 2003

REPORTS

PAN booklets and reports
"My Sustainable T-shirt"
"The Deadly Chemicals in Cotton", 2007
"Organic Cotton: From Field to Final Product", 1999
"White Gold: The True Cost of Cotton", Environmental Justice Foundation

"Fashion Victims: The True Cost of Cheap Clothes at Primark, Asda and Tesco", *War on Want*, 2006
"Fashioning Sustainability: A Review of the Sustainability Impacts of the Clothing Industry", *Forum for the Future*, 2007
"Low Cost Clothing Waste", *Salvation Army Trading Company and Oakdene Hollins*, 2006
"Report on Sustainability", *Design Council*
"Well Dressed? The Present and Future Sustainability of Clothing and Textiles in the United Kingdom", *Cambridge University Institute for Manufacturing*, 2006
Baden, Sally and Barber, Catherine, "The Impact of the Secondhand Clothing Trade on Developing Countries", *Oxfam*, 2006
Co-op Bank Ethical Consumer Reports with the National Economic Foundation, 2005–2006

Text by Sandy Black

Edited by Raven Smith

Designed by
Marion Mayr
with Delphine Perrot
and Matthew Pull

Black Dog Publishing
Limited
10A Acton Street
London
WC1X 9NG
UK

info@blackdogonline.com
www.blackdogonline.com

British Library
Cataloguing-in-
Publication Data.

A CIP record for this book
is available from the
British Library.

ISBN: 978 1 906155 09 4

Black Dog Publishing
is an environmentally
responsible company.
*Eco-Chic: The Fashion
Paradox* is printed on
Munken Lynx and Arctic
the Volume, respectively
uncoated and coated FSC
certified papers.

Printed in Latvia.

architecture art design
fashion history photography
theory and things

www.blackdogonline.com